GIS

AND THE
2020
THE
CENSUS

Modernizing Official Statistics

AMOR LAARIBI • LINDA PETERS

Esri Press, 380 New York Street, Redlands, California 92373-8100
Copyright 2019 Esri
All rights reserved.
23 22 21 20 19   1 2 3 4 5 6 7 8 9 10
Printed in the United States of America
Library of Congress Cataloging-in-Publication Data

Library of Congress Cataloging-in-Publication Data
Names: Laaribi, Amor, author. | Peters, Linda.
Title: GIS and the 2020 census : modernizing official statistics / Amor
Laaribi, Linda Peters.
Description: Redlands, California : Esri Press, 2019.
Identifiers: LCCN 2018060051 (print) | LCCN 2019007152 (ebook) | ISBN
9781589485051 (electronic) | ISBN 9781589485044 (pbk. : alk. paper)
Subjects: LCSH: Census--Methodology. | Census--Geographic information systems.
Classification: LCC HA179 (ebook) | LCC HA179 .L33 2019 (print) | DDC
352.7/50285--dc23
LC record available at https://urldefense.proofpoint.com/v2/url?u=https-
3A__lccn.loc.gov_2018060051&d=DwIFAg&c=n6-cguzQvX_tUIrZOS_4Og&r=qNU49__SCQN30XC-f38qj8bYYMTIH4VCOt2
Jb8fvjUA&m=N9LDm816lpUOSrnLbGNLKNGC9sSQOOxCGez3LIoTHM&
s=IU2vJ0BdojtLU_0AhLGaxkrJaFhjH2348dHKCFbJlUA&e=

The information contained in this document is subject to change without notice.

Ask for Esri Press titles at your local bookstore or order by calling 1-800-447-9778. You can also shop online at www.esri.com/esripress. Outside the United States, contact your local Esri distributor or shop online at eurospanbookstore.com/esri.
Esri Press titles are distributed to the trade by the following:

In North America:
Ingram Publisher Services
Toll-free telephone: 800-648-3104
Toll-free fax: 800-838-1149
E-mail: customerservice@ingrampublisherservices.com

In the United Kingdom, Europe, the Middle East and Africa, Asia, and Australia:
Eurospan Group
3 Henrietta Street
London WC2E 8LU
United Kingdom
Telephone 44(0) 1767 604972
Fax: 44(0) 1767 6016-40
E-mail:eurospan@turpin-distribution.com

Contents

Foreword

Timothy Trainor, former chief geospatial scientist, US Census Bureau; former co-chair, UN Committee of Experts on Global Geospatial Information Management

Having worked on five decennial censuses in the US for a large and diverse population within a varied landscape, I have experienced many challenges, difficulties, successes, and celebrations in census taking. In the US, each decade provided opportunities for change and advancement. The 1980 Census experienced inconsistencies between changed boundaries, an outdated road network, and miscoded addresses. There also were demands for data at lower levels of geography to help local and state governments in their responsibilities. In response, the 1990 Census saw the development of a single database with GIS applications from which all geographic products were derived so that changes could be applied consistently. Changes also included a nationwide geographic framework for small areas. To address calls for a more complete statistical frame, the 2000 Census focused on creating a national address list that helped assure a more complete count. The next logical requirement, knowing and using the location of the addresses, was a major focus of the 2010 Census and was made possible by the growing use of GPS technology. As the 2020 Census nears, the use of satellite imagery to aid in address verification and the correct alignment of roads (and thereby many boundaries) is helping to assure solid geospatial information in support of the census.

A census is a primary source of data for each country. The data collected is usually part of a full census in which every household participates in the count. It is not a sample survey, it is not secondary or tertiary data; rather, it is the raw data that is then tabulated and aggregated to levels that are important to data users, leaders, decision-makers, and, in many cases, the law. The framers of the US Constitution outlined the importance of a census by calling for an enumeration every ten years in Article I, Section 2. Its importance was further acknowledged by assigning responsibility as the director for the first census in 1790 to Thomas Jefferson. For many countries, a census is foundational—it provides data and information on current conditions as well as future opportunities and challenges.

However, the numbers on their own are not relevant without an association to location. This is where geography plays its vital role. It answers the question "where" for a summary of people within a household, their age, their gender, their relationship to each other within the household, their health, economic condition, employment, and whatever other question may be included in a country's census count. Knowing the "where" of a population's characteristics offers an important and interesting view on a community's conditions and trends.

A census provides the data that allows us to begin the determination of a cause-and-effect relationship to important questions posed by "why." Why so many people in this area and so few in that area? Why are there greater health issues in this area? Why is employment high or low here? Why are schools here and not there where school-age children live? Why is crime more prevalent in this one particular area? Why does this area appear healthy while that area doesn't? The questions are boundless, and the answers are enlightening. Based on these realizations, more "where" questions can lead to solutions, growth, and planning. Where are new or better transportation facilities in demand? Where is a new hospital or health-care unit required? Where are the best building locations for new schools or refurbishing of existing schools?

The data collected during a census, when combined with location, starts the journey of a transformation to valuable information. The statistics about the nation, its regions, its subnational governments and possibly even its communities and neighborhoods open the door to expanding knowledge of its inhabitants. That often leads to a better understanding of the conditions and opportunities in each of these areas. New development, improvements to services, correction to problems, innovation, and improved economic prospects are examples of potential outcomes resulting from the availability of complete and accurate census statistical data.

Geospatial information is needed for each phase of the census—collecting the data, tabulating the counted household numbers, disseminating aggregated tabulations, and analyzing the results of the census. National Statistical Offices (NSOs) may have a small cadre of geographers to support statistical work. Conducting a census requires geospatial information normally maintained by a National Mapping Agency (NMA) or National Geospatial Agency (NGA). For this reason alone, a national census is a collaborative effort. It is best for NSOs and NMAs or NGAs to work together on this common national goal.

The United Nations is leading efforts on the importance of data. In 2011, it formed a Committee of Experts on Global Geospatial Information Management (UN-GGIM). NGAs and NSOs actively work together on important topics to advance their mandate (http://ggim.un.org/). Since its inception, much good work has been done that helps nations plan and conduct their national census. Topics like global fundamental geospatial data themes, the integration of statistical and geospatial information, geodetic reference frames that contribute to data quality, and geospatial information supporting the Sustainable Development Goals, for which significant amounts of census data are required, are examples of work underway.

To ensure that each household is included in the census, the country usually is divided into some type of enumeration area (EA) or enumeration district (ED). No area is left out of this delineation. Enumerators are then assigned to one or more EAs and they conduct the count. Enumerators must know *where* the EA is and what its boundaries are so that they neither undercount nor overcount within their assignment area. A census map that shows the details of an EA is needed to ensure that assignments are known and clear. This minimally includes the EA boundary, roads, paths, and observable features like rivers as well as geographic names for orientation.

Today, technology has simplified past practices in census taking. A phone or tablet enabled with GPS can assist enumerators in knowing where they are relative to their assignment area, which is depicted on a map on their mobile device. Systematically walking to each household, recording its location, and recording answers to the census questionnaire links the important raw data offered by the respondent to a geographic location. The confidentiality of each household's response is paramount in gaining support from respondents for their participation in a census. Security of the data takes on new forms with each technological development.

The confidentiality of responses is assured through various statistical techniques and checks. A household's response with its location is used in adding that response to others within the EA, thereby aggregating the results to a larger geographic area. Using the geographic code of the response (geocode) makes this possible. This allows us to aggregate the data together with other responses within predefined geographic areas that are deemed important for various uses of census data—for example, the combined numbers for the EA or a village or city. This begins the tabulation phase of a census.

It is crucial that data disseminated from a census offer complete and accurate results. While important, having results only at a national level is extremely limiting to the value of a census. The more data that is available and the smaller the level of geography in which data is made available multiplies the positive benefits to the residents of a nation and its communities.

In 2015, the UN Sustainable Development Agenda was agreed to by nations of the world. With 17 goals, 169 targets, and over 230 indicators, the need for small-area data is now paramount if we are to realize the vision of leaving no one behind. The availability of statistical data from the census aligns with determining the appropriate level of geography to meet not only the basic indicator framework but also, ultimately, the intersection of targets and indicators for more complex relationships.

The notion of counting people seems fairly simple. While the basic task of enumerating the population is manageable, many factors complicate this important government function. Counting everyone, regardless of how difficult or how remote; completing census operations and tabulating results in a short time frame; assuring the security of enumerators and the census process; hiring and assigning sufficient numbers of census takers and supervisors; counting everyone once, only once, and in the right location; applying tested cost-effective technologies; evaluating coverage and accuracy of the census; assigning the results to the correct meaningful geography; and widely disseminating results in a timely way are but a few of the challenges in planning and implementing a national census.

Not many books tell you how to conduct a census. In fact, no single book can serve as a recipe for conducting the census. Each country differs in its circumstances. Mandates to carry out censuses vary. The readiness and preparations needed for embarking on a census differ. Even with these diverse variables, important references such as *GIS and the 2020 Census: Modernizing Official Statistics* offer guidance and help in this critically important government responsibility. Sources like this book help countries account for basic functions and address evolving technologies that can simplify and improve the inordinate scope of conducting a census.

A census is, without question, the largest civilian activity for a nation, larger than a national election or any similar activity. Because it is household based, knowing the geographical location of each household is important to ensure that everyone is included. It consists of many linked operations that span multiple activities for planning, for conducting the census, for processing the numbers, and for disseminating the results. Each activity offers opportunities for problems and challenges. The effective use of GIS technology minimizes risks associated with traditional manual approaches that oftentimes are related to those problems and challenges. As census workers encounter questions or seek solutions to a problem, or look to technology to solve a challenge, reaching for *GIS and the 2020 Census: Modernizing Official Statistics* is a good first step toward realizing a positive outcome.

Preface

GIS and the 2020 Census: Modernizing Official Statistics is designed with National Statistical Offices (NSOs) in mind and is meant to provide guidance in conducting GIS-based census and survey work. It is intended to address technical and practical issues concerning statistical organizations as they prepare for the 2020 Round of Censuses and beyond. This book is not meant to be a geographic information systems (GIS) textbook. Esri offers many different textbooks and training materials that can be used to learn the GIS functions and concepts presented in this book.

The term *country* as used in this publication also refers to territories or areas, as appropriate.

Many GIS terms are used throughout this book. If you are unfamiliar with any GIS term, please refer to the Esri GIS Dictionary at https://support.esri.com/en/other-resources/gis-dictionary. This online dictionary contains thousands of terms and definitions. Esri teams manage this resource and keep it current.

In addition, online ancillary material for this book is provided at esri.com/Census2020. The ancillary material includes the following resources:

- Chapter 2—UN recommendations on geographic products
  - Source: *UN Handbook on the Management of Population and Housing Censuses*, rev. 2, available at https://unstats.un.org/unsd/publication/seriesF/Series_F83Rev2en.pdf
- Chapter 4—updated census data model
- Chapter 6—characteristics of the main commercial earth observation satellites
- Chapter 7—"ArcGIS Secure Mobile Implementation Patterns" (Esri white paper also available at http://downloads.esri.com/resources/enterprisegis/Esri%20Whitepaper%20-%20ArcGIS%20Secure%20Mobile%20Implementation%20Patterns.pdf)
- Global Statistical Geospatial Framework referenced throughout the book (available at http://ggim.un.org/meetings/GGIM-committee/8th-Session/documents/Global-Statistical-Geospatial-Framework-July-2018.pdf)

Contributions and acknowledgments

Designer: Steve Pablo
Editors: David Oberman, Sasha Gallardo, and Stacy Krieg
Project director: Linda Peters

Other contributors included Andre Nonguierma, Bolaji Taiwo, Charlie Frye, Donald Steinmetz, Jean-Michel Durr, Kurt Schwoppe, Roberto Bianchini, and Timothy Trainor.

This book features the work of several Esri colleagues, including cartographers and data scientists. Thanks to Adam Mollenkopf, Andrew Skinner, Gerry Clancy, Greg Pleiss, Jennifer Bell, Jim Herries, Lisa Berry, and Mark Romero.

Special thanks to Albania Institute of Statistics, Central Agency for Public Mobilization and Statistics Egypt, Central Bureau of Statistics Nepal, Central Statistics Office Ireland, Department of Statistics Jordan, Instituto Nacional Estatística Portugal, Philippine Statistics Authority, and Statistics Canada for sharing their case studies so others can learn.

Thanks to Barbara Shields, Brian Beha, Carmelle Terborgh, Catherine Ortiz, Charles Brigham, Clint Brown, David Oberman, Deepti Kochhar, Eric Laycock, Gerry Clancy, Ismael Chivite, Jeanne Flores, Jeanne Foust, John Day, Kathleen Ojo, Leslie Barlow, Mike Livingston, Richard Ybarra, Stacy Krieg, Steve Pablo, and Thomas Sweet for project support, feedback, guidance, and input.

Finally, thanks to the worldwide GIS user community and NSOs around the globe for doing amazing work with ArcGIS technology.

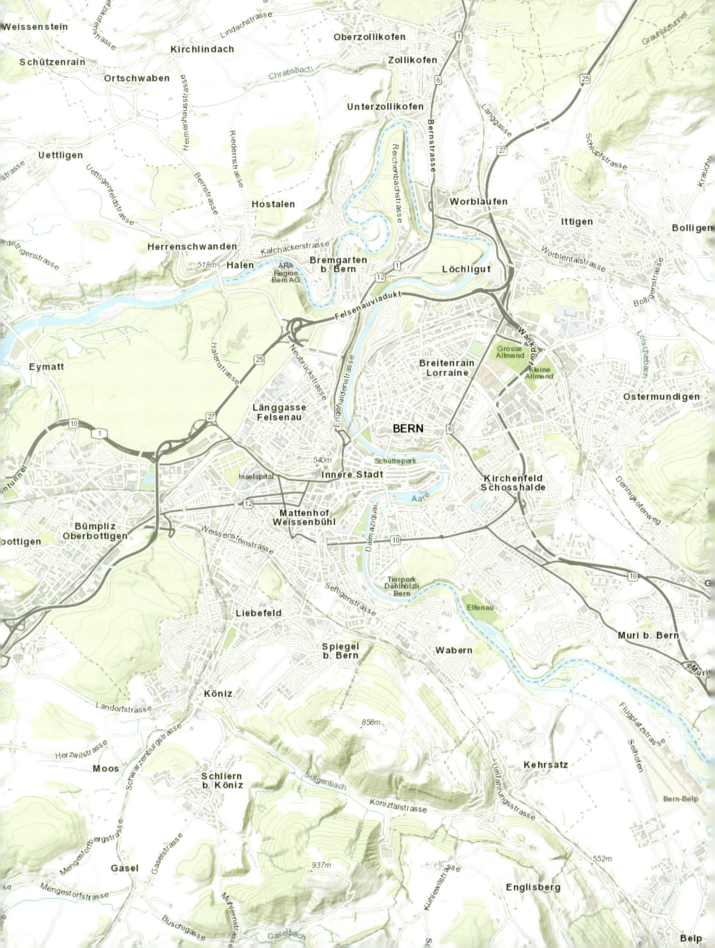

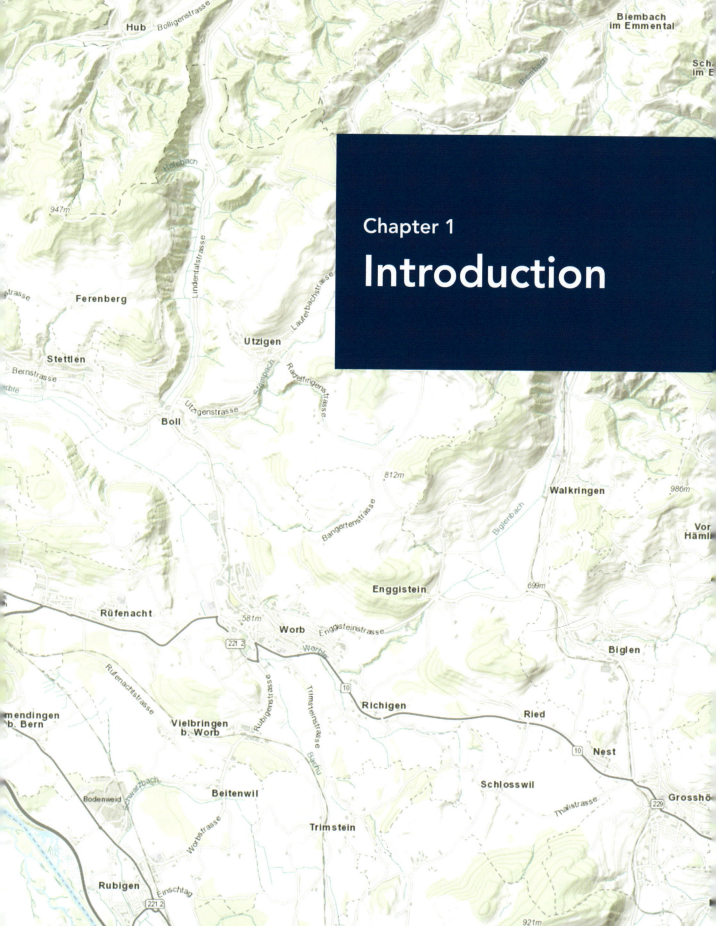

Chapter 1
Introduction

Rationale, scope, and purpose

GIS and the 2020 Census: Modernizing Official Statistics supports the transformation of countries' censuses with the use of geographic information systems (GIS) and related geospatial technologies to improve data collection, analysis, and dissemination and to enable agencies to build accurate, authoritative, actionable data. The book is specifically intended to provide an up-to-date reference and guide for using geospatial methodologies and techniques to support census and statistical operations.[1] A comprehensive user-oriented guide, the book addresses the needs of census geographers, planners, and managers at all the stages of a census and caters to the needs of the various users of statistical and geospatial products and services.

The increasing use and application of modern geospatial technologies[2] worldwide, particularly during the upcoming round of censuses, have opened a new chapter in all phases of population and housing censuses, improving the efficiency in pre-enumeration, enumeration, and post-enumeration phases. This statement can be attested by Esri through its involvement in many census mapping projects and confirmed by the United Nations (UN) *Principles and Recommendations for Population and Housing Censuses*, the outcomes of a global consultation for the 2020 Round of Census. Rapid changes in technology have brought about improvements in many areas such as computing power, storage, speed, and analytics. Recently, a paradigm shift in the acquisition, resolution, storage, analysis, and distribution of imagery has brought raster analytics to the forefront of projects, offering exponential advances in speed, accuracy, and cost reductions. Digital transformations such as these will have a huge impact on the work of the National Statistical Office (NSO).

A new pattern emerged in conducting censuses during the last decade—a pattern that has ushered in the recognition of the central role of geography to census operations.[3] Geography is increasingly acknowledged as key to virtually all national statistics systems, providing a structure for collecting, processing, aggregating, managing, analyzing, sharing, and disseminating data. In its digital form, geospatial information is exchanged more rapidly, used and reused at will, duplicated without alteration, and easily disseminated to end users. In addition, this geospatial data needs to adhere to the wide variety of security and privacy concerns that are also at the heart of most censuses.

The UN recommended the necessity for countries to keep abreast of technological advances made since the previous round, especially in GIS and Global Positioning Systems (GPS). The UN also recommended that, for the 2020 Round of Censuses, the adoption of GIS should be a major strategic decision.[4] The UN Statistical Commission (UNSC) and the UN Committee of Experts on Global Geospatial Information Management (UN-GGIM) recognized the crucial importance of the integration of statistical and geospatial information for decision-making and have recently recommended the development of a Global Statistical Geospatial Framework (GSGF).[5]

In recognition of this important recommendation, the UNSC and the UN-GGIM began to address the challenges of managing and effectively integrating geospatial and statistical information nationally and globally. They established in 2013 the Expert Group on the Integration of Statistical and Geospatial Information (EG-ISGI). The Expert Group was tasked with developing and advancing the implementation of a GSGF as a basis for the integration of statistical and geospatial information and supporting the building of a statistical-geospatial infrastructure, especially in the context of the 2030 Agenda for Sustainable Development. This importance was also recognized by UN-GGIM regional committees, where it is considered a key priority.[6]

Global Statistical Geospatial Framework

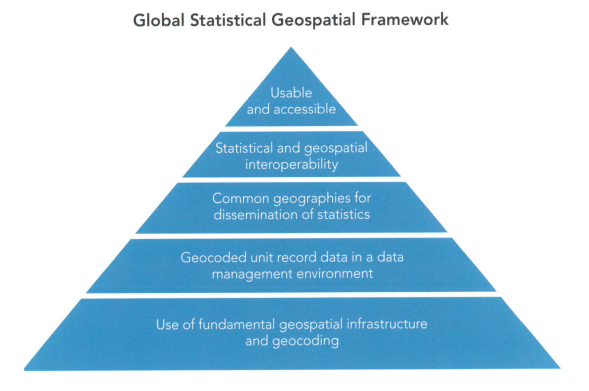

Figure 1.1. The Global Statistical Geospatial Framework (GSGF).

These recent technological developments have already been adopted by many NSOs, including some developing countries. The wealth of national experiences demonstrates that the use and application of GIS is without exception beneficial to the efficiency and quality of the population and housing census. It is understood, however, that a single solution will not fit all national circumstances; hence, there is a need to present various options with guidance to NSOs, allowing them to choose the appropriate solution for their national and local conditions or policies. This book provides guidelines for NSOs to make informed decisions on appropriate GIS technology and how to efficiently use GIS in statistical business processes, taking into consideration different procedures, workflows, organization capabilities, budgets, census timelines, security and application needs, and best practices.

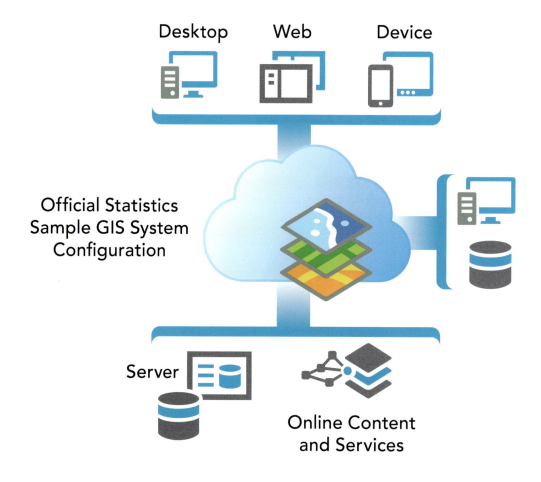

Figure 1.2. Example of a GIS with various types of connections (web, desktop, and mobile).

Importance of the integration of statistical and geospatial data

The rapid development of modern geospatial technologies has created unprecedented opportunities for geospatial data, and GIS has drastically increased the quantity and quality of geospatial data being collected from a variety of sources. For example, users have access today to imagery that would have been expensive and limited in the past.[7] Geospatial information is becoming a major economic activity with applications across many sectors, bringing increased utility to these sectors and impacting business decisions (Foresman and Luscombe 2017).

With the increasing complexity of national and global challenges, the need to understand interrelationships across the economic, social, and environmental dimensions is crucial for sustainable development at all levels, and the integration of information by geography is critical to designing holistic solutions for any locale. The demand is growing for information on small geographic areas to monitor the development goals and indicators at local and community scales. The integration of statistical and geospatial information has become a significant way to unlock new insights that would otherwise not have been possible by looking at socioeconomic or geospatial data in isolation. It is now understood that the integration of geospatial data with statistics provides significant benefits for nations, as opposed to one-dimensional traditional approaches.

For example, such integration has proved to be critical in achieving improved operational readiness and responsiveness to disasters. By using satellite imagery, scientists and demographers can compare images and statistics taken before and after earthquakes or flooding to estimate the amount of aid to be allocated to populated areas or select safe places in which to temporarily settle the affected population. Using statistical analysis and statistical mapping to study the patterns of urban or rural poverty is a well-established way to provide useful, policy-relevant insights into the patterns of social exclusion and deprivation for local governance policymakers (Baud et al. 2009). Many such examples are related to the increased use of geospatial data in socioeconomic, demographic, and environmental analysis.

Knowing where people and things are and their relationship to one another provides context and improves understanding, aiding in evidence-based decision-making. The geocode is considered one of the basic uniting elements in statistics to which characteristics of persons, households, and enterprises can be attributed.

In this digital-economic age, geospatial technologies are expanding the power of geography and location, from the limited geographical proximity object of Tobler's First Law of Geography to a richer research frontier, enabling us to explore the economic and social impacts of location and spatial relationships. This power is leading geographers to cogitate about a Second Law of Geography for a spatially enabled economy, allowing us to understand why spatial enablement increases functional utility across sectors (Foresman and Luscombe 2017).

The First Law of Geography states that "everything is related to everything else, but near things are more related than distant things."

Waldo Tobler

It is worth noting that the integration of statistical and geospatial information should be seen in the context of a wider integration of data from a variety of sources. This integration reflects the trends of today's data-driven society through the big data revolution, characterized by satellite imagery, unmanned aerial vehicle (UAV) data, GPS, mobile technology and GIS surveying, volunteered geographic information (VGI) and crowd-sourced data, real-time data streams, cloud-based computing, open data, the Internet of Things (IoT), and geoblockchain. Most studies have stated that spatially enabled data represents at least eighty percent of all data generated within the big data revolution (Foresman and Luscombe 2017).

In today's global community, there is a clear recognition of the need to integrate geospatial and statistical information;[8] the challenge being faced is how best to achieve this integration in an effective and consistent way. It was noted that many NSOs are already transforming, or are planning to transform, their statistical infrastructure, offering an opportunity to embed geography into their national systems and processes. NSOs have been moving from the census mapping approach, limited to the use of GIS for some mapping and dissemination operations, to a GIS-based approach where geography is the foundation of the census, with the use of GIS and other core geospatial technologies at all stages. There is an increasing recognition that the adoption of a geographic-based approach with full integration of statistical and geospatial information has an important role in the modernization of statistics.[9]

GIS can help NSOs realize benefits in terms of reduction of cost and time required, accuracy and quality improvements, and efficiencies in collecting, processing, and communicating information, which all greatly increase the return on investment.[10]

The initial chapters of this book consider the role of GIS in the census, including planning and establishing a full digital GIS-based census program, as well as the importance of geodatabase development. GIS topics relevant to pre-enumeration and enumeration, including the benefits of a digital approach in using GIS throughout statistical business processes, are also addressed. More specifically, for data collection purposes, the book addresses how in a census NSOs need to look at the finest level of geography possible (dwelling and unit level) and capture information at that level. Other chapters focus on post-enumeration GIS tasks and the use of digital mapping in presenting, analyzing, and disseminating census data and marketing geographic products and data. A final chapter presents next-generation trends, focusing on big data and geoanalytics.

The book provides statistical organizations with the contemporary methodologies to address user needs at all stages of a census during the 2020 round. Readers will learn how to plan and carry out work using GIS in all phases of a census.

References

- Baud et al. 2009. "Matching Deprivation Mapping to Urban Governance in Three Indian Megacities." *Habitat International*.
- GI for Census by the Program Review of the 2010 Round of Censuses carried out by the US Census Bureau for the UNSC in 2015.

- Report on *National Statistical and Geographical Institute of Brazil: Global Geographic Information Management*, presented at the forty-first session of the UN Statistical Commission. 2010. E/CN.3/2010/13. Available at https://unstats.un.org/unsd/statcom/doc10/2010-13-Brazil-GGIM-E.pdf.
- Tim Foresman and Ruth Luscombe. 2017. "The Second Law of Geography for a Spatially Enabled Economy." *International Journal of Digital Earth*.
- UN Economic Commission for Africa/African Centre for Statistics (ACS). 2010. *The 2010 Round of Population and Housing Censuses: A Guide on Census Planning and Enumeration for African Countries*.
- UN Expert Group on the Integration of Statistical and Geospatial Information. 2016. *Background Document on Proposal for a Global Statistical Geospatial Framework*. Available at http://ggim.un.org/docs/meetings/Global%20Forum/Summary-report%20of%20the%20Global%20Forum.pdf.
- United Nations Statistics Division. 2017. *Principles and Recommendations for Population and Housing Censuses*, rev. 3. New York: United Nations Publication. Available at https://unstats.un.org/unsd/publication/seriesM/Series_M67Rev3en.pdf.
- US Census Bureau. 2015. *New Technologies in Census Geographic Listing: Select Topics in International Censuses*. Available at https://www.census.gov/content/dam/Census/library/working-papers/2015/demo/new-tech-census-geo.pdf.

Notes

1. While the main focus of the book is on field-based census approaches and operations, similar GIS techniques can be applied in register-based censuses as well.
2. Geospatial technologies refer to all the means used for the measurement, analysis, and visualization of features or phenomena that occur on earth. They include three core technologies that are all related to mapping features on the surface of the earth: remote sensing (RS), Global Positioning System (GPS), and GIS.
3. The objective of a census is to "count everyone, count them once only, and count them in the right place," according to Preston Jay Waite (US Census Bureau), former associate director for decennial census, US Department of Commerce.
4. See *Principles and Recommendations*.
5. See details on the GSGF in chapter 2.
6. See details at http://ggim.un.org/regional-entities/.
7. See *National Statistical and Geographical Institute of Brazil: Global Geographic Information Management*, a report presented at the forty-first session of the UNSC (E/CN.3/2010/13) in February 2010. Available at https://unstats.un.org/unsd/statcom/doc10/2010-13-Brazil-GGIM-E.pdf.
8. See *Principles and Recommendations*, para. 3.49: "To ensure complete integration of statistical and geospatial information."
9. See the UN Economic and Social Council's *In-Depth Review of Developing Geospatial Information Services Based on Official Statistics: Note by the United Kingdom Office for National Statistics*. CES. ECE/CES/2016/7.
10. See UNECA/ACS' *The 2010 Round of Population and Housing Censuses: A Guide on Census Planning and Enumeration for African Countries*.

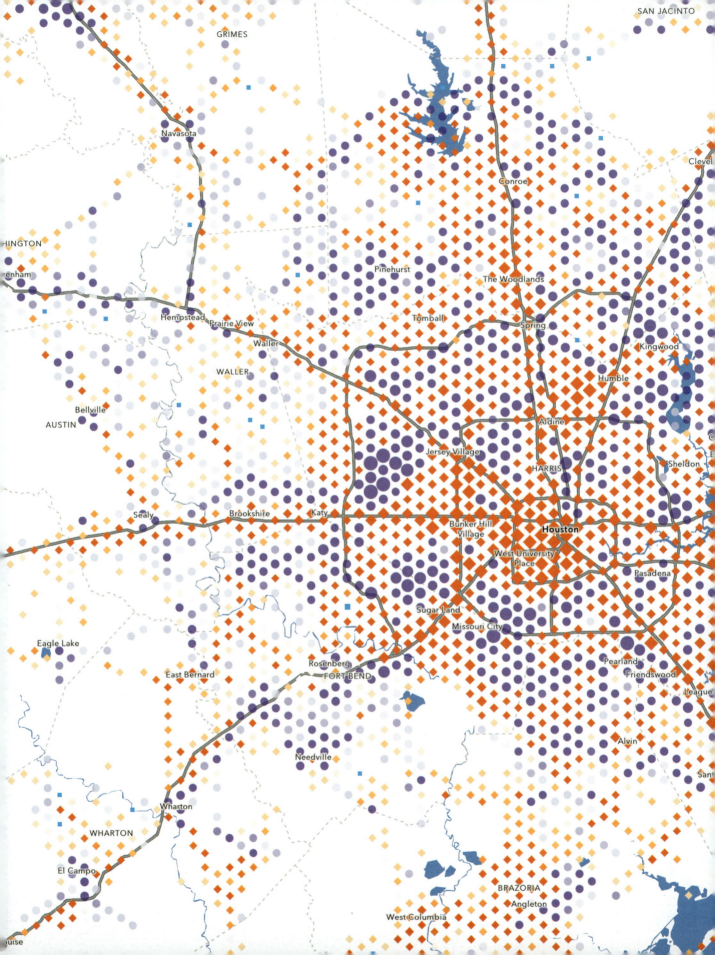

Chapter 2
The role of GIS in census

Planning the census process with GIS

Census geography program

In most countries in the world, a population and housing census is conducted periodically, at least once every ten years in accordance with the UN *Principles and Recommendations*.[1] A population and housing census is considered the greatest democratic operation because it is conducted at the individual or household level, providing information on the main characteristics of a country's entire population in terms of size, geographic distribution, and demographic, social, economic, housing, and living conditions.[2]

Mapping is generally recognized as one of the most crucial activities of a census, playing a critical role in providing the geographic basis used during the actual process of enumeration. Owing to recent technological developments in GIS and other geospatial technologies, the scope of census mapping has been extended to census data analysis and dissemination, with greater efficiency in data collection and enumeration. However, there are some challenges in opting for a full digital census-mapping approach; the use of these technologies has crucial impacts during mapping activities, data collection, processing, analysis, dissemination, evaluation, and archiving, and should therefore be taken into account at an early stage of census planning. Embarking on a GIS-based census should be planned and implemented in a consistent and timely manner.

GIS should be considered an integral part of the census process and carried out continually as a long-term strategy rather than a set of short-term stand-alone mapping and dissemination operations (figure 2.1).

A GIS-based census program aims to achieve the following objectives:

- Support the census planning process.
- Support fieldwork, field operations, and operations management.
- Improve the efficiency and accuracy of the data collected.
- Contribute to analysis.
- Contribute to the dissemination of the census data.
- Integrate statistical and geospatial information for data analysis and evidence-based decision-making and for future censuses and surveys.[3]

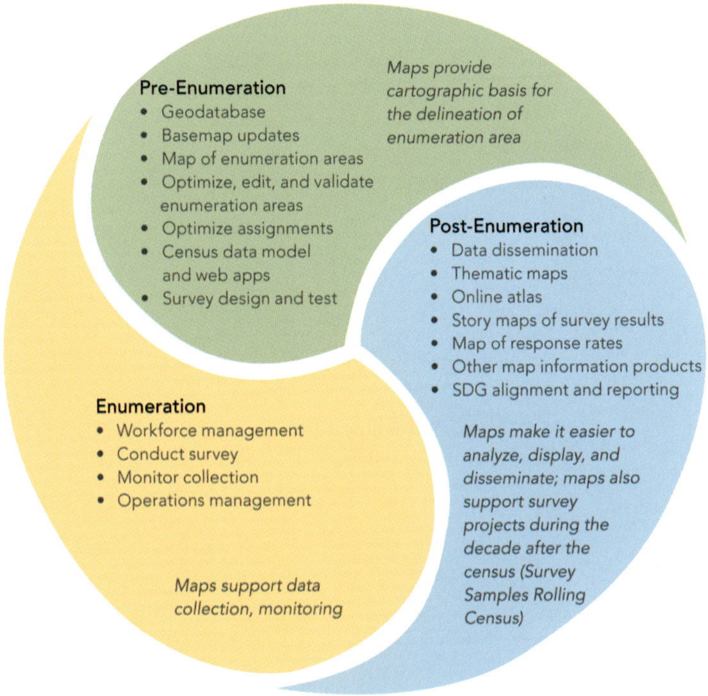

Pre-Enumeration
- Geodatabase
- Basemap updates
- Map of enumeration areas
- Optimize, edit, and validate enumeration areas
- Optimize assignments
- Census data model and web apps
- Survey design and test

Maps provide cartographic basis for the delineation of enumeration area

Post-Enumeration
- Data dissemination
- Thematic maps
- Online atlas
- Story maps of survey results
- Map of response rates
- Other map information products
- SDG alignment and reporting

Maps make it easier to analyze, display, and disseminate; maps also support survey projects during the decade after the census (Survey Samples Rolling Census)

Enumeration
- Workforce management
- Conduct survey
- Monitor collection
- Operations management

Maps support data collection, monitoring

Figure 2.1. The evolving GIS role in census phases.

Quality Management / Metadata Management							
Specify Needs	Design	Build	Collect	Process	Analyse	Disseminate	Evaluate
1.1 Identify needs	2.1 Design outputs	3.1 Build collection instrument	4.1 Create frame & select sample	5.1 Integrate data	6.1 Prepare draft outputs	7.1 Update output systems	8.1 Gather evaluation inputs
1.2 Consult & confirm needs	2.2 Design variable descriptions	3.2 Build or enhance process components	4.2 Set up collection	5.2 Classify & code	6.2 Validate outputs	7.2 Produce dissemination products	8.2 Conduct evaluation
1.3 Establish output objectives	2.3 Design collection	3.3 Build or enhance dissemination components	4.3 Run collection	5.3 Review & validate	6.3 Interpret & explain outputs	7.3 Manage release or dissemination products	8.3 Agree on action plan
1.4 Identify concepts	2.4 Design frame & sample	3.4 Configure workflows	4.4 Finalise collection	5.4 Edit & impute	6.4 Apply disclosure control	7.4 Promote dissemination products	
1.5 Check data availability	2.5 Design processing & analysis	3.5 Test production system		5.5 Derive new variables & units	6.5 Finalise outputs	7.5 Manage user support	
1.6 Prepare business case	2.6 Design production systems & workflow	3.6 Test statistical business process		5.6 Calculate weights			
		3.7 Finalise production system		5.7 Calculate aggregates			
				5.8 Finalise data files			

Figure 2.2. GSBPM, version 5.0, with a description of phases and subprocesses.[4]

Supporting the census planning process

GIS can be applied across the Generic Statistical Business Process Model (GSBPM), shown in figure 2.2. One of the primary objectives of a GIS-based census program is to support the census planning process.

The support includes maximizing coverage while avoiding coverage errors such as noninclusion or double inclusion of units that may result in undercounting or overcounting, respectively. It is important to define explicitly the census geography in terms of hierarchical subdivision of the whole territory into administrative, geographic, and statistical areas, including enumeration areas (EAs) and groups of EAs under the responsibility of supervisors. These geographies are used to estimate the staffing and materials needs and logistics requirements and define the operational zones (or census management areas) for the data collection.

As recommended by *Principles and Recommendations*, the GIS-based census program should be developed at an early stage of census planning to allow sufficient time to produce full national coverage maps (including map services and mobile map packages, which are covered in chapter 6) well before the census date and before the initiation of field-training exercises. Developing a timetable for the GIS and mapping activities is of paramount importance; it's a time-bound operation with the critical date being the date that all enumeration-related maps and map services must be made available to the census field enumeration. This requires the identification of the technical, operational, and institutional tasks to be carried out through the planning process. These tasks include the evaluation of available geographic and technological resources and the critical design issues that determine the nature of the census GIS, with a focus on its core geospatial database and the range of applications that it will support. Of importance is the inventory of existing data, maps, and other geographic data sources such as imagery. Data conversion and integration processes should also be understood—all of these depend on a well-designed environment and a well-planned operational strategy.[5]

The stages for planning geographic work for the census are shown in detail in figures 2.3a and 2.3b.

The planning stages are divided here into institutional issues, such as the user needs assessment, the determination of the GIS strategy, and the scope of census-mapping activities. The stages also include technical issues such as the explicit definition of census geography, the design of the geospatial database, and the development of clear protocols for data collection. These stages can be carried out more or less simultaneously using organizationally approved methodologies, and many of the choices depend also on the chosen data-integration strategy.[6]

These planning steps may seem difficult to follow or be considered costly by some NSOs. However, once a fundamental geospatial infrastructure is established and GIS is integrated into the statistical business process, the efficiencies gained and benefits realized far outweigh any initial costs. Each country needs to have guiding policies in place to tailor the technological options according to its needs and availability of resources. To justify the investments involved, the strategies of the pre-enumeration mapping program by many NSOs are designed to produce the geographical outputs suitable not only for the census enumeration but also for the operational requirements of data collection activities, dissemination activities, and other user applications such as demarcation of electoral boundaries, defining catchment areas of various public services, monitoring and reporting

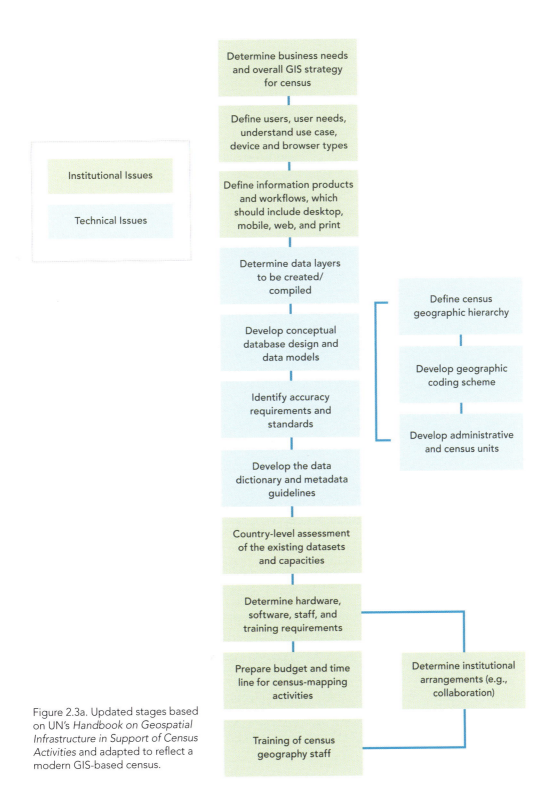

Determine business needs
and overall GIS strategy
for census

Define users, user needs,
understand use case,
device and browser types

Define information products
and workflows, which
should include desktop,
mobile, web, and print

Institutional Issues

Technical Issues

Determine data layers
to be created/
compiled

Develop conceptual
database design and
data models

Define census
geographic hierarchy

Develop geographic
coding scheme

Identify accuracy
requirements and
standards

Develop administrative
and census units

Develop the data
dictionary and metadata
guidelines

Country-level assessment
of the existing datasets
and capacities

Determine hardware,
software, staff, and
training requirements

Prepare budget and time
line for census-mapping
activities

Determine institutional
arrangements (e.g.,
collaboration)

Training of census
geography staff

Figure 2.3a. Updated stages based on UN's *Handbook on Geospatial Infrastructure in Support of Census Activities* and adapted to reflect a modern GIS-based census.

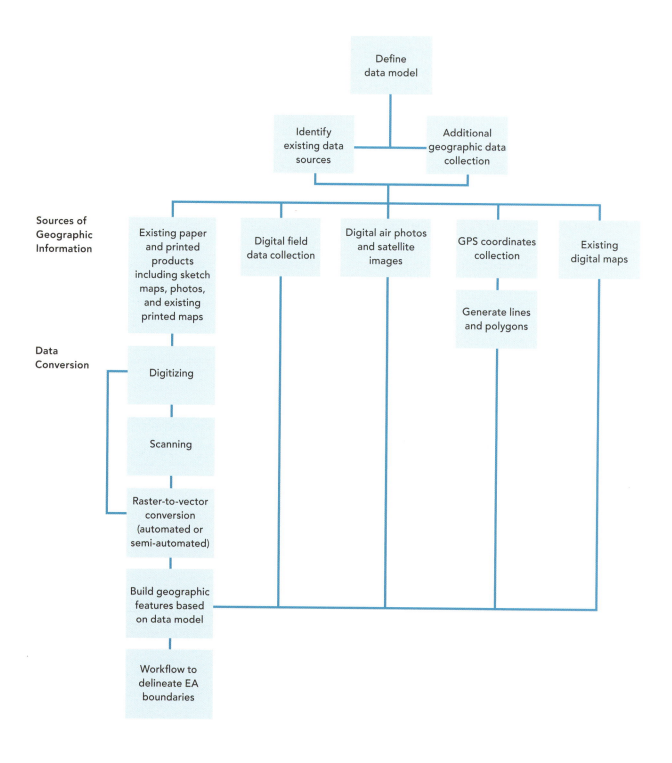

Figure 2.3b. Census planning stages—additional technical issues.

on the Sustainable Development Goals (SDGs), and more. To maximize return on investment in GIS, NSOs should actively participate with other national authorities, including the National Mapping Agencies (NMAs), in establishing a National Spatial Data Infrastructure (NSDI).

GIS planning considerations

The shift from limited census-mapping operations to an entirely GIS-based digital approach that spans across all stages of the census requires the implementation of an enterprise GIS. The planning and implementation of an enterprise GIS for the census should include a cost-benefit analysis to justify the long-term investment in building a GIS infrastructure. It should also require a comprehensive user-needs assessment; lessons learned from many GIS projects show that a GIS is successful when it provides outputs that meet well-defined user needs. The user-needs analysis should also assess the available technology in the market and allow the evaluation of different GIS software options to define the most suitable GIS capabilities for census purposes. More specifically, understanding the user needs requires understanding the appropriate hardware, software, and related integrated systems that will provide the specific digital products and services needed. Those products and services can range from interactive ad web-based mapping applications, map services, map packages, cloud computing, and mobile apps to spatial analysis and advanced analytics.

GIS-based planning considerations include the preparation of a detailed implementation plan that corresponds to the different operational phases of the census process. In line with the GSBPM and its equivalent for geospatial applications (see figure 2.4), such a plan should address issues related to

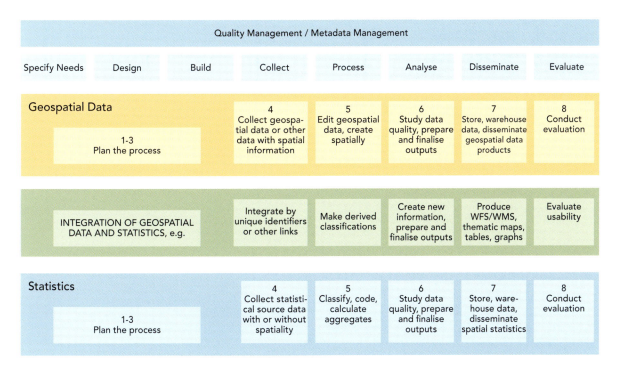

Figure 2.4. The GSBPM and its equivalent dimensions in the production of geospatial data. *Source: A Point-based Foundation for Statistics—Final Report from the GEOSTAT 2 Project.*

the design of the geospatial database, data conversion and integration, and all the other phases of geospatial data production.

Because GIS was not traditionally considered part of the core business of the NSO, awareness workshops about the benefits of GIS should be organized to win executive support for the program. Technical trainings and workshops about the use of GIS should be provided to the staff involved in the census and supporting functions. In addition, the plan should also involve workshops for the major data users about the potential of GIS and draw on institutional mechanisms to mobilize cooperation among all stakeholders to establish a GIS infrastructure at a national level.

GIS can be leveraged to support a wide variety of activities across the entire census process. Following are some examples of how GIS is being applied today in census preparation. These activities will create the foundation for all census work to follow:

- Creation or updates to geodatabase and basemaps.
- Creation or updates and validation of EAs.
  - Production of digital EA maps for fieldwork and operations.
  - Use of remote-sensed data in EA creation or update.
  - In-office address canvassing can be done using imagery where applicable and where quality data is available.
  - Where in-office validation is not possible, maps can be used in field verification or *in situ* validation.
  - Integrating fieldwork using remote-sensed data.
- Conducting GIS analysis to ensure complete and balanced coverage. Overlaying EA maps on a

scaled national basemap to ensure the absence of omissions or duplications.
- Applying GIS analysis to facilitate efficient census operations.
  - Using GIS analysis to determine the most efficient placement of field offices.
  - GIS-based analysis to optimize allocation of field-workers to EAs based on various criteria such as language, distance, hours of work, and more.
- Creation of map services (the way maps are made available to the web).
- Creation of mobile map packages (the way maps are made available on a mobile device in an offline mode).

More details are provided in the following sections and subsequent chapters.

Needs assessment

It is generally recognized that a well-defined plan that involves various users with different data needs should be prepared at an early stage. Using geospatial information technology in all the stages of a census requires even more focus and the need to identify, understand, and plan how to address the specific GIS and mapping needs and expectations of the main user groups, as well as the census geographic products required.

The needs assessment plan should include strategies on the content to be discussed during the consultations with users, questions on the ways census products will be accessed (device type) and used as well as their presentation, and the kind of training that needs to be provided to users.

Conducting a comprehensive needs assessment with a business need–driven approach rather than a technology-driven approach helps to define user needs. The assessment should also identify any available resources within the NSO (and in the country), such as maps suitable for the census operations, existing software packages and related equipment, qualified staff in GIS, and financial resources for the GIS-based census program. This identification will assist in reconciling user expectations with what is feasible given available resources, working backward from final products and services to requirements.[7]

The next section will elaborate on the needs assessment of the main user groups: (a) major users of census data, (b) persons and institutions participating in the census operations, and (c) the general public and civil society.

Major users of census data

A user-oriented census provides major data users—governmental departments, local administrations, the academic and research sector, and the private sector—with easy access and clear understanding of the statistics available, enabling them to benefit from census results. One of the major impacts of a GIS-based census is the extension of the community of users, interested in statistics with a geographic dimension. The assessment of needs in this case includes consultation on demographic and geographic content desired, geographic structures such as administrative hierarchies or geographic units needed for data collection or data aggregation,

and geographic base products (maps, imagery, and other remotely sensed data) that support analysis and dissemination of census data. A consultation of the needs of these major users is necessary to determine the form and scope of data to be disseminated and to ultimately understand their expectations in terms of census geographic data products.

Persons and institutions participating in the census operations

Evaluating the needs for census-mapping activities is equally important for the persons (employees and contractors) and institutions participating in the census operations. To obtain an understanding of existing resources and requirement gaps, the NSO must carry out a survey of available human resources, hardware, and software, and must conduct an inventory of existing data (in digital format and on paper) and any requirements for data conversion. The NSO should also understand any ongoing or planned relevant GIS-oriented activities by other public and private entities. The purpose of this assessment is to avoid duplicating efforts, which is key to reducing the cost of census geographic operations and delivering census products on time.[8]

Conducting a comprehensive needs assessment to answer some of the critical questions shown in the following table will help the NSO consider which new technologies to adopt to modernize the census process.

Figure 2.5. Critical questions that NSOs should consider for a needs assessment.

Critical questions	Example areas to be considered
What strategy will be adopted for the use of geospatial technology?	Will the agency use GIS technology throughout the statistical process and across the organization? Or will it be used only in certain functional areas (e.g., if GIS is adopted it can serve as the base for future surveys beyond population and housing such as agriculture, labor force, etc.), thereby improving return on investment for the organization?
What are the costs involved?	What are the costs required to adopt the geospatial technology, including costs for new hardware, upgrades of hardware, or existing software and any data needed? This should include an understanding and consideration of ongoing needs to maintain the systems whether purchased outright or built in-house.
What advantages are expected to be realized?	Identify the benefits that the use of geospatial technology will bring to the census (e.g., improved accuracy, efficiencies in operations, cost savings, or delivery of data in a timelier manner).
What are the costs or benefits of implementing this new system or method for the agency?	Proceed with a cost-benefit analysis to justify the GIS-based method.
What is the ease or difficulty of installing and maintaining hardware or software?	Ease of installation and maintenance are concerns for many NSOs because they may not have technical expertise on staff to support. NSOs may need to consider outsourcing or cloud-based deployments, for example.
Are both the software and the database scalable? To what extent can the system manage peak loads?	The performance of both the GIS software and the geospatial database should be scalable: able to grow and be used for multiple purposes. Appropriate system sizing and scaling will need to be done to consider peak upload periods across all systems.
What type of users will access the system?	Some types may include employees, field supervisors, area managers, executives, contractors, citizens, and application developers. How will their identity be defined, and what will they have access to?

Figure 2.5. Critical questions. (continued)

Critical questions	Example areas to be considered
What types of accessibility?	• What type of device(s) will be used to access? • What functionality is required or allowed by the user? • Will workers be both online and off-line?
What kind of mapping, GIS, and imagery capabilities are needed?	• Do executives, field supervisors, or area supervisors (for example) need different tools? • Are there plans to use a street basemap or an image basemap or both? • What scale or resolution is required? • What geographic reference layers (infrastructure, natural environment) are needed?
What other data should be considered?	• How will administrative data be used? • Are geographic names or searches required? • What point of interest (POI) data is needed (hospitals, schools, etc.)?
What measures should be taken for geocoding?	• What level of accuracy is needed in geocoding? • What geocodes will need to be captured, updated, and used?
What support will be required?	• Documentation and reference manuals. • Help and vendor support: o Availability of local support from the vendor to provide any needed support in a reasonable amount of time.

What are the staff training needs?	• Is this existing workforce adequately trained? If not, can training be provided in time frames needed?
	• More specifically:
	  o Are staff trained in the production of maps and cartographic databases?
	  o Are staff trained in the creation of map services?
	  o Are staff trained in basic GIS concepts, implementation, and data management?

Figure 2.5. Critical questions. (continued)

Critical questions	Example areas to be considered
What are additional key considerations about EA maps, devices, imagery, and GPS?	• Device needs should include GPS and built-in maps based on current available digital geography. • Device or application needs to allow for edits to census geography in the field. • Device needs to allow for secure capture of survey data in the field in both online and offline modes. • EA maps should be designed for ease of use by enumerator. • EA maps should be designed for efficiency. • Use of satellite imagery to verify boundaries and identify new buildings and housing locations. • Use of GPS to georeference points including housing location and important landmarks.
What security needs should be considered?	Can the GIS integrate with existing security systems and does it allow for industry-standard security principles and controls to be applied at all levels?

Cost-benefit analysis

An important component of needs assessment is to proceed with a cost-benefit analysis. A consideration of the costs and benefits of using GIS (and other geospatial technologies) across all stages of the census is essential for making informed decisions about how much to invest and showing the benefits from GIS use. The costs, as stated earlier, include the acquisition of equipment, software, maintenance, services, hiring additional staff or training existing staff, acquiring data from outside the NSO, and data conversion costs. Benefits can be achieved in many areas including time and cost savings, improvements in staff effectiveness and efficiency, improvements in accuracy, and the earlier dissemination of finished products.

Country experiences have shown that the benefits derived from the use of GIS include productivity gain and time savings; cost savings; cost avoidance; greater credibility and authority of geographic and map products and survey data; better service; increased accuracy; improved consistency; income generation; improved analysis; improved policy-making; improved data sharing; and improved outreach.[9] While measuring all the expected benefits can be difficult because they are only partially quantitative, their impact in terms of improvement of data accuracy and data quality—the ultimate purpose of a census—is recognized by countries that use a comprehensive, large-scale GIS in their censuses.

General public and civil society needs

Rapid changes in technology, combined with the growing demand by the public and civil society for data and information access and transparency, are shaping the needs of users in the community. In some cases, it is necessary to provide specific data or access to meet the needs of these users, as individuals or communities. Community engagement is key for organizations as producers of official statistics. Citizens and civil society alike need to fundamentally understand the issues of the day and where change is needed, which comes from NSO authoritative data.

Modern geospatial platforms provide easy-to-use tools (e.g., apps) for data sharing and collaboration, which allow for even more citizen engagement. NSOs may need to educate the general public about the power of geospatial tools in conveying census information to users, and how spatial analysis related to GIS capabilities allows users to analyze and visualize data, leading to a more meaningful interpretation of results. For example, census data is essential and most relevant in public safety efforts. NSOs must also keep abreast of and anticipate the general public demand for their data, including the need for data to support the understanding and reporting on the UN SDGs (see the case study on Ireland and SDGs in chapter 8).

Information product needs

The ultimate purpose of conducting a comprehensive needs assessment of the three user groups is to determine the range of output or information products that need to be completed both throughout and at the end of the GIS-based census program. This determination allows the NSO to rethink the geographic products from the users' perspective, and how to make them available in a form suited to their needs supplemented by proper and useful documentation, including metadata.

Generally, the geographic information products include digital EA maps for the creation of aggregate dissemination areas; geographic boundary files in digital format that provide statistical reporting units used for census dissemination and spatial analysis; a road network file in digital form representing the country's national road network and containing information on street names and types for all major urban areas;[10] and correspondence files that indicate how current reporting units relate to those used in previous censuses and facilitate a comparison between sequential censuses (see the online ancillaries at esri.com/Census2020).

Other information products may include the list of changes to municipal boundaries showing the

Volunteered geographic information

Public demand for information is expanding rapidly, as is "citizen science"—the scientific research conducted, in whole or in part, by amateur scientists. A widespread community engagement called volunteered geographic information (VGI) is popularizing the creation, sharing, and use of geospatial data, often through smart phones, social media, and online mapping tools, and acting as a valuable mechanism to encourage public participation and citizen engagement in geospatial information. VGI, crowdsourced data, and social media may provide essential information to citizens and local knowledge to communities on their neighborhoods, health facilities, zoning conditions, or even the damage from flooding or some other local disaster. Citizens and particularly some focus groups may need statistical data to combine with field data to create community mapping. Even though the quality or accuracy of such mapping may not be high, the speed of collection and mapping of the data can be performed easily, making it useful for an early response.

changes brought to municipal boundaries, status, and names that occurred between the current and previous census; a set of vector layers containing feature data, such as landmarks, roads, schools, health facilities, etc., which can be used for population-based spatial analysis; centroids/point-based files (point data based on GPS coordinates or individual addresses) that provide respectively geographic point reference for each reporting unit and other geographic features (such as dwellings, places, etc.); and gazetteers that provide geographic coordinates and naming for all population settlements and other important geographic entities in the country (such as administrative units, places, and census units).[11] Modern systems also allow for the creation of operational dashboards which can be useful during the full census cycle, giving transparency and increasing communication and collaboration across teams. Finally, in dissemination, many different types of information products may be required, including maps, story maps, atlases, online web applications, and more (more details are provided in chapter 9).

Success factors

Besides conducting a comprehensive needs assessment that helps adequately define the user needs and identify the available resources within the NSO and in the country, particularly the funding requirements, we need to consider critical factors to succeed in a full digital GIS-based census program. Chief among these factors are: (1) ensuring commitment from senior management for building a long-term digital program; (2) building technical and human capacities required for sustaining the GIS-based systems and databases and setting up an independent unit for cartography/GIS activities within the NSO; (3) using technical standards; (4)

developing a partnership for cooperation with the NMA and other organizations involved in geospatial information activities; and (5) choosing the appropriate methodology of integration of the new geospatial technologies with the census-mapping operations (compatibility). These factors are findings revealed by survey-based studies and lessons learned from country experiences during the last 2010 Round of Censuses.[12] We will elaborate on them in the following sections.

Human factors

While a GIS-based census project may be perceived as technical in nature, what ultimately drives its success often hinges on human factors, particularly in terms of ensuring commitment from senior management for building a long-term program and the true integration of geospatial and statistical data. It is critical, as stated earlier, to consider the GIS-based census program as a long-term program that benefits not only the national census office but also other government agencies and ministries as well as census data users. Approaching GIS as an integral part of the process and knowing that it requires an important initial investment can help achieve a return on investment in the long term.

With any new methodology with little critical mass of experiences known by policy makers and good practices confined to specialists, a promoter and a champion are needed. These people will not only steer the GIS-based census process but will also reach out to the decision makers, advocating for the benefits of using this new approach. A champion can communicate and demonstrate the power of GIS to visualize, explore, and analyze data related to development, ensuring appropriate and timely government support for all aspects of the program.

IT and human capacity building

A GIS-based census program carried out as a continuous process requires an independent geographic information unit to be set up within the NSO, with a permanent staff that can carry out the geospatial analysis and census-mapping tasks spanned over all census stages and between censuses. A permanent unit that can develop partnerships, understand and adhere to data standards and interoperability requirements, forge agreements and contracts for data collection and sharing, and cooperate with the other major actors in building the NSDI of the country is a valuable asset for success. In the absence of in-house GIS capabilities, it becomes difficult for the census office to make qualitative checks on the data created and delivered by the contracted companies. This difficulty may result in the delivery of inaccurate and deficient data, which in turn affects the quality of the geospatial data and map products used for the census.

Building technical and human capacities required for sustaining the GIS-based census program is a recurrent issue to be addressed. Building this capacity requires training personnel with appropriate skills in GIS to serve all census geography needs. A well-trained staff is a key factor for the success of GIS-based census-mapping projects. Country experiences have shown that retaining skilled GIS staff within NSOs is a major issue, particularly with the proliferation of numerous GIS applications unrelated to the census and often commercially more attractive and lucrative. To retain trained qualified staff, NSOs need to provide significant incentives and ensure continual training to keep employees abreast of advances in technology.

Use of standards

Standards are important to every industry and GIS is no exception. The benefits of developing, adopting, and implementing technical standards and common metadata have been recognized by both statistical and geospatial communities. Those benefits enable interoperability and facilitate the integration and use of diverse sources of statistical and geospatial data and services in all sectors of a global economy. It is recognized that the development of common standards and metadata would specifically make statistical and geospatial information more usable and relevant to a wider range of users.

Implementing geospatial databases for the census and related geographic products requires the creation and maintenance of metadata guidelines and a data dictionary. The metadata standard and its use beyond the census would increase the usability and relevance of this data and enhance the ability to compare data both within and across geographies. NSOs should adhere to applicable standards established for the country because they are necessary to ease the effort of sharing census data and understanding between organizations and between applications. Many applications extend beyond national borders, including those related to disaster management, spread of infectious diseases, humanitarian assistance, migration, and cross-border displaced population, for which it is necessary to integrate datasets across national borders.

Geospatial standards and metadata are not always available in countries. When they are unavailable, it is recommended that NSOs follow published basic standards and definitions, especially about the geospatial features used in statistical operations, such as boundaries of statistical units, buildings, private dwellings, and collective living quarters.

As stated previously, work led by the UN has resulted in the development of a Global Statistical Geo-spatial Framework (GSGF) used as a guideline for integrating statistical and geospatial information. An overview of this framework is presented in the box.[13] The development of an overarching statistical-geo-spatial framework, as part of an overall information architecture at both the national and global levels, is needed for enhancing the common understanding of concepts such as geocoding, georeferencing, and other terminology; sharing common standards; and fostering collaboration between both statistical and geospatial communities. This recognizes that when statistical and geospatial information is integrated within a statistical-geospatial framework, the geostatistical results can significantly improve the quality of official statistics and population and housing censuses and support the measuring and monitoring of the SDGs. This also explains and justifies the shift from census mapping to GIS-based approaches, with full use of GIS and geospatial technologies across all stages of the census and beyond.

What is the GSGF?

The GSGF, developed under the auspices of the EG-ISGI, is a high-level framework that consists of five broad principles that are considered essential for integrating geospatial and statistical information (see figure 2.6).

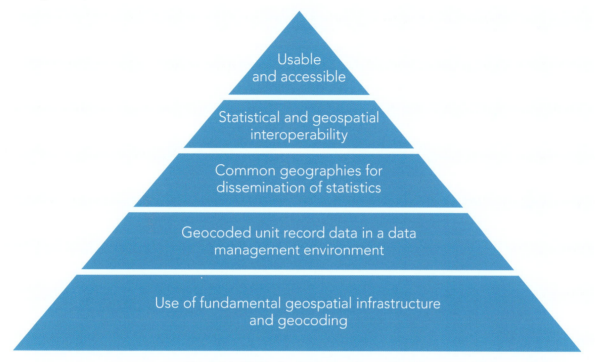

Figure 2.6. GSGF—five fundamental principles.

The GSGF principles—goals and objectives

Each of the high-level principles* in the GSGF is defined by a set of goals and objectives and is supported by international, regional, and applicable national standards and best practices. At its sixth session in 2016, UN-GGIM adopted the following five principles:[14]

Principle 1: Use of fundamental geospatial infrastructure and geocoding

This foundational principle is about the fundamental geospatial infrastructure. In this context, it refers to those geospatial datasets that underpin the core business of NSOs. The requirement is about "a common and consistent approach to establishing the location and a geocode for each unit in a dataset, such as a

---

* This text explaining the principles is mainly derived, with some adaptations, from the background paper *Proposal for a Global Statistical Geospatial Framework*, available at http://ggim.un.org/meetings/GGIM-committee/documents/GGIM6/Background-Paper-Proposal-for-a-global-statistical-geospatial-framework.pdf. Also used is the *Global Statistical Geospatial Framework: Linking Statistics and Place* document, available at ggim.un.org/meetings/GGIM-committee/8th-Session/documents/Global-Statistical-Geospatial-Framework-July-2018.pdf.

person, household, business, building or parcel/unit of land. . . . The goal of this principle is to obtain a high quality, standardized physical address, property, building identifier, or other location description in order to assign accurate coordinates and/or a small geographic area or standard grid reference to each statistical unit (i.e., at the microdata level)." The fundamental geospatial infrastructure will differ between countries, but "the process of obtaining locations and geocodes should use relevant, fundamental geospatial data . . . from the National Spatial Data Infrastructures or other nationally agreed sources." In some nations, it is likely to include national address lists, land parcel databases, road networks, business registers, and building footprints. In other nations, it is likely to include national and regional boundaries, town and locality locations, etc. However, the EG-ISGI recognizes that geocoding of statistical units using point referencing is highly preferable when compared with merely associating statistical units with a geographic region (i.e., a polygon).

Principle 2: Geocoded unit record data in a data management environment

This principle focuses on the requirement that the linkage for each statistical unit record should occur within a data management environment to allow all statistical data to be applied to any geographic context (i.e., in aggregating data into a variety of larger geographic units), including future changes to geographies over time, and enable data-linking processes that aim to integrate information of varying nature and sources by so-called linked data techniques. This principle is underpinned by two combined factors: (1) key to geospatial enablement and flexibility, the finer the better; and (2) statistical data management ensures confidentiality. While principle 1 is about geocoding infrastructure, principle 2 is about applying this geocoding infrastructure to unit records and ensuring that the statistical infrastructure can use geospatial infrastructure and standards for geocoding.

Principle 3: Common geographies for dissemination of statistics

This principle is about the enablement of comparisons across datasets from different sources, which requires using a common set of geographies for the display, reporting, and analysis of social, economic, and environmental information. The goal of this principle is to provide the tools for integration of aggregate data on common geography and for the dissemination of data. In addition to the recognized importance of traditional statistical and administrative geographies, NSOs should consider the benefits of grid-based statistical systems because gridded data can be both a rich source of information and a consistent geography for disseminating and comparing information.

Principle 4: Interoperable data and metadata standards

This principle aims at greater efficiency and simplification of the creation, discovery, integration, and use of geospatially enabled statistics and geospatial data; increasing the potential application of a larger range of data and technologies; and a wider range of data available and accessible for use in comparisons and analysis in decision-making: "Both the statistical and the geospatial data communities operate their own general data models and metadata capabilities; however, these models are often not universally applied.

The statistical community uses the Generic Statistical Information Model (GSIM), the Statistical Data and Metadata eXchange (SDMX), and the Data Documentation Initiative (DDI) mechanisms. The geospatial community uses the General Feature Model (GFM) and the ISO19115 metadata standard, plus a number of application-specific standards." Within the statistical community, there is a need to build geospatial processes and standards into statistical business processes in a more consistent manner. In consequence, the EG-ISGI has recognised that a top-down approach is required, incorporating geospatial frameworks, standards, and processes more explicitly into the Common Statistical Production Architecture and its components. Work has started internationally on how to better enhance interoperability between statistical and geospatial metadata standards.

Principle 5: Accessible and usable geospatially enabled statistics

This principle is about the ultimate purpose of developing this GSGF: Informing decision-making in a more flexible, agile approach using new and existing data and reassuring custodians of safe release (i.e., release of their data with confidence, privacy, and confidentiality protected) while enabling users with discovery and access of geospatially enabled statistics. More specifically, this will consist of identifying or, where required, developing policies, standards, and guidelines that support the release, access, analysis, and visualization of geospatially enabled information. In addition, data users can undertake analysis and evaluation. Web services enable machine-to-machine access and dynamic linkages of information. As stated in principle 4, this will allow data to be accessed and used efficiently and ultimately support the modernization agenda of many NSOs and NMAs.

The UNSC adopted the framework at its forty-eighth session in March 2017, and subsequently the Committee of Experts endorsed it at its seventh session in August 2017.

The standards and best practices that will form the detailed guidance for countries implementing the framework are still under consideration by the EG-ISGI and will be brought to the UNSC and UN-GGIM for consideration when finalized.

Where standards, policies, or datasets required to support the framework do not currently exist, the framework provides a clear mandate for their establishment. Collaboration between countries and within the EG-ISGI provides a mechanism to assist with the formation and establishment of these standards, policies, or fundamental datasets both within member states and internationally. A number of areas of further work have been identified and are under consideration by EG-ISGI.

The framework is driven by strong principles but remains broad enough that countries can adapt it to their local conditions and needs. Many members agreed to prepare country-level examples detailing their application of the GSGF principles to their national conditions in preparation for broader global community input. In this regard, a template for country examples for each of the five principles has been prepared by the Australian Bureau of Statistics and available for use by countries.

Other countries such as Sweden are now beginning to share their interpretations on how they will implement the GSGF within their organization.

Collaboration

As stated previously, NSOs need to be aware that the challenges involved in introducing GIS and other geospatial technologies are not only technical, but more often institutional and organizational. Mobilizing cooperation among all stakeholders and building partnerships right from the beginning of the census-planning phase is essential to implement a GIS-based census program catering to the needs of all major users.

For example, since producing basemaps is not a core competency of the NSO, developing a partnership for cooperation with the NMA can be mutually beneficial: the NMA provides the NSO with basemaps updated and appropriate for the census operations, and, in return, the mapping agency may benefit from the improvements provided by the fieldwork undertaken by the NSO and the geographic products derived from the census.

Other examples include the selection of GIS data or systems that should be made considering the use by other government departments, allowing that the construction of a national census geospatial database can be employed in many different national contexts for numerous purposes. Institutional arrangements facilitate partnership for data standards and interoperability, agreements and contracts for data collection and sharing, and collaboration across government at a variety of levels including national, regional, and local, thus contributing to the building and development of the national geospatial information infrastructure of the country.

Figure 2.7. Collaboration across agencies and the community.

Geography and Statistical Data Are Foundational
An Integrated Data Model Is Essential

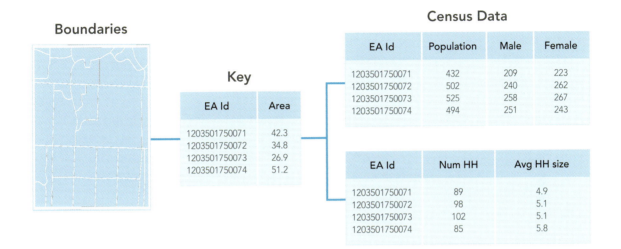

Boundaries

Census Data

Key

EA Id	Area
1203501750071	42.3
1203501750072	34.8
1203501750073	26.9
1203501750074	51.2

EA Id	Population	Male	Female
1203501750071	432	209	223
1203501750072	502	240	262
1203501750073	525	258	267
1203501750074	494	251	243

EA Id	Num HH	Avg HH size
1203501750071	89	4.9
1203501750072	98	5.1
1203501750073	102	5.1
1203501750074	85	5.8

Figure 2.8. Integration of geospatial and statistical data. Statistical data can be easily mapped by using geographic information such as geocodes, EA codes, and EA boundaries.

Compatibility—methodology of integration

Choosing the appropriate methodology of integration of the new geospatial technologies with the census operations is another central factor in the adequate integration and optimal use of geospatial technologies. Given the different approaches and national experiences, it is generally recognized that no universal solution fits all; in deciding what approach to adopt, the NSOs should be guided by their needs, policies, and availability of resources allocated to the census in their countries.

Lessons learned from different experiences point to challenges in integrating existing census or geographic data with newly collected data and converting the data into digital form. Consideration should be given to the construction and implementation of a geospatial database, required data models, and maintaining standards, metadata guidelines, and data dictionaries.

For example, the NSO may need to extract, transform, and load (ETL) some data received from other agencies or sources owing to variations in file formats. By considering standards, system requirements, data gaps, and other key issues, the NSO will be better prepared for success.

Considerations for rapid changes in technology

How do NSOs keep abreast of technology changes and understand what and when to implement? Artificial intelligence (AI), machine learning (ML), IoT, and smart devices hold the promise for an intelligent future. The challenge will be understanding and leveraging these new technologies in both a timely and cost-efficient manner and mapping the NSO's business needs and workflows to these potential new technologies.

Understanding new ideas such as this, in addition to continuous adaptive security or microservices, will be critical to future success. Intelligent applications (apps) and analytics are another key trend we must be prepared for. Intelligent apps have the potential to transform the nature of work and the structure of the workplace. While NSOs are conducting their work today, they must at the same time plan for the future.

The GIS industry is no stranger to this transformation, according to Jack Dangermond, president and founder of Esri: "The geospatial industry is quickly evolving because the capabilities of digital connectedness and collaboration are moving ahead exponentially. In fact, the five biggest trends in the area of geographic information system (GIS) technology are centered on making data more accessible and creating context to visualize this data in an age when fast, easy access to information is taken for granted."

Figure 2.9. Jack Dangermond, president of Esri, addresses a conference audience.

Location as a Service

Advanced Analytics

Big Data Analytics

Real-Time GIS

Mobility

Figure 2.10. Top five trends in GIS technology today.

According to Dangermond, the top five trends in GIS technology today are as follows:

1. Location as a service
2. Advanced analytics
3. Big data analytics
4. Real-time GIS
5. Mobility

Dangermond continues: "The last leap in computing was the shift from the server to the cloud. Software as a service (SaaS) opened a world of opportunities for GIS, as shared map services like the World Imagery basemap are no longer separate from the unique services offered to users. GIS users can share data, collaborate, make mashup maps in the server, and then connect to the cloud.

The next leap in GIS technology and computing is connecting to the vast network of devices providing data in real time. This technology is a revolutionary change and brings great opportunity. The more accessible data is, the more important it will be to understand it. And maps are the visual language for understanding the context of data."

An example of these technologies coming together today is the Esri World Population Estimation model. Chief Cartographer Charlie Frye leads this project on behalf of Esri.

Esri World Population Estimate

Figure 2.11. Image of the Sinai Peninsula. Courtesy of MDA NaturalVue.

MDA NaturalVue is imagery processed with natural colors (RGB channels) to reflect the earth's true colors. This cloud-free imagery is available even for areas with persistent cloud coverage.

As methods like these become more repeatable and proven, it will influence the way we conduct our own census and survey work.

This project brings together big data, advanced analytics, and location as a service. In December 2014, Esri published the initial version of the World Population Estimate (WPE) image service on ArcGIS Online. The service represented a global estimate of the 2013 population of the earth as a footprint at 250-meter resolution. The WPE is a dasymetric raster surface in which each cell represents an estimated count of people living in the location the cell represents. The same method is applied globally, which means the values in each of the cells are intended to be comparable. Data used includes Landsat8 panchromatic imagery, classified land cover from MDA Information System's BaseVue® 2013, and a global dataset of road intersections. A texture-detecting model is used to locate settlement in the rural areas beyond where the urban classes from BaseVue 2013 exist. Because land cover data inherently includes information about surface water, agriculture, and permanent ice, some of these factors can be eliminated because there is a high level of certainty that people as a rule do not live in these locations.

Esri's purpose in creating the WPE is to facilitate population-based spatial analysis—specifically, providing a footprint for ArcGIS tools to perform the following:
- Provide a basis for estimating redistributions of other population characteristics with higher geographic fidelity than traditional choropleth mapping techniques. These characteristics include demographic variation, economic behaviors, political attitudes, and cultural characteristics.
- Support cross-boundary estimation of populations that:
  o Are affected by natural disasters and complex humanitarian emergencies (for mitigation, response, and recovery).
  o Live within high-risk environments, such as areas prone to flooding or forest fires.
  o Are exposed to disease (to prevent transmission).
  o Are affected by disease outbreak (to direct resources to support effective treatment efforts).
- Estimate human impact on the environment for purposes of sustainability, resilience, and planning along the lines of green infrastructure.

In summer 2016, Esri published an update representing the estimated footprint and population for 2015. The 2015 estimate included additional image services for population density and confidence. The 2015 services were all based on 150-meter resolution.[15]

In early 2018, Esri published a population 2016 estimate that included an improved confidence score. This work continues, and Esri is now collaborating to further this research in a consortium called POPGRID (https://www.popgrid.org). Hosted by the Center for International Earth Science Information Network (CIESIN) at Columbia University, this group works on a voluntary basis to share and document techniques for producing global gridded dasymetric redistributions of population, to foster greater awareness of gridded population estimates, and to produce comparisons of the global gridded products. The POPGRID participants include Oakridge National Laboratory, Esri, CIESEN, the Joint Research Centre (JRC), the European Commission, WorldPop (University of Southampton), the German Aerospace Center (DLR), ImageCat, Inc., the US Census Bureau, the World Bank, Facebook®, and Google®.

Using imagery and other data sources and analyzing them using machine learning and AI, each of these organizations is working to innovate and create a global mosaic of high-resolution settlement layers that will provide an increasingly higher quality estimate of human population distribution.

References

- Andrea Gros and Tobias Tiecke. 2016. *Connecting the World with Better Maps*. Available at https://code.facebook.com/posts/1676452492623525/connecting-the-world-with-better-maps/.
- Charlie Frye. 2015. *Map Gives New Insights into Global Population*. Available at https://medium.com/esri-insider/map-gives-new-insights-into-global-population-d7b1902f7c15.
- Charlie Frye. 2016. *Updated Population Dataset Sharpens Focus on the Human Footprint*. Available at https://blogs.esri.com/esri/esri-insider/2016/03/30/updated-population-dataset-sharpens-focus-on-the-human-footprint/#more-6823.
- Jack Dangermond. 2017. *Five GIS Trends Changing the World According to Jack Dangermond, President of Esri*. Available at http://geoawesomeness.com/five-gis-trends-changing-world-according-jack-dangermond-president-esri/.

Notes

1. Since its inception, the UN recommends that each country conduct a population and housing census at least once every ten years, usually within the so-called census round. The 2020 census round covers the ten-year period 2015–2024.
2. The UN *Principles and Recommendations* defines the population census as "the total process of collecting, compiling, evaluating, analyzing and publishing or otherwise disseminating demographic, economic and social data at the smallest geographical level appropriate pertaining, at a specified time, to all persons in a country or in a well-delimited part of a country." In the case of a housing census, this same process focuses on "statistical data relating to the number and condition of housing units and facilities as available to the households pertaining, at a specified time, to all living quarters . . . and occupants thereof in a country or in a well-delimited part of a country."
3. These objectives sum up the findings of the UN regional workshops held worldwide during the 2010 Round of Censuses and presented at the 2015 International GIS Workshop in China.
4. See https://statswiki.unece.org/display/GSBPM/GSBPM+v5.0.
5. See details in the UN Department of Economic and Social Affairs Statistics Division's *Handbook on Geospatial Infrastructure in Support of Census Activities*, 2009. Available at https://unstats.un.org/unsd/demographic/standmeth/handbooks/series_f103en.pdf.
6. See *Handbook on Geospatial Infrastructure*.
7. See *Handbook on Geospatial Infrastructure*.
8. See *Handbook on Geospatial Infrastructure*.
9. See *Handbook on Geospatial Infrastructure*.
10. For example, Statistics Canada has its boundary files and the road network files available in three formats: ArcGIS® shapefile (.shp), Geography Markup Language (.gml), and MapInfo® (.tab).
11. See *Handbook on Geospatial Infrastructure*.

12. See details in *Australia Programme Review* and the related background paper on *Developing a Statistical Geospatial Framework in National Statistical Systems: Survey of Linking Geospatial Information to Statistics—Analysis of Questionnaire Responses* (2013), available at https://unstats.un.org/unsd/statcom/44th-session/documents, and the UNSD report on the *Results of a Survey on Census Methods Used by Countries in the 2010 Census Round*, available at https://unstats.un.org/unsd/censuskb20/KnowledgebaseArticle10696.aspx.

13. For details, see the report of the UN Expert Group on the Integration of Statistical and Geospatial Information, 2015, E/CN.3/2015/37, at https://unstats.un.org/unsd/statcom/46th-session/documents.

14. See *UN Expert Group on the Integration of Statistical and Geospatial Information Background Document on Proposal for a Global Statistical Geospatial Framework*. Available at http://ggim.un.org/meetings/GGIM-committee/documents/GGIM6/Background-Paper-Proposal-for-a-global-statistical-geospatial-framework.pdf.

15. See the Esri story map "We Are Everywhere" available at https://landscapeteam.maps.arcgis.com/apps/MapJournal/index.html?appid=23d43b031a4d47629c511909188cfefd.

Chapter 3
Changing technology

Five key trends in GIS

As mentioned in the previous chapter, there are five key trends in the GIS industry today. In this section, we will explore each of these in more detail. We will also discuss other technologies key to the census process, such as GPS, cloud computing, sensor networks, imagery, and analytics.

There was a time when GIS use in general was limited. The use and application of GIS have expanded dramatically as academia, business, and government agencies alike have seen the benefits of under-standing data geospatially. The fundamentals of GIS and what it can do have also evolved substantially. We are entering an era of services-based GIS. This means the GIS professional connects with citizens or consumers directly through web-based applications that provide easy-to-access visualizations. GIS also has huge implications for the enterprise user at a business or a government organization, where departments have enormous amounts of geographic data. Performing spatial analysis on the web and having access to distributed servers where different layers of data exist allow users to bring this data together, fuse it, and analyze it across the network.

Location as a Service

Advanced Analytics

Big Data Analytics

Real-Time GIS

Mobility

Figure 3.1. Five key trends in the GIS industry (also shown in figure 2.10).

Location as a service (LaaS)

Location as a service (LaaS) is a new concept that combines the three main categories of cloud computing services: infrastructure, software, and platform as a service. Location provides a platform to develop, run, and manage analytics and embedded applications without needing to build analytics and data mainte-nance infrastructure into other enterprise apps and systems. LaaS is the best infrastructure to manage, store, and share location-specific capabilities between different departments and organizations. It's a service provisioned and scaled on demand. LaaS delivers software and apps on a centrally hosted basis that can be used by the entire organization anywhere, anytime, and by anyone. LaaS provides a way to more widely leverage location to understand data through knowledge-focused workflows and on-demand analytics and provide insight.

   LaaS is a location data delivery model in which data acquired through multiple sources is available via a simple application programming interface (API). By implementing LaaS, organizations can realize greater operational efficiencies, increase security, reduce costs, and optimize citizen engagement, all while achiev-ing a higher return on investment.

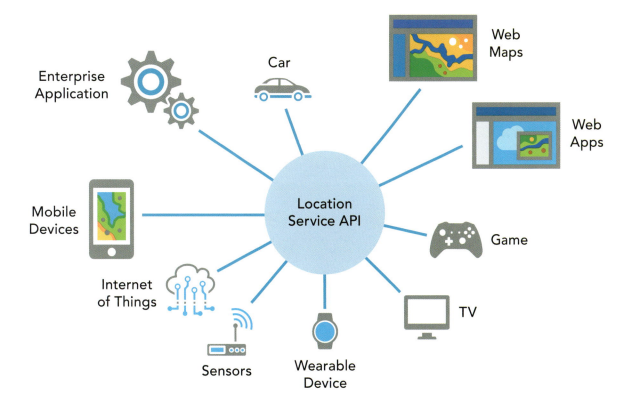

Figure 3.2. Location service API.

Advanced analytics

Spatial analysis is important to any business that values location as a variable to success. EA planning is an example of a crucial function that depends on geospatial analysis. When counting a population, a planner needs to understand where the population is, what challenges the physical geography or terrain brings, and how the transportation network and built environment work. All this data can be overlaid onto a map to perform statistical analysis to optimize and create efficient EAs. This same type of advanced analytics can be applied to other areas of census workflows such as workforce optimization and management.

Maps communicate this information well, and in a web services environment, professionals will be able to make maps, graphs, and charts and perform analytics easily. Accessible from an organization's cloud, the power of GIS, mapping, and spatial analytics is opened across the enterprise.

Figure 3.3. Spatial analysis example: EA optimization.

Big data analytics

The term *big data* refers to datasets that are so large or complex that traditional data-processing applications are inadequate to handle them. The ability to access vast amounts of data has changed the way all organizations function and has evolved to include the integration of big data operations into spatial analysis.

Today, anyone in the enterprise can access billions of observations or tens of thousands of raster images from spacecraft and analyze them quite easily. Data from sensor networks, radio-frequency identification (RFID) tags, surveillance cameras, UAV, and geotagged social media posts also all have geographical components to them. This big data, combined with the right tools, will greatly expand what traditional GIS has provided.

Tools such as ArcGIS® GeoAnalytics, Image Analytics, and GeoEvent™ Server all use the power of distributed computing to speed up geospatial analysis and make us more productive. GeoAnalytics Server works with existing tabular and geospatial data so a user can find hot spots, analyze patterns, aggregate and summarize data, and visualize results over time.

GeoEvent Server can track dynamic assets that are constantly changing location, such as vehicles, people, and vessels, or stationary assets, such as weather and environmental monitoring sensors. In addition, it provides real-time situational awareness for coordinated field activities. The spatiotemporal big data store makes it possible to work with observational data such as moving objects, changing attributes of stationary sensors, or both. The spatiotemporal big data store also enables the archiving of high-volume observation data, sustains high-velocity write throughput, and can run across multiple machines (nodes).

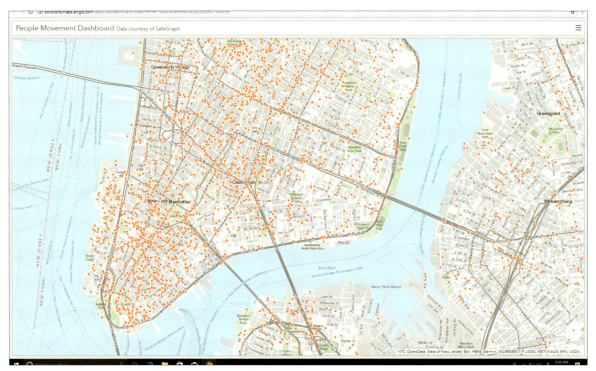

Figure 3.4. GeoEvent Server is being used to display aggregate, anonymized location events sourced from SafeGraph, a geospatial data company that builds and maintains ground truth sets on places and human movement. This exemplifies both big data and real time coming together to inform decision-making.

With ImageAnalytics Server, raster analytics quickly extracts information from very large images or image collections. Highly scalable raster analysis models, with distributed computing and storage, get traditionally large and slow analytical tasks done in a fraction of the time. Similarly, dynamic image services provide on-the-fly processing and mosaicking capabilities to make it easy to access both new and existing imagery.

On-the-fly processing transforms source imagery into a wide range of on-demand products, reducing the amount of imagery needed to process and maintain. Enterprise users can build their own imagery and raster analytics workflows for fast, multi-CPU, parallel processing of massive imagery collections. (Detailed information on imagery and analytics is presented in chapter 5).

Real-time GIS

The world is already interconnected digitally—people are connected with one another and with their government. According to the 2017 *Measuring the Information Society Report* from the International Telecommunications Union (ITU), the latest ITU data estimates that more than half of the world's households (53.6 percent) now have access to the Internet at home, compared with less than 20 percent in 2005 and just over 30 percent in 2010. Globally, the number of mobile cellular subscriptions grew from 2005 to 2017, from 33.9 per 100 inhabitants to an estimated 103.5. In the least developed countries (LDCs), the growth has been more impressive, increasing from 5.0 in 2005 to an estimated 70.4 in 2017. Worldwide, active mobile-broadband subscriptions increased from 11.5 per 100 inhabitants to 56.4 in only seven years. Here as well, growth in LDCs was even stronger, from 0.4 in 2010 to 22.3 in 2017, offering hope that they are on a path to catch up with the rest of the world (ITU Telecommunication Development Sector [ITU-D]).

This trend will continue as companies like Google, together with South Africa's Convergence Partners and other investors, announced recently they will invest as much as USD$100 million in metro fiber networks in key parts of Africa. Google and partners signed an agreement to invest in CSquared, a broadband infrastructure company focused on building wholesale metro fiber-optic networks and enabling Internet access in Africa. CSquared has operational networks in Uganda and Ghana and will operate as an independent company headquartered in Nairobi, Kenya, with plans to deploy networks in more countries.[1] This is just one example of the investments being made across the region to improve access for LDCs.

Leveraging this vast network of devices is the latest trend and priority for organizations that want to keep ahead in terms of having a comprehensive enterprise GIS for the future.

Mobility

Mobile devices continue to advance and offer more processing power. This advancement is triggering a proliferation in types of applications that allow for the capturing of location. Today, a simple user experience is possible with apps and app builder tools for mobile devices. These devices can be used to collect geospatial data anywhere at any time.

GIS allows you to connect to virtually any type of streaming data feed and transform your GIS applications into frontline decision applications, showing the latest information as it occurs. Smartphones are being used to integrate real-time data from the IoT directly into a GIS where that data can be analyzed and visualized. We are now starting to talk about the Location of Things (LoT).

Other key trends

Imagery and drones

As NSOs plan and execute their national census efforts, up-to-date imagery is proving to be a critical source of information. No other source of geospatial content provides the timeliness, context, and comprehensiveness of high-resolution imagery. When integrated as part of a modern GIS, imagery becomes a data backbone capable of supporting the entire enumeration framework. Imagery can be used in pre-enumeration planning to do in-office address canvassing or to validate existing EAs. Imagery analysis can also be conducted to understand areas of change, such as agricultural or forested areas.

Imagery use in visualization is also on the rise, particularly on tablets and mobile devices. Today, there are two ways of serving imagery for use in web and mobile applications. The first is a cached map service or raster tiles. This is a regular map service that has been enhanced to serve maps very quickly using a cache of static images. The map cache is a directory that contains image tiles of a map extent at specific scale levels. Returning a tile from the cache takes the server much less time than drawing the map image on demand.

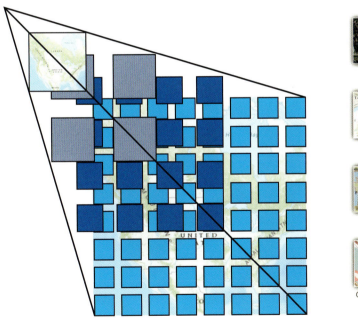

Select a basemap

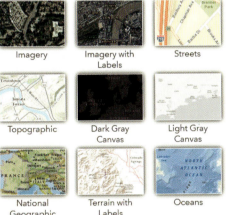

Imagery   Imagery with Labels   Streets

Topographic   Dark Gray Canvas   Light Gray Canvas

National Geographic   Terrain with Labels   Oceans

OpenStreetMap   USA Topo Maps   USGS National Map

Figure 3.5. Basemaps available from ArcGIS include both raster (left) and vector.

The second way—vector tiles—contains vector representations of data across a range of scales. Unlike raster tiles, they can adapt to the resolution of their display device and even be restyled for multiple uses. They can be published as a vector tile package. A corresponding vector tile layer is created when you publish the package that can be added to a web map online.

Thanks to emergent technologies such as high-resolution sensors and small or miniature satellites, modern sources of imagery have reduced costs, improved accuracies, and thus have a growing applicability for statistical processes. The use of imagery in analytics has risen substantially in recent years and will continue to do so with the proliferation of data from new sensors such as UAVs or drones.

The adoption of drone technology across industries leapt from the fad stage to implementation fairly quickly as more and more businesses realize the benefit of this new technology. Known by many names including *UAVs*, *miniature pilotless aircraft*, and *flying mini robots*, drones are quickly growing in popularity. Drones are proving to be extremely beneficial in places where people cannot reach or are unable to perform tasks in a timely and efficient manner. New technologies such as Drone2Map® for ArcGIS allows users to create orthomosaics, 3D meshes, and more from drone-captured still imagery in minutes, not days. Tools like this allow one to view locations from all angles and inspect buildings or locations that may be difficult to access, visualizing imagery from multiple points of view.

Figure 3.6. The imagery demonstrates the feasibility of using drones to replace or augment surveys using high-resolution 3D mapping. The drone is a 3DR® Site Scan with a Sony® R10C camera. Images courtesy of 3D Robotics®. Drone image courtesy of McKim & Creed.

GPS

GPS is a piece of this equation, and whether needed for the collection of ground control points for imagery capture or simply to use the built-in GPS on a cell phone to capture location or get directions, both are possible and affordable today. Everyone has access to highly accurate GPS tools and workflows without any middleware. According to industry experts, several things led to this access, including a long list of technological standards that have been adopted and institutionalized in a relatively short time—Bluetooth®, REST, 3G, LTE, Wi-Fi, USB, and many more.

GPS, owned by the US government, is the world's most popular satellite navigation system. Because of its widespread popularity, it is sometimes used interchangeably or confused with Global Navigation Satellite System (GNSS). GNSS is a general term for any satellite constellation that provides accurate positioning, navigation, and time information on a global basis. Other global navigation systems include Russia's Global Navigation Satellite System (GLONASS), Galileo (European), BeiDou Navigation Satellite System (Chinese), and some regional systems. GPS originated in 1973 and was exclusively used by the military; it became fully operational in 1995. Originally, the signal quality was intentionally degraded under a program called Selective Availability (SA).

Brent Jones, a lifelong surveyor and land records/cadaster industry manager for Esri, says that since the year 2000, when "President Clinton intentionally turned off [SA], [accurate] GPS signals [have been] accessible to the public. Designed to make GPS more responsive to civil and commercial users, Clinton's executive decision immediately improved GPS accuracy for the entire world and opened a market for lower-cost GPS devices and solutions. As a result, GPS manufacturers expand-

ed by building and selling GPS components (e.g., modules or chipsets) not just end-user devices. This created competition for components that could be embedded into all kinds of solutions in a multitude of areas, such as precision agriculture, logistics, and machine control. It also allowed entrepreneurs to apply GPS in innovative ways, such as installing it in . . . the now-ubiquitous smartphones and tablets for location services."

The UN-GGIM EG-ISGI calls out in principle 1 ("Use of fundamental geospatial infrastructure and geocoding"):

"The global framework requires a common and consistent approach to establishing the location and a geocode for each unit in a dataset, such as a person, household, business, building, or parcel/unit of land. A corresponding record of the relevant time or date for each instance of location information recorded should also be associated with each unit record. The goal of this principle is to obtain a high-quality, standardized physical address, property or building identifier, or other location description, in order to assign accurate coordinates and/or a small geographic area or standard grid reference to each statistical unit (i.e., at the micro-data level). Time and date stamping these locations will place the unit both in time and in space. An alternative approach to geocoding for recording location is to use direct or indirect capture of coordinates (e.g., from GPS and maps, respectively) from fieldwork."

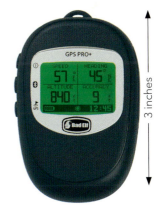

Figure 3.7. The Bad Elf GPS Pro + is a Bluetooth GPS + GLONASS receiver and data logger, accurate up to 2.5 meters. It quickly acquires satellite lock without cell tower assistance.

Jones wrote: "We have highly accurate stand-alone GPS devices, such as the one-meter Bad-Elf® GNSS Surveyor, the submeter Trimble® Navigation R1, the Spectra® Precision Mobile Mapper 300, the Geneq® iSXBlue, the single-centimeter Eos® Arrow 200, and the super-accurate geodetic Septentrio® Altus NR2 . . . These devices don't come with heavy desktop software to process data; they just produce a highly accurate position that you can use in your own technology or solution. This modularization represents the virtual deregulation of accuracy."

GPS systems, once expensive and complicated, have become commonplace. Today, one can simply decide on the accuracy level needed, choose the device desired, and get to work.

Cloud computing

Cloud computing is growing in importance for GIS professionals. Reasons include cost, scalability, flexibility, and rapid deployment. Two specific scenarios for GIS in the cloud are particularly compelling: increasing operational efficiencies with on-demand

GIS and streamlining application development and deployment. Traditional desktop deployment and single-threaded processing architectures that traditionally dominated GIS tools are not sufficient to analyze web-scale data, much less the flood of data from the IoT.

Cloud technology can be leveraged in many ways and depends on organizational needs. Some organizations opt to use a private cloud, some use cloud offerings such as those available via Amazon Web Services (AWS) or Microsoft Azure, some may choose to use Esri's ArcGIS Online, and others may use a hybrid combination of these.

Enterprise GIS can allow one to quickly deploy ArcGIS Server applications and services to the cloud rather than buying and maintaining infrastructure. The advantages of this in census operations can be key owing to the huge swell of temporary part-time workers and peak loads that are large and not representative of the day-to-day needs of a statistical organization. In this case, leveraging cloud infrastructure can prove to be extremely cost-effective.

Figure 3.8. GeoHive portal combines data from Central Statistics Office Ireland and Ordnance Survey Ireland to provide a simple, easy-to-use interface for citizens and researchers alike to find the data needed to understand such issues as society, economy, and environment.

Open data

This section would not be complete without mentioning the open data movement. Open data is the idea that some data should be freely available to everyone to use and republish as desired, without restrictions from copyright, patents, or other mechanisms of control. The UN Statistics Division organized a meeting at the Statistical Commission in March 2017 with the goal of exploring how open data initiatives can provide advantages to NSOs operating in both advanced and less advanced statistical systems, including in countries with limited resources.

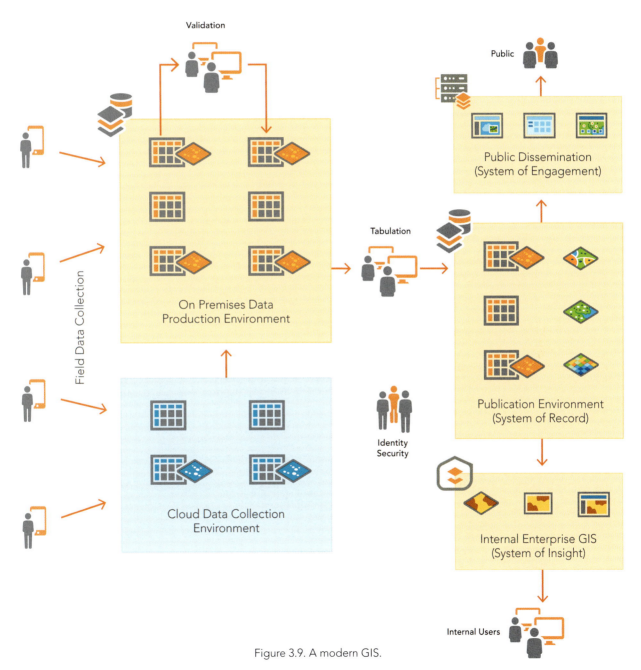

Figure 3.9. A modern GIS.

According to the UNSD, vast numbers of datasets that do not contain information on an individual or organization (such as weather data, GPS data, school enrollment, transport schedules, and many others) are routinely made available as open data. However, other data (such as microdata from population, economic, or agricultural censuses, household surveys, and others) can only be part of the public domain if proper precautions are taken to protect the privacy and confidentiality of individuals and organizations. In a similar sense, data generated by civil, business, or building registers could be made public under strict ethical and security protocols and secure technology platforms. Nontraditional data sources from civil society or the private sector could also be useful for research and daily decision-making purposes.

Modern GIS platforms provide the capabilities to publish data openly and securely based on the needs of the organization. With changing technology, data security and confidentiality will continue to evolve. Some of these technologies will be expanded on in the following chapters.

References

- Brent Jones. 2015. *The Democratization of Accuracy*. Available at https://blogs.esri.com/esri/esri-insider/2015/09/03/the-democratization-of-accuracy/.
- International Telecommunications Union. 2017. *Measuring the Information Society Report 2017*. Available at https://www.itu.int/en/ITU-D/Statistics/Documents/publications/misr2017/MISR2017_Volume1.pdf.
- Moneyweb. 2017. *Google, Partners to Invest R1.3bn in Africa*. Available at https://www.moneyweb.co.za/news/tech/google-partners-to-invest-r1-3bn-in-africa/.
- UNSD. 2017. *Open Data: Adding Value by Matching Access with Privacy and Security*. Available at https://unstats.un.org/unsd/statcom/48th-session/side-events/20170303-1M-friday-seminar-on-emerging-issues/.

Note

1. See https://venturebeat.com/2017/05/16/google-and-partners-commit-100-million-to-african-broadband-project-csquared.

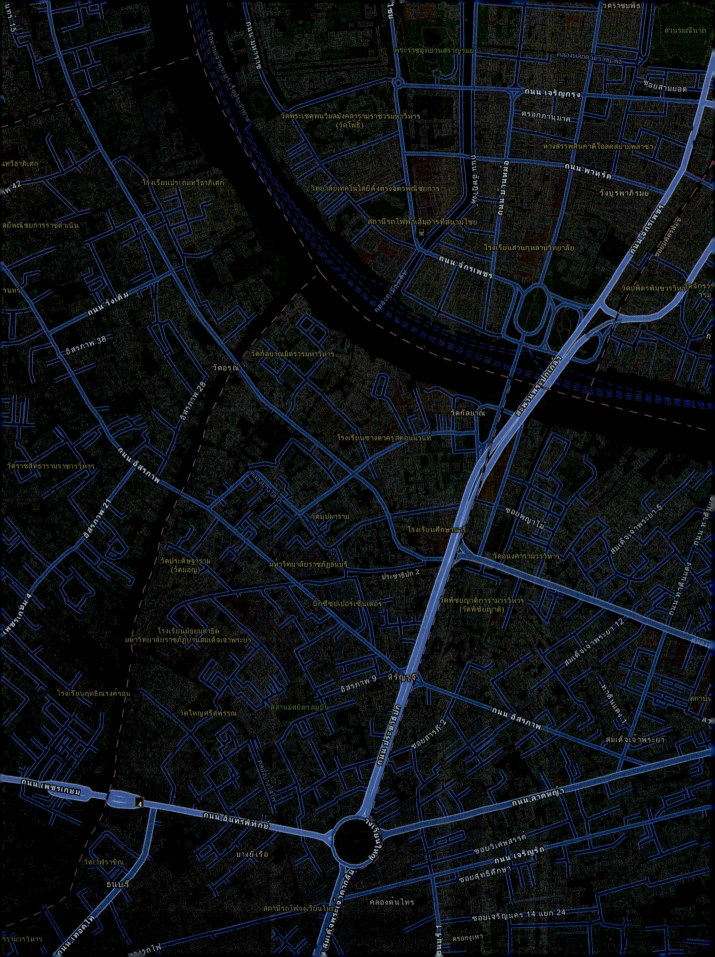

Chapter 4

Establishing the foundation—the geodatabase

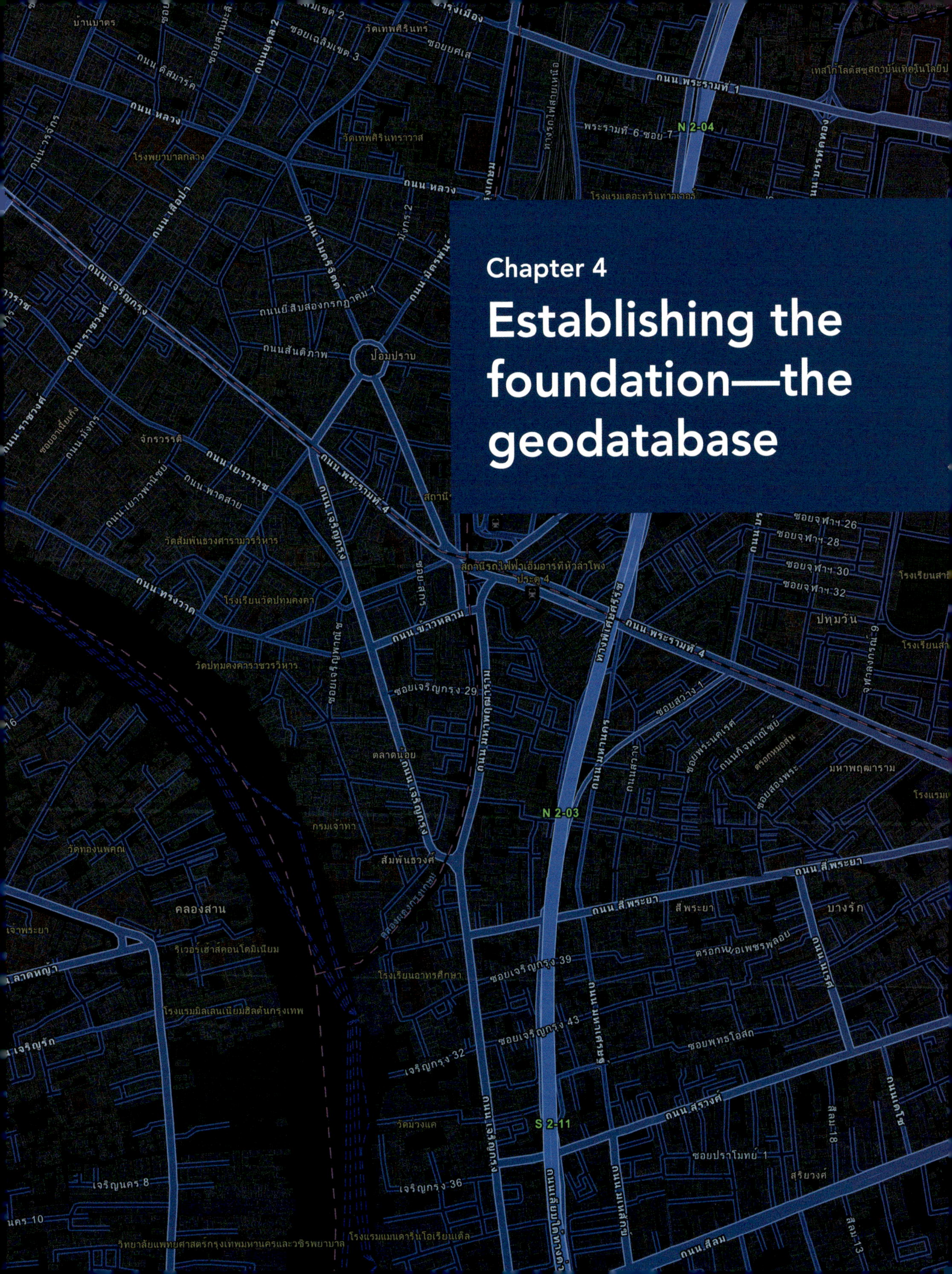

What is a geodatabase?

This chapter is about establishing the foundation of any GIS—the geodatabase. It provides an overview of the process of building a geodatabase by outlining some basic concepts on spatial data structure, spatial data modeling, and the design of the database itself. The chapter highlights the geospatial data sources needed in a census and the related geographical classifications in census geography that allow the identification of the geographic features and core objects of the census geodatabase. The chapter particularly emphasizes the geocoding concept and its central role in linking statistical data with geography, including a clarification about its association with the georeferencing concept.

At its most basic level, a geodatabase is a collection of geographic datasets of various types held in a common file system folder or a multiuser relational database management system (RDBMS) such as Oracle®, Microsoft SQL Server, PostgreSQL, or IBM DB2®. Geodatabases come in many sizes, have varying numbers of users, and can scale from small, single-user databases built on files up to larger workgroup, department, and enterprise geodatabases accessed by many users.

But a geodatabase is more than a collection of datasets. The term *geodatabase* has the following meanings in ArcGIS:

- The geodatabase is the native data structure for ArcGIS and the primary data format used for editing and data management. While ArcGIS works with geographic information in numerous GIS file formats, it is designed to work with and leverage the capabilities of the geodatabase.
- The geodatabase is the physical store of geographic information, primarily using an RDBMS or file system. Accessing and working with this physical instance of a collection of datasets can be done either through ArcGIS or through a database management system (DBMS) using Structured Query Language (SQL).
- Geodatabases have a comprehensive information model for representing and managing geographic information.
- Geodatabase software logic provides the common application logic used throughout ArcGIS for accessing and working with all geographic data in a variety of files and formats. This functionality supports working with the geodatabase and includes working with shapefiles, computer-aided design (CAD) files, triangulated irregular networks (TINs), grids, imagery, Geography Markup Language (GML) files, and numerous other GIS data sources.
- Geodatabases have a transaction model for managing GIS data workflows.

Geodatabase design is based on a common set of fundamental GIS design steps, so it's important to understand these GIS design goals and methods.

GIS design involves organizing geographic information into a series of data themes—layers that can be integrated using geographic location. So it makes sense that geodatabase design begins by identifying the data themes to be used and then specifying the contents and representations of each thematic layer.

This approach involves defining the following:

- How the geographic features are to be represented for each theme (for example, as points, lines, polygons, or rasters[1] along with their tabular attributes
- How the data will be organized into datasets, such as feature classes, attributes, raster datasets, and so forth
- What additional spatial and database elements will be needed for integrity rules, implementing rich GIS behavior (such as topologies, networks, and raster catalogs), and defining spatial and attribute relationships between datasets

Spatial data structures

This section will focus on the characteristics of a spatial database structure, highlighting the fundamental concepts used to represent and organize geographic features and their spatial relationships in a computer system. It includes some basic spatial concepts to allow the user to understand what characterizes geospatial information and distinguishes the structure of a spatial database from a conventional database. The aim here is to understand the fundamental concepts useful to grasp what is needed for building a geospatial database for census, using specific examples related to census and statistical contexts.

Geospatial data

The core element of a GIS is geospatial data[2]—that is, data about objects[3] located on the earth's surface. What distinguishes geospatial data from conventional data is that, in addition to the descriptive attributes that characterize conventional data (such as demographic characteristics or time), geospatial data is inherently described by its position on the earth (through geographic coordinates latitude and longitude; Cartesian coordinates x,y,z; address; place-name, etc.) and its geometric form (such as boundaries of a country).

For example, a parcel of land can be described as follows:

- Geometrical data
  - Position
    - Located at 100 Nelson Mandela Ave.
    - X=a; Y=b within system (X,Y)
  - Form
    - Dimensions (sides and arcs constituting a polygon)
- Attribute (descriptive) data
  - Landowner
  - Land use
  - Condition
  - Area
  - Date last sold

In other words, geospatial data has two dimensions: the "where" (spatial component) dimension and the "what" (attribute) dimension, the only one for the conventional data. Attribute data can be stored as different field types in a table or database: character, numeric (integer or floating), date/time, and binary large objects (BLOB).

Examples of geospatial data include roads, rivers, pipelines, cities, administrative units (province, county, ward, district, etc.), crop coverages, mountain ranges, and more. Examples of spatial attributes (or properties) include the width of a river, length of a road, or the boundary of a given country. Often it is also desirable to attach nonspatial attribute information such as the name or the type of road (e.g., Primary, Secondary, Highway), place, and city names, to the spatial data.

Spatial data structure definition

The formal organizational structure of geospatial data in a computer system is generally called a *spatial data structure*. Since the inception of GIS, many approaches have been proposed to represent as accurately as possible geographic features of the real world with their geometric aspects. For example, three of the most common representations of the basic features in maps are points, lines, and polygons (areas or regions).

Spatial data structures aim to organize geometry in 2D, 3D, or higher (e.g., time) for a faster processing of user spatial queries and other geometric operations. The selection of a specific spatial data structure, also called *low-level data structure* because it deals closely with implementation and execution at the machine level, may considerably influence the processing of spatial queries.[4]

A key geodatabase concept is the dataset. It is the primary mechanism used to organize and use geographic information in ArcGIS. The geodatabase contains three primary dataset types:

- Tables
- Feature classes
- Raster datasets

Table
A collection of rows, each containing the same fields. Feature classes are tables with shape fields.

Feature Class
A table with a shape field containing point, line, or polygon geometries for geographic features. Each row is a feature.

Raster Dataset
Contains rasters which represent continuous geographic phenomena.

Figure 4.1. Geodatabase primary database types.

Feature classes are homogeneous collections of common features, each having the same spatial representation, such as points, lines, or polygons, and a common set of attribute columns (e.g., a line feature class for representing road centerlines). The four most commonly used feature classes are points, lines, polygons, and annotation (a term for map text).

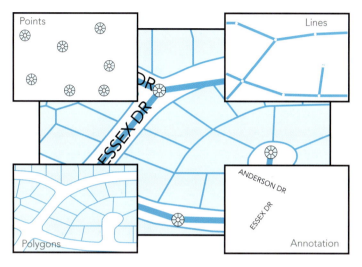

Figure 4.2. Feature classes.

In the geodatabase, attributes are managed in tables based on a series of simple yet essential relational data concepts:

- Tables contain rows.
- All rows in a table have the same fields.
- Each column has a data type, such as integer, decimal number, character, and date.
- A series of functions and operators is available to manage tables and their data elements.

Creating a collection of these dataset types is the first step in designing and building a geodatabase. Users typically start by building a number of these fundamental dataset types. Then they add to or extend their geodatabases with more advanced capabilities to model GIS behavior, maintain data integrity, and work with an important set of spatial relationships.

Owner

Field: Add Delete Calculate Selection: Zoom To Switch

OBJECTID	PARCEL_ID	Owner_Name	DEED_BOOK	SALE_PRICE
1	5491	Doyle, Joanne	14256	57000
2	5492	Smith, Christine	14669	75000
3	5506	Beard, Collin	14927	75861
4	4970	Willams, Miranda	14310	67500
5	5148	Welbon, Conrad	14550	56000
6	5091	Paulman, Joyce	14310	36439
7	5144	Roberts, Julie	14977	37448
8	5497	Moldes, Bradford	14646	34439

Figure 4.3. Table attributes.

Spatial data models

Earlier, *spatial data structure* was defined as what is needed for data to be organized and implemented on computer systems, but we should consider the higher level of abstraction, independent from the implementation and physical aspects.

A spatial data model reflects the conceptual view of the user to the "geographic reality" or "real world" in consideration. This has the advantage of adding and updating the components of the "geographic reality" under consideration for representation, independently from the GIS software in use or to be used.

In a GIS, as a computer system, space would be represented either as a continuum (or surface) or in a discrete manner, with both representations having their advantages and disadvantages for specific applications—hence the representation of spatial data respectively in a raster or vector mode.

Vector vs. raster

The spatial data model used to represent the world as a surface divided into a regular grid of cells (i.e., arranged in rows and columns) is the *raster data model*. The raster model is useful for storing data that varies continuously, as in an aerial photograph, a satellite image, or an elevation surface. A raster data model describes how an image is stored. A raster defines the pixels (cells) in rows and columns, the number of bands, and the bit depth that compose the image. When you view a raster, you are viewing an image of that raster data.

All images are rasters, but not all rasters are considered images. For example, a digital elevation model (DEM) is a cell-based raster dataset but is typically not considered an image. Other types of rasters that are not considered images per se

are magnetic data, interferogram, bathymetric data, and other grid-based datasets.

Each cell (pixel) contains an attribute value and location coordinates. Unlike a vector model, which stores coordinates explicitly, raster coordinates are contained in the ordering of the matrix. Groups of cells that share the same value represent a geographic feature.

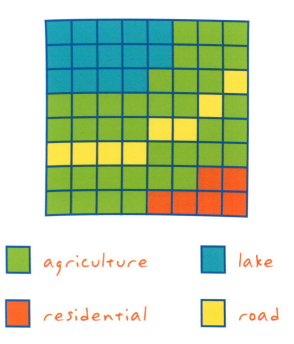

agriculture   lake

residential   road

Figure 4.4. Raster—each cell contains an attribute value and location coordinates.

However, the resolution of the raster depends on its pixel size: the smaller the pixel size, the higher the resolution, but also the larger the data volume (hence a trade-off to be made about the size versus the cost of storage and processing).

A *vector model* is a coordinate-based data model that represents spatial objects or geographic features using a data structure whose geometric primitives are points, lines, and polygons. This allows the representation of discrete objects defined by their coordinates with a precision that depends on the number of coordinates in consideration.

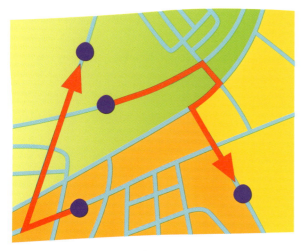

Figure 4.5. Vector—a coordinate-based data model that represents geographic features as points, lines, and polygons.

The vector model is appropriate for the representation of point-based features such as wells, dwellings, schools, landmarks, urban centers at small scale, line-based features (such as roads, railways, rivers, pipelines, boundaries, etc.), and polygon-based features (such as lakes, forests, cities at large scale, administrative units, provinces, countries, or regions). Other popular data structures like the irregular tessellations are also used in some vector-based models, such as TINs, contour lines, Thiessen or Voronoi polygons, and so on.

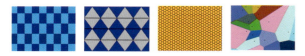

Figure 4.6. Irregular tessellations—tessellation is the tiling of a plane using one or more geometric shapes, with no overlaps and no gaps.

The vector model would be suitable for census data collection units at point level as well as at EA. We will expand on the vector model when we use it for the building of a census geospatial database

at the EA level because it's a vector-oriented model database.

Let's first illustrate the vector versus raster models, representing the same geographic feature.

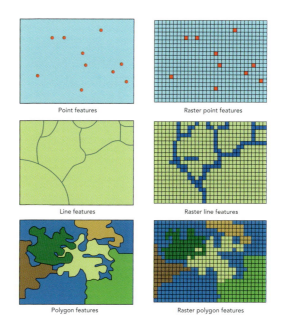

Figure 4.7. Vector versus raster—representation of points, lines, and polygons in vector and raster formats.

Topology

Topology in GIS is generally defined as the spatial relationships between adjacent or neighboring features. If features are coincident and share the same location of coordinates, boundaries, or nodes, chances are that geodatabase topology can help better manage geographic data.

Geodatabase topologies help ensure data integrity. Using a topology provides a mechanism to perform integrity checks on data and helps to validate and maintain better feature representations in a geodatabase. For example, making sure that a feature set that represents an EA completely covers the area and leaves no gaps or overlaps is a function of topology.

In addition, topologies can be used for modeling numerous spatial relationships between features. These topologies enable support for a variety of analytic operations, such as finding adjacent features, working with coincident boundaries between features, and navigating along connected features. The geometric primitives of the vector data model are represented in a computer database as follows: a point is represented by one pair (x,y); a line (a set of connected points) is represented by a sequence of x,y coordinates with the starting and ending points called *nodes*; and a polygon (a set of connected lines) is represented by a set of x,y coordinates in which the starting point coincides with the ending point of the loop.

Topology is the arrangement for how point, line, and polygon features share geometry. Topology is employed to do the following:

- Constrain how features share geometry. For example, adjacent polygons (such as parcels with shared edges, street centerlines, and census blocks) share geometry and adjacent soil polygons share edges.
- Define and enforce data integrity rules: no gaps, overlapping features, or slivers should exist between polygons.
- Support topological relationship queries and navigation, such as identifying feature adjacency and connectivity.

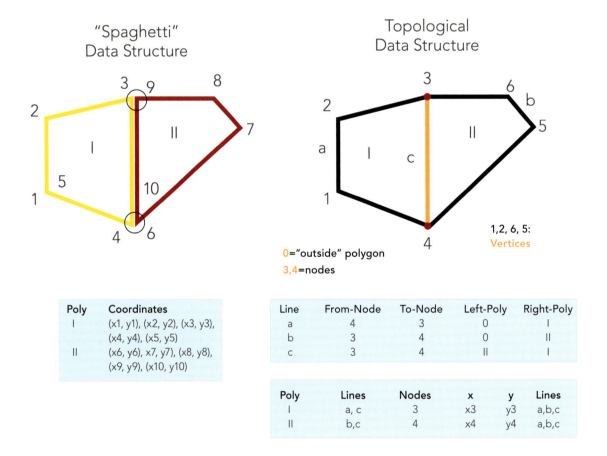

Figure 4.8. Comparison between topological and spaghetti data structures. Topology is the arrangement that constrains how point, line, and polygon features share geometry. Without this, you have a spaghetti data structure.

- Support sophisticated editing tools that enforce the topological constraints of the data model.
- Construct features from unstructured geometry, such as creating polygons from lines.

Topology explicitly stores the relationships among the geometric primitives. As shown in figure 4.8, it represents the polygons in an optimal way.[i] Topology is defined as the mathematics branch that deals with the spatial relationships (connectivity, adjacency, etc.) among the geographic features represented by the primitives (point, line, polygon) in a GIS. The topological data structure determines explicitly, for example, how and where points and lines connect and whether polygons are adjacent. In short, topology describes the geometric relationships of the geographic features of a given space.[ii]

The use of topology distinguishes a GIS database because it allows users to make spatial queries. This capability is useful for network analysis and necessary for various spatial analyses, all of which constitutes the power of GIS.

It is worth mentioning that a simple vector model, used by CAD systems, stores vector data without establishing relationships among the geographic features. It is called the *spaghetti model*. With this model, vector data consists of simple lines with no topology and usually no attributes. For example, spaghetti lines may cross but those crossings are not recognized as intersections (see figure 4.8, which compares the spaghetti and topological models).

Geospatial database design

Earlier, we defined geospatial data and the models to represent geospatial data to structure them in a way that would allow their implementation in a computer system. The next step is to create and maintain a database to help organize and manage geospatial data. What distinguishes a GIS from a CAD system is that a GIS relies on a DBMS, constituting an integrated software that allows users to store, manipulate, and retrieve data from a geospatial database.

Database modeling

Using abstraction from concepts by humans to their implementation in the machine, database modeling relies generally on a three-tier model:

1. A **conceptual model** involving the identification of the geographic features to be included in the database as entities/objects, the definition of their attributes, and how they relate to one another. An abstraction and objective representation of the real world independent from the DBMS software to be used.

2. A **logical model**, a resulting outcome from the transformation of the conceptual model using the DBMS data model techniques (e.g., relational, object, or object-relational).

3. A **physical model**, a resulting outcome from the transformation of the logical model, dealing with storage devices, file structure, and access methods that sort data records. A physical model deals with the storing and encoding of data—the lower-level data structure of the database.

Many GIS databases within NSOs are created without necessarily going through the modeling process. Some organizations tend to select the GIS technology first and then proceed with the creation of the database in accordance with the selected software requirements. NSOs, particularly in developing countries, often do not have the time or the expertise required to understand how to establish their geodatabase. The challenge here is that this work is fundamental to success and will have an effect across all business processes. Diligence in creation of the database model and developing guidelines and best practices are recommended for building a comprehensive and sustainable geospatial database that can respond to the needs of the census and beyond. Database modeling would lead to the preparation of a detailed data dictionary that guides the database development process and serves as documentation in later stages, justifying any additional investment the NSO would need for the creation of its geospatial database.

Database designers tend to give attention to the DBMS data model techniques used for the geospatial database creation. An array of techniques has evolved from the flat file, hierarchical, and network models, to the relational and the object-oriented models. However, the relational and, to a lesser degree, the object-oriented and the hybrid object-relational are the most used, but with the relational still prevailing and dominating the field. The dominance of the relational (RDBMS)

in the database field would be arguably attributed to the many resources invested in its development, its massive installed base that developed even before the appearance of the object-oriented, and particularly to its close ties with SQL,[5] the standard database query language adopted by virtually all mainstream databases.

Some would even ask that if object-oriented programming languages like Java or C# (C++) are so popular, why aren't object-oriented database management systems (OODBMSs) more popular, too? The debate between relational and object-oriented within the database community, paralleling the debate of vector versus raster in GIS,[6] does not seem to be going away soon; it is, however, tempered by the increasing use of the hybrid object-relational approach. We will elaborate more on the relational model and provide an overview on the object-oriented model as well.

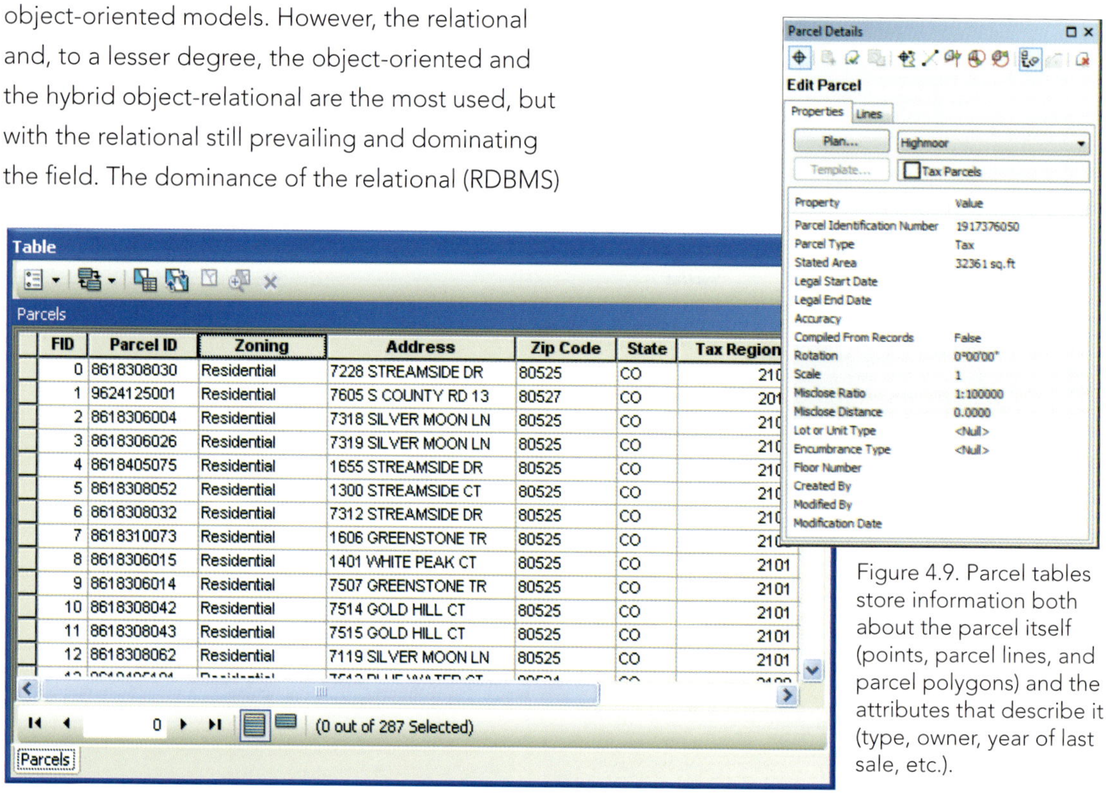

Figure 4.9. Parcel tables store information both about the parcel itself (points, parcel lines, and parcel polygons) and the attributes that describe it (type, owner, year of last sale, etc.).

Relational database model

In a relational database model,[7] the geographic features and their relationships are represented by tables of data (files). The relational database model is used to store, retrieve, and manipulate tables of data that refer to the geographic features (see the example of a parcel table in figure 4.9). The focus is on the potential relation between any two features, which is defined by a name and a list of attributes, including a key identifier that characterizes the relation. The manipulation of relations, suitable for mathematical operations, would thus allow queries and reports; this gave the model its "relational" name.

The relational model, dealing with the formats of the attributes and the relations that link the geographic features and used at the implementation level of the database, is based on the entity-relationship (E/R) model, developed by P. Chen in 1976[8] as an abstract concept of the database.

Census GIS database: Basic elements

In creating the census GIS database, we start by identifying the components of a census geographic database and stress the different stages in its development, including geographic data inventory for EA delineation; geographic data conversion through scanning, digitizing, or use of earth observation data; construction and maintenance of topology; integration of various digital data; implementation of an EA database; metadata development; and data quality control.

The basic elements of the census database include the following:
- Boundary database—including polygons that represent the census units
  - Administrative units
  - Census units/EAs

Parcels feature class

Shape	ID	PIN	Area	Addr	Code
	1	334-1626-001	7,342	341 Cherry Ct.	SFR
	2	334-1626-002	8,020	343 Cherry Ct.	UND
	3	334-1626-003	10,031	345 Cherry Ct.	SFR
	4	334-1626-004	9,254	347 Cherry Ct.	SFR
	5	334-1626-005	8,856	348 Cherry Ct.	UND
	6	334-1626-006	9,975	346 Cherry Ct.	SFR
	7	334-1626-007	8,230	344 Cherry Ct.	SFR
	8	334-1626-008	8,645	342 Cherry Ct.	SFR

Related ownership table

PIN	Owner	Acq.Date	Assessed	TaxStat
334-1626-001	G. Hall	1995/10/20	$115,500.00	02
334-1626-002	H. L Holmes	1993/10/06	$24,375.00	01
334-1626-003	W. Rodgers	1980/09/24	$175,500.00	02
334-1626-004	J. Williamson	1974/09/20	$135,750.00	02
334-1626-005	P. Goodman	1966/06/06	$30,350.00	02
334-1626-006	K. Staley	1942/10/24	$120,750.00	02
334-1626-007	J. Dormandy	1996/01/27	$110,650.00	01
334-1626-008	S. Gooley	2000/05/31	$145,750.00	02

Figure 4.10. Parcel table with map and example of linking to attribute data via unique ID or PIN.

- Geographic attribute tables
- Census data tables—nonspatial attributes including a unique ID that allows for the link to the corresponding geography
- Other vector data—e.g., points of interest, landmarks, transportation or water features

The geodatabase storage model is based on a series of simple yet essential relational database concepts and leverages the strengths of the underlying DBMS. Simple tables and well-defined attribute types are used to store the schema, rule, base, and spatial attribute data for each geographic dataset. This approach provides a formal model for storing and working with your data. Through this approach, SQL can be used to create, modify, and query tables and their data elements.

You can see how this works by examining how a feature with polygon geometry is modeled in the geodatabase. A feature class is stored as a table, often referred to as the base or business table. Each row in the table represents one feature. The shape column stores the polygon geometry for each feature. The contents of this table, including the shape when stored as a SQL spatial type, can be accessed through SQL.

Object-oriented model

An object-oriented model represents the "real world" in the form of a set of objects. Each object is associated with a unique identifier, encapsulating attributes defining its characteristics, and methods defining its behavior. Objects sharing the same set of attributes and methods are grouped in classes, and new classes can be derived from the existing classes through inheritance (the new class inherits all the attributes and methods of the existing class and may have additional attributes and methods).

Objects are at the core of the object-oriented model (as tables are at the core of the relational data model), but they seem to be more natural to represent the real world. The OODBMS, supported by the oriented-object programming languages such as Smalltalk, C++, Java, and others, was created to overcome the shortfalls of the RDBMS. But, mainly for lack of agreement on a standard for object-oriented database and the strong implementation of RDBMSs, the OODBMSs have been used more frequently to complement the RDBMSs than to replace them.

In this regard, superimposing the object-oriented database concepts on relational databases is more commonly used by the commercial GIS products. The Esri geodatabase[9] is object-relational and illustrates the object-oriented concepts extension brought to relational-based databases. The subsequent examples will rely on the use of this geodatabase.

Administrative Areas

Enumeration Areas

Field Offices

Building Footprints

Basemap

Orthophoto

Figure 4.11. Thematic layers are one of the main organizing principles for GIS database design.

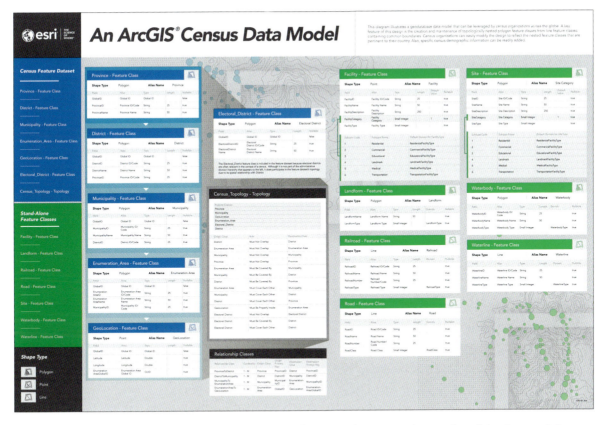

Figure 4.12. Census data model (see the online ancillaries for a complete, up-to-date version of the data model).

Worth noting is that to provide a complete description of the reality to be represented in a database and ultimately allow the programmer or developer to maintain a sustainable database, the data models must be completed by a data dictionary. Usually, the data dictionary contains all the necessary metadata about the name and definition of the entity types and attributes included in the data model as well as any codes used to identify the entities and their attributes—the type of each attribute and the domain of its values. (More information on metadata will be provided in chapter 6, and on metadata for dissemination in chapter 9).

Basemap considerations

A comprehensive GIS-based census database should have at its foundation the smallest statistical unit for data collection, be it an EA, a census tract, a block group, a census block, a dwelling or housing unit, or an address. Basemaps constitute one of the main sources of data for the delineation of EAs, but they need to meet some requirements to support the EAs' delineation process.

All census geographers should consider specific factors as part of their basemap inventory process, such as the types of basemaps, either available or to be created eventually, required for the census purposes. NSOs are not typically the custodians of the basemaps in the country because their creation may require a national mandate. Often a NMA takes on this role and has staff with surveying and cartographic skills and equipment necessary to build a complete national digital basemap. Thus, NSOs would most likely need to acquire various basemaps from different outside providers or use map services, requiring national institutional coordination and collaboration.

NSOs need various up-to-date basemaps at different scales,[10] the master data from which enumeration and publication maps are made. They primarily need national base data covering the whole country, at small scale, showing the major administrative area boundaries and the location of major reference features. NSOs also need topographic data at large and medium scales, generally produced by their NMAs, which show elevation and other major topographic features needed for demarcation. They also need city and cadastral data at large scales showing land parcels, streets and roads, city buildings and important landmarks, or any features that may be useful for census mapping in urban areas. In addition to this base data, NSOs need maps showing population distribution from the previous census, or any features that may be useful for GIS-based census purposes. (This will be further covered in chapter 6.)

Because the information will be incorporated into the GIS-based census database, the legend and metadata about the sources should be well documented to be part of the data dictionary. Maps or map services should include the sources of data, the geographic referencing information, and the scale, including consistent map projection, but also the other cartographic parameters like map datum, grid, and any other information helpful to map users. These parameters should fully match those adopted in the new technologies (GIS and GPS) before trying to use this data in a GIS project.

Quality control and quality improvements to basemaps

The quality of geospatial data, including maps that are used in the census, has a major influence on the quality and reliability of the census data to be collected. Striving for high accuracy may be costly, but adequate activities need to be carried out that go beyond data conversion in terms of quality control, quality review, and editing of the maps used during the enumeration. Problems and inconsistencies must be resolved before the final products can be generated.

Specific measures help to ensure the data quality of the final maps used by the enumerators. One such measure is to ensure the consistency of the geospatial database that will be the basis for the creation of digital maps. We should, for example, check that two adjacent EAs actually connect on the map with no overlapping, or that a supervisory area (SA) correctly includes the assigned EAs. The aim is to make sure that full and unduplicated coverage of the country's territory exists by correctly delineated EAs (i.e., without undercoverage or overcoverage).

In addition, we need to check that the metadata (map scale, data sources, date of production, etc.) is properly attributed. Because the digital map is composed of a set of data layers, checking their organization is very important to avoid any overlay in which a top geographic data layer would hide features of a layer in a lower level. While most of the consistency checks are increasingly done interactively on computers, the quality control of the cartographic work may still require, for some developing countries, printing of the updated maps and organizing them by administrative unit. Traditionally, NSO census geographers gave the maps to local administrators for final checking and corrections, including the accuracy of the directional positioning of localities and the area coverage—a kind of peer review. Indeed, involving local authorities provides some ownership to the data and ultimately builds confidence in the results. Today, this process is changing with the use of a digital approach to map production.

Many country experiences have proven that the use of GIS, integrated with remotely sensed data and GPS, facilitates the quality control of the field data and in turn increases its quality. More specifically, with GIS and its geospatial database, the delineation of EAs can be substantively improved because a number of questions about the EA will be addressed (such as total number of dwellings/households per EA or locality) and also with regard to updating data on roads, streets, and reference points for map orientation. Actually, map updating and improvements refer to the activities aimed at updating data on housing units for the organization of field census operations, making the list of buildings and housing units up-to-date. We will see in later sections how the logistics of fieldwork activities will be better planned, managed, and monitored with this same data.

Earth observation data

As noted earlier, population and housing censuses require up-to-date and detailed basemaps for the accurate delineation of EA boundaries. But in many instances, basemaps suitable for a census are either outdated or inaccurate when they are available, or in some cases simply do not exist. Modern satellite imagery, digital aerial photography, and GPS, combined with GIS, have been increasingly used to overcome the lack of

appropriate basemaps for the EA demarcation.

In the last few decades, the integrated use of remotely sensed data[11] (aerial photos and satellite imagery) and GPS has been practiced to field-validate EA boundaries that were created in the office using available GIS-based maps from the previous census or sometimes as a substitute for up-to-date basemaps when they were not available.

NSOs have many more imagery-based options than they had just a few years ago. Digital aerial photography, known for its high resolution and accuracy, can obviously be used for census mapping. While its acquisition cost and particularly the expertise and equipment needed for the additional processing required to produce orthophoto[12] maps used to be prohibitive for the NSO to pursue, imagery costs have decreased and continue to do so today. Some aerial imagery providers, such as Woolpert, have begun to provide orthorectified imagery at very competitive rates. This trend is reinforced by aerial photography and imagery captured from drones that can be processed much faster and easier than ever before. Similarly, high-resolution satellite imagery (providing geographic details that are quite comparable to digital orthophoto maps) are also decreasing in costs and increasing in coverage and accessibility. Today, some cost-free initiatives[13] are available. Satellite-based remote sensing and GPS technologies constitute a viable alternative in support of EA delineation (more details on the use of earth observations are in chapter 5).

Defining census geography

Census geography refers to how the country is geographically divided prior to the actual census enumeration to facilitate field operations, data processing and analysis, and ultimately reporting and disseminating census results. In this section, we will elaborate on the various geographic classifications, including the enumeration geography (administrative areas approach), the grid- and point-based approaches, and the spatial register–based approach.

Geographic classifications
One of the key issues a NSO faces when it starts to prepare for a census geography program is choosing the geographic classification approach to determine the geographic units for census enumeration, as so many other operations depend on this choice—in other words, what would be the geographic level or scale to which statistical data will be linked, as the "geography on which the census is collected will determine the geography

on which the census data can be disseminated."[14] An increasing number of approaches are being used and are outlined in the following paragraphs.

Administrative areas approach/enumeration geography
The traditional administrative areas approach involves the use of existing administrative boundaries to provide the basis for the geographic areas, representing the smallest area for which population information is available. It consists of the creation of a list of all administrative and statistical reporting units in the country, with the relationships between all types of administrative and reporting unit boundaries being defined.

Most countries have their own specific administrative boundary hierarchy, generally a nested administrative hierarchy (see figure 4.13) by which

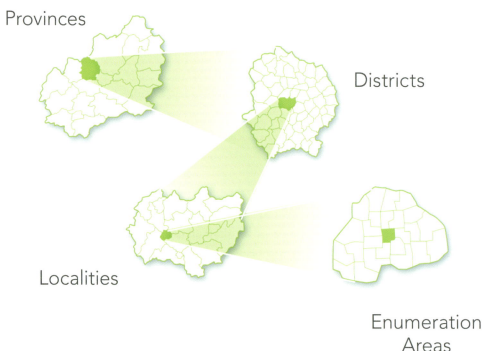

Figure 4.13. Nested administrative hierarchy.

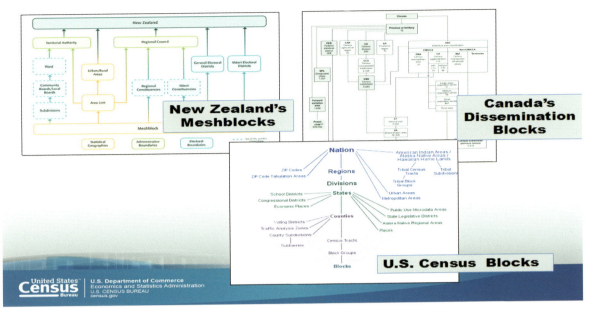

Figure 4.14. Geographic hierarchies based on census blocks. *Source*: US Census Bureau.[16]

the country and each lower-level set of administrative units (except the lowest) are subdivided to form the next lower level; the lowest level often constitutes the EA. The numbers of boundaries vary between countries depending on the physical size, population, and population distribution of each country. The number of boundaries is also influenced by the number of tiers of government with countries having national, state, and local governments (see the following example of administrative hierarchy from the UN workshops for the 2010 Round of Census).

However, this approach makes it more difficult to provide statistical information describing other geographic areas. (In certain countries, EAs are further subdivided into blocks[iii] bounded by physical features such as streets or rivers; see figure 4.14.)

This process of division of a country into areas for census purposes is also known as *enumeration geography*. Relying on the boundaries of administrative areas is considered for some a natural and

more appropriate approach for surveying populations, housing units, and geographic areas because they conform to the boundaries of the physical features on the ground (i.e., roads, railroads, rivers, lakes) and on urban development patterns.[15]

Grid-based approach

Enumeration geography relies on administrative areas aligned with physical boundaries for census purposes. But some would argue that a reliance on physical boundaries that have the potential to change is precisely the reason not to use administrative areas in favor of other geographic classifications. In this regard, the statistical grid is proposed as an alternative, especially in Europe,[iv] where a big advantage of the grid-based statistical system is seen to be the application across boundaries. Grids are stable over time and not affected by frequent administrative boundary changes. Indeed, grids offer a great potential for cross-border studies needed by the global community to tackle environmental, health, socioeconomic, population, urban planning, emergency management, and national security concerns. It also offers the potential for studies of indicators where the data heavily depends on the spatial entity to which it relates.[17]

While the boundaries of administrative areas are often irregular, statistical grids, used as geographies for population and census information, are fundamentally spatial units with equal size and even distribution. Moreover, grid-based statistics offer flexibility in the size of the grids, starting with relatively small grids and increasing in size to larger and larger grids (e.g., from 100 m × 100 m to 10 km × 10 km or bigger) and constituting a nested framework. These grid cells provide a great potential for comparable spatial statistics and statistical time series.

One major criticism with grids is that they are not population-centric, meaning that there will be a different number of people in the same-sized grid cell, depending on urban or rural locations. However, statistical grids offer a spatial reference system that can serve as the smallest statistical area unit for which—respecting statistical confidentiality—data may be provided to the user, providing an effective approach for environmental and other non-population-based statistics. The most important advantage of statistical grids is the independence of administrative (national or international) boundaries. Furthermore, being a spatial reference system, statistical grids provide a mechanism for integrating data from other sources and are suitable for GIS-based overlaying capabilities

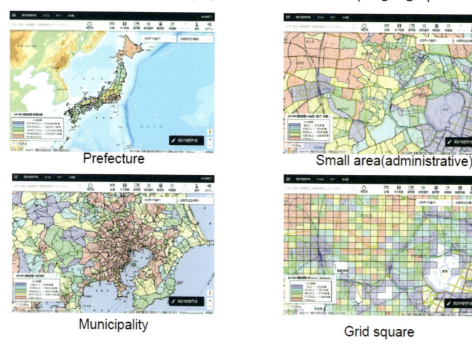

Figure 4.15. Example of data displayed in grids and other geographic units.[vi]

and other spatial analysis. They can serve as the smallest statistical area unit with better solutions for statistical disclosure control. In this regard, grid statistics are being increasingly adopted in some national statistical institutions, particularly in Europe, as an alternative to census blocks.[18]

The debate of grid-based approach versus population/administrative areas approach has been recurrent for some time now. The UN-EG-ISGI[19] discussed the issue thoroughly in several meetings and conducted a comparative study, highlighting advantages and disadvantages of the two approaches. The conclusion is that the solution is not either/or and that statistical grids can complement traditional statistics based on administrative/statistical units, and thus, when needed, a mixed approach[20] that combines administrative areas with grids is advisable. Since statistical grids can be used for many purposes, such as regional/spatial analysis and planning, research, environmental, and other telecommunications purposes, some efforts are being made to develop standards to consolidate the use of grid-based areas.[v] National Statistics Center of Japan (NSTAC) has been working with grid data for some time and is providing population census data in multiple geographic units.

Point-based approach

Another approach dealing with higher geographic levels consists of geocoding statistical units associated with unreferenced location information (address, property, or building) to the level of single coordinates (e.g., x,y,z coordinates). This point-based location has the advantage of increasing the spatial resolution of the statistical data and provides considerable flexibility when linking the statistical information to any type of geographic area of interest and delivering aggregations at any spatial unit. It

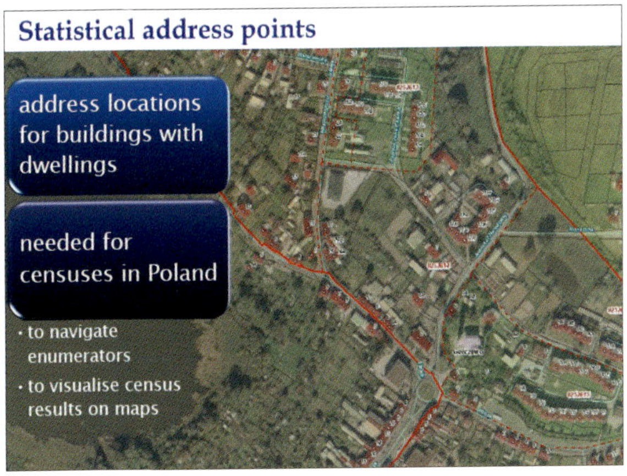

Figure 4.16. Statistical address points database excerpted from the Polish Modern Census, Example of Statistical Address Points, Poland. See *The Polish Modern Census: Incorporating Geospatial Technology and Data with Administrative Information.*[23]

allows for considerable adaptability to changes in the geographic areas over time or to adapt to new geographies that emerge. Another advantage of a point-based location of people and dwellings is that it increases the spatial relevance of statistical information, particularly in crisis management, as in the case of flooding and other natural disasters.[21]

The point-based approach is increasingly used through the direct capture with GPS of the coordinates (latitude and longitude) of point-based features such as dwellings or other features of interest. Some countries are embarking on capturing a latitude-longitude for every housing unit, building their geospatial infrastructure, known as the dwelling frame.[22]

Spatial register–based approach

An alternative that has been used particularly in Europe and Nordic countries[24] is the register-based approach. The register-based approach involves the full use of the existing administrative sources related to individuals, households, dwellings, and addresses. Some cases extend to other relevant registers providing information on business units, tax, education, and employment.[25] Usually, administrative records are data collected as part of the management of federal, state, or local governmental programs.

Countries using administrative registers expect to reap the following benefits: reduced costs; no burden of massive responses; reduced time to produce census outputs; and better coverage and quality of census data. However, coverage and data quality depend on the quality of registers, including reliable information related to households and addresses. In addition, some preconditions related to the use of administrative data should be met. They include the existence of a legal framework allowing their use for census purposes with adequate protection of privacy and the availability of comprehensive and reliable registers (population, buildings/dwellings, and addresses). Institutional cooperation is also required because of transparency issues, such as, generally, several institutions being custodians of the registers, easy access to the registers, and acceptance from the people as the data is at the individual level (e.g., using a nationwide unique ID).

Some countries are even using spatial-based registers. For example, in Netherlands, two important geographical registers became accessible for statistical use because of the new law governing Statistics Netherlands. These registers contain information on roads, from highways to streets, and data on address-location—that is, x and y coordinates. The Dutch census of 2011 was carried out almost entirely by collecting data from registers, such as the housing registry, in combination with other sources, such as the land registry and the central bank. Studies show that in the absence of geocoded population registers, disaggregation and spatial modeling techniques can help to fill the gaps.[26]

Enumeration areas[27]

We have outlined the different geographical classifications used for census purposes. A common central piece is the need to identify the statistical unit required for census data collection. In the following paragraphs, we will focus on the design of the still most used one: the EA that is used with the traditional administrative areas approach.[vii] The UN *Principles and Recommendations* defines EA as the operational unit for data collection during the census that comprises the lowest level of the geographic hierarchy of administrative and statistical units.

As stated previously, the delineation of the EAs for census purposes is a defining step of the census geography program, carried out at an early stage of the census process. Taking into consideration a certain number of critical design criteria, EAs should do the following:

- Cover the whole country—by showing clearly that there are no gaps in the territory to be enumerated—and not overlap.
- Fit within the national administrative hierarchy and be consistent, as much as possible, with other relevant geographic units (needed for education, health, environmental, and development purposes).
- Have clearly observable and easily identifiable boundaries on the ground—enumerators need to be able to find the boundaries of the area for which they are responsible (use preferably physical features such as rivers, lakes, roads, railroads, parcel boundaries, or any other visible feature that defines a sharp boundary, and try to ensure that these features are shown and named on the updated maps).
- Have populations of approximately equal size.
- Be small enough and accessible to be covered by an enumerator during data collection but

large enough to guarantee confidentiality of personal information.

- Be consistent (to a larger extent) with EA boundaries used in the previous census to allow comparability over time.
- Be small and flexible enough to respond to the dissemination demands for small-area data and the ability to be aggregated to present information on larger geographic units, and be useful for other types of data collection activities.[28]

Practically, the design of EAs is guided by two major needs: on one hand, it should facilitate the census data collection and the related field operations, and on the other hand, it should

allow the production of useful census output products for various census data users.

It is important to stress that the size of the EA is of utmost importance for the field operations because it affects the way the census is conducted. The size of EAs should be defined by simultaneously considering population size and surface area. The chosen population size (most important in terms of censuses) varies from country to country and is determined based generally on pretest results and estimates from the previous census. However, for most practical purposes, the population size of an enumeration is generally in the low to mid- hundreds. As per surface area and accessibility, the main criterion is to ensure that one enumerator can count the population within the EA in

Figure 4.17a. Enumeration area showing a boundary line cutting through a building.

Figure 4.17b. Enumeration areas showing significant change since the previous survey.

the time scheduled for data collection, knowing that enumeration can proceed more quickly in towns and cities than in rural areas.

We have just set the guiding principles that NSOs need to follow for EA design. In chapter 6, we will present how we use geospatial technology to help delineate them. After the delineation of EAs, we need to proceed with the design of SAs, which is usually straightforward. SAs provide the means for crews of enumerators to be effectively guided and managed, given that experience has shown that supervision of the enumerator's work is an essential requirement for the success of any census. Each SA contained usually a group of eight to ten contiguous EAs to facilitate the enumeration and assignment of workloads. Indeed, the EAs assigned to the same SA must be compact to minimize travel times (allowing the supervisor to travel to the field to observe enumerators and ensure accuracy in recording information, resolve problems, and conduct verifications) and of approximately equal size. They should be delineated to be included in the same field office area, which is usually defined according to administrative units, and thus their boundaries must not cross administrative boundaries.

Census management areas consist in turn of aggregations of SAs and are defined for facilitating the management of the census enumeration. They might relate to either administrative regions or statistical areas because they are devised as operational zones, driven by the need of management for the most efficient data collection. GIS spatial analysis tools can be used in this process to create efficient EAs that help reduce costs and save time.

Geographic coding

The creation of the traditional geographic classification system includes two processes: dividing a country into smaller geographic areas and assigning a code to each of the resulting geographic areas. This geospatial enabling process constitutes one of the major approaches to what is known as *geocoding*. The purpose of the following section is to introduce the geocoding concept relevant for census mapping and its different approaches related to data collection. We will further clarify the difference between geocoding and georeferencing.

Coding scheme

Generally, the NSO is the custodian of a coding structure, a system that uniquely identifies each level of the administrative hierarchy, including the assignment of a unique code (alphanumeric or preferably numeric) to each EA, called the *coding scheme*. This unique code (a series of numbers) is used to ensure unique enumeration during the census data collection and is used in data processing to compile enumerated information for households in each EA and to aggregate this information for administrative or statistical zones for dissemination.

Geographic units are numbered at each level of the administrative hierarchy—usually leaving gaps between the numbers to allow for the future insertion of newly created zones at that level. Indeed, the coding scheme should be flexible and expandable to accommodate any changes in the structure of the administrative hierarchy and the EAs.

For example, at the province level, units may be numbered 5, 10, 15, and so on. A similar scheme would be used for lower-level administrative units and for EAs. Since there are often, for example, more districts in a province than provinces in a country, more digits may be required at lower levels.

The unique identifier for each smallest level unit—i.e., the EA—then consists simply of the concatenated identifiers of the administrative units into which it falls.

- An EA code of 01-07-22-018-076392 means that enumeration area 076392 is located in region 01, province 07, municipality 22, Barangay 018.

A prerequisite to the building of a GIS database at the EA level is the development of a geocoding scheme in which the unique code can be used to

Region (2 digit)	0 1
Province (2 digit)	0 7
City/Municipality (2 digit)	2 2
Barangay (3 digit)	0 1 8
Enumeration Area Number	0 7 6 3 9 2

Geographic units are numbered at each level of the administrative hierarchy—usually leaving gaps betwen the numbers to allow for future insertion of newly created zones at that level.

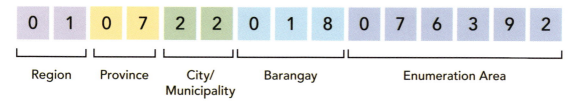

Figure 4.18. Example of an enumeration area coding scheme from Philippine Statistics Authority.[29]

link the digital EA boundary (geographic features) to the aggregated census data (attributes recorded for them). The development of a coding scheme is therefore necessary to assign a unique code to each EA, needed for data processing. When we assign geographic identifiers, such as latitude-longitude coordinates, to the boundaries or the centroid location of the EAs, the resulting codes, referred to as *geocodes*, will allow data to be linked geographically and displayed on a map and therefore establish a link between GIS boundaries and tabular census data. Some NSOs are going even further than EAs to geocoding street addresses, landmarks, buildings, and dwelling and housing units. For some data users, geocoding is referring more specifically to this latter operation.

Definitions of geocoding

Geocoding (geographically enabling unit records) is defined as the process of finding associated geographic coordinates (expressed in latitude and longitude) from other geographic data for the statistical units, such as street addresses or postal codes. (Geocoding is a way to ensure that the data "knows" where it is.)

In other words, geocoding involves taking location information for these statistical units (such as address) and linking this information to a location coordinate (i.e., x,y,z coordinates) and/or a small geographic area. The geocodes (the location coordinates and geographic areas codes) obtained from this process can be stored directly on the statistical unit record or linked in some way to the record. There is a common misunderstanding between geocoding and georeferencing, so it is important to emphasize that while they are related, they are quite different. Georeferencing is often done, for example, with raster images. Georeferencing is the process of referencing data against a known geospatial coordinate system by matching to known points of reference in the coordinate system so that the data can be analyzed, viewed, and queried with other geographic data.

In the GIS industry, geocoding is synonymous with address matching, which is the process of assigning map coordinate locations to addresses in a database.[30] A GIS is capable of doing this by comparing the elements of an address or a table of addresses with the address attributes of a reference dataset—the GIS data layer used as the geographic reference layer (e.g., a city's street centerlines layer)—to find a match (i.e., to determine whether particular address falls within an address range associated with a feature in the reference).

But the concept of geocoding goes beyond address matching. It covers a continuum of spatial scales: from individual housing units to EA levels, up to higher administrative or national levels. The use of GPS, directly capturing precise data at the level of point locations (latitude and longitude coordinates), allows the coding of centroids, building corners, or building point-of-entry coordinates for a unit such as a block of land, building, or dwelling.

A look at the main geocoding methods used by many countries during the 2010 Round of Censuses is informative. In this regard, at the forty-fourth session of the UNSC held in February 2013, the commission discussed the program review *Developing a Statistical-Spatial Framework in National Statistical Systems*, which was based on the outcomes of the *Survey of Linking Geospatial Information to Statistics*, led by the Australian Bureau of Statistics (ABS) in September–October 2012 and had fifty-two NSOs complete the survey. Participating countries recognized, among other things, that adding a geospatial capability to statistics requires the codification of location attributes linked to socioeconomic statistical informa-

Main geocoding methods	Percentage using this method	Comments
Enumeration geography	31%	This is a traditional approach that takes the geospatial reference from the geography that the data is collected within, but forces enumeration geography and dissemination geography to be tied together.
National registers	23%	Strong in Europe.
Address coding	9%	The major countries using this method are Australia, New Zealand, USA, UAE, Poland and Portugal.
Block, locality, and community coding	8%	Stronger in the Americas and Asia, and similar to enumeration geography but generally the areas are larger.
Direct capture (via GPS)	6%	This method is being used in a number of developing countries througout the world, where these countries may be leapfrogging older methods.

Figure 4.19. Main geocoding methods in the 2010 Round. *Source:* Final report for the Expert Group on the Integration of Statistical and Geospatial Information.[31]

tion, known under the concept of geocoding. The results are summarized in figure 4.19.

Additional reference information

The provision of geocoded statistical data for small areas has become a new challenge for NSOs. On the one hand, the demand for spatial data and especially for data related to small areas has increased. On the other hand, the technical possibilities to collect and process georeferenced data using geospatial information technology, including geographical information systems, have also greatly increased. Statistical data is increasingly collected or organized in such a way as to be linked to

a georeference system, most preferably a coordinate-based system, and structured in a geospatial database. This database benefits from being developed with an extended scope, encompassing the foundational elements related to the smallest statistical unit (e.g., EA), but also incorporating other reference information, such as topography, elevation, land parcels, transport networks, etc.

The added value of establishing detailed geographic databases of EAs that would encompass the needs for census data collection, support the processing of census data, and be directly linked to data dissemination for small areas is incalculable. These databases need to consistently integrate their database structure's census data with other geographic reference data, such as roads, rivers, landmarks, and settlements, thus providing a critical base for disaster preparations. The partic-ipants noted that the geographic presentation of statistical data significantly increased the interest of users, resulting in a better appreciation of statis-tical products and statistical work in general.

Case study: Albania

The National Institute of Statistics of Albania (INSTAT) is the main producer of official statistics in the country and responsible for the coordination of the Albanian statistical system.

The production of official statistics in Albania is regulated by the "Law on Official Statistics" that follows the Fundamental Principles of Official Statistics of the United Nations and the European Statistics Code of Practice. Albania is a candidate for membership in the European Union and, as such, is committed to put in place standards in line with the *acquis communautaire*. The European Union directive Infrastructure for Spatial Information in Europe (INSPIRE) requires member states to share spatial themes through a network of services and to adopt its set of rules.

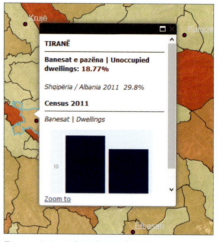

Figure 1. A widget lets administrators geospatially monitor census coverage.

To build its GIS, the institute partnered with two Italian agencies, TeamDev and CIRPS—University of Rome. They determined census methodologies and introduced GIS technology into the 2011 census process.

INSTAT's expectations for GIS included supporting processes for a complete census count, making data easily available, and providing a foundation for future statistical surveys. Albania's statistics department launched an enterprise GIS that enabled the country to meet these requirements, as well as complying with statistical standards. The system was used to complete the 2011 Albania Population and Housing Census and continues in place today, supporting the agency and the community.

GIS became an agent of transformation. INSTAT integrated geospatial processes with official statistical production to make its data location-based. The system improved continuity by connecting workflows and outputs. GIS also improved the quality of the institute's data by running built-in processes that verified and checked accuracy.

INSTAT increased the value of its GIS by extending its usefulness beyond the initial census project, and the institute is now using it for planning and implementing current statistical operations. INSTAT's digital data and maps are interoperable with other institutions' digital maps and geographic data resources. Statistical information from INSTAT is readily available via a Web GIS application that is open, allowing users to gain access to information. "The statistical maps can be created by our

Figure 2. INSTAT web application.

users themselves with specific classification as per needs or specifics of the studies or phenomena," according to Ervin Shameti, head of cartography and GIS sector.

System rollout

Pre-enumeration phase

To begin, the GIS team built an enterprise geodatabase that various team members could access. Using geodatabase tools, they digitized building footprints and street lines from high-resolution orthophotos to create basemaps of the entire country. Because the digitization process would follow a complex workflow for managing vector and raster data, the team developed specific tools for quality and topology control that reduced editing errors and inconsistencies.

Next, the team customized software tools to delineate census enumeration area (EA) boundaries and codes. To reduce human error, the team built an algorithm that partially automated workflow procedures for mapping the physical morphology of the territory (ridges, slopes, streams), the boundaries of administrative units, the location and shape of roads and streets, and buildings.

Census controllers and supervisors began asking for EA and administrative maps. To produce these products, the team used a GIS tool to create a series of layout pages from a single map document quickly. A feature layer, or index layer, divided the map into sections based on each index feature in the layer and generated one page per index feature. This allowed them to create a multipage map series from a single map document.

Enumeration phase

The team developed an innovative custom application to monitor census coverage in real time during data collection operations. Enumerators transmitted data, such as the number of interviews completed, the number of households, and persons and housing units enumerated, via mobile texts. Located at the INSTAT headquarters, the GIS server mapped the data and made the maps accessible through its web service.

Managers could monitor census progress by date and location. The web service included widgets specific to tracking and visualizing census operational data such as a daily completion count. One widget compared the number of population, households, and housing units estimated prior to the field data collection with the actual number of census units that enumerators had surveyed that day. Another widget allowed users to query the same data and graphically display survey completions by groups, individual census takers, and administrative units.

Managers could use alphanumeric codes to access coverage data by unique identifiers of the census and administrative units. They could also choose to use a map interface to select and visualize data in its geographic context.

Post-enumeration and dissemination phase

To make the census data accessible online, the team developed GIS web applications. Users could interactively select a specific classification method to display the data (manual, natural breaks, equal interval, quantile, geometrical interval). They could also select the number of class breaks, apply transparency, and choose different color ramps. The web application was prepared and published in Albanian and English. Users accessed the app from their computers, tablets, and smartphones at www.instat.gov.al.

GIS technology

INSTAT uses ArcGIS software. The prevailing criteria that led the agency to choose ArcGIS were that it is simple and ready to use. Users can work in a single integrated environment, which reduces system implementation time.

ArcGIS ensured functional workflows between desktop and server environments. System administrators easily configured the system to support multiple departments and business processes without compromising the underlying data. It provided users with census data integrated with spatial dimensions, ensuring that everyone who needed data could access it using a map interface.

The team implemented the ArcGIS geodatabase on a Microsoft® SQL Server to store census data, administrative and statistical boundaries, and orthophotos.

Web GIS developer tools helped the team customize editing operations. Staff performed multiuser edits and digitized building boundaries, EAs, and street lines. An ArcGIS extension processed data from the digital elevation model (DEM) required for delineating EAs.

ArcGIS server technology acted as a dedicated geospatial data engine to support the enterprise. Using its development tools, the team built web applications, such as the mobile app that monitored field operations, and developed client applications in JavaScript™ and HTML. The technology provided a platform for web services that published geospatial information.

Business value gains

By implementing ArcGIS, INSTAT generated high-quality authoritative datasets and published census map products that it shared across the agency and with Albania's citizens via the web.

Time savings. INSTAT estimates that ArcGIS saved it twenty weeks for print map production and four weeks for data dissemination. The agency also reduced quality assurance activities by ten weeks.

Labor efficiency. The enterprise geodatabase centralized information and automated controls, so the institute needed only two operators to perform quality assurance activities. This allowed managers to concentrate personnel resources on the massive activity of data entry.

Integrated systems. Application programming interfaces (APIs) and developer tools drove rapid application development. The apps were easier to integrate with other systems used during the survey.

Increased data value. Web GIS has made data more accessible, and therefore more people use it. They simply use a search tool to find what they need. Data contains location information so that it can be mapped, which makes the data easier to interpret and analyze. Also, different systems can use the same data for other purposes, which broadens the opportunity to map nonspatial data and analyze it.

Efficient data distribution. Production costs had always limited the number of printed atlases that INSTAT published. Now anyone can access the maps from a browser. INSTAT continues to print an atlas, but new versions include maps with QR codes that link to digital online interactive maps.

Web capability. Departments connect and share data on an enterprise-wide platform. Mobile apps connect field and office staff members. Managers no longer need technicians to make their maps. Rather, they can access GIS in their browsers, create their own statistical maps, and integrate them into their work.

Archival reduction. Digital maps have solved storage space concerns that come with paper maps.

Albania's INSTAT successfully implemented GIS to modernize its procedures and data system, making the census process more effective and efficient. Most importantly, Albanians now have census information at their fingertips.

References

i. For example, the Esri approach uses nodes, arcs, and polygons as primitives for its vector data model. The first step is to record the location of all nodes—that is, endpoints and intersections of lines and boundaries. Based on these nodes, arcs are defined. (This is why Esri GIS software was initially called ArcInfo and then ArcGIS.) These arcs have endpoints, but they are also assigned a direction indicated by the starting point of the arc, which is referred to as the *from node* and the destination point as the *to node*. The orientation of a given arc can be assigned in either direction as long as this direction is recorded and stored in the database. The intermediary points of the lines are called *vertices*.

ii. See the *UN Handbook on Geospatial Infrastructure in Support of Census Activities*: "A topologically structured database stores not only individual features but also how those features relate to other features of the same or different feature class. For example, in addition to a set of lines representing a road network, the system will store the nodes that define road intersections, which allows the system to determine routes along several road segments. Or, instead of storing polygons as closed loops, where the boundaries between neighbouring polygons would be stored twice, a topologically structured GIS would store each line only once, together with information on which polygon is located to the left and to the right of the line. This avoids redundancy and facilitates the implementation of many GIS and spatial analysis functions."

iii. It is worth noting that administrative boundaries such as the block level serve as the smallest area definition for geographic hierarchies in some countries such as New Zealand, Australia, Japan, the US, and Canada. The main reason is that small size and utility of census blocks make them good candidates to serve as a unit for acquiring, managing, and using spatial statistics.

iv. Over two dozen countries and institutions worldwide have already begun the transition to a grid-based statistical system for statistical reporting (i.e., some countries in the European Union since 1970). See, for example, Japan's experience in *Geographic Boundaries of Population Census of Japan*, presented at the first meeting of the EG-ISGI at the UN Headquarters in New York, November 2013. Available at http://ggim.un.org/meetings/2013-ISGI-NY/documents/ESA_STAT_AC.279_P20_Geographic%20Boundaries%20of%20Population%20Census%20of%20Japan02.pdf.

v. Recent global efforts have culminated in the development of a discrete global grid systems (DGGS) abstract specification that has been developed under the auspices of the Open Geospatial Consortium (OGC). This system offers further options in the use of grids within the context of the principle of common geographies and in geospatially enabled statistics. See http://www.opengeospatial.org/projects/groups/dggsdwg and http://www.opengeospatial.org/pressroom/pressreleases/2656.

vi. National Statistics Center of Japan (NSTAC) presentation on *Utilizing Grid Square Statistics* at Esri UC 2018.

vii. UNSD conducted a survey on the main sources of census statistics that are used by countries or areas for producing the total population count for their censuses of the 2010 round of censuses.

The compiled information indicates that the traditional census, based on full field enumeration, is still the predominant source of data for producing the total population count. Out of the 138 countries or areas that responded to the survey, 115 (83 percent) use the traditional census. Virtually all the countries or areas in Africa, Latin America, and the Caribbean and Oceania are using the traditional census as the main source of data for the total population count. In Asia, all countries or areas except four—Bahrain, Israel, Singapore, and Turkey—have the traditional census as the main source. Among the North American countries or areas that responded to the survey, Greenland has a register-based census while the rest rely on the traditional census. In Europe, 54 percent of the countries or areas use the traditional census while the rest are using alternative sources to generate the total population count. This report on the results of a survey on "Census Methods Used by Countries in the 2010 Census Round" is available at http://unstats.un.org/unsd/census2010.htm.

Notes

1. The "raster" concept will be defined in the next section.
2. The GIS community has used interchangeably the terms *geographic*, *spatial*, and *geospatial* to designate the data about objects on the earth's surface. Geospatial data and information are more and more predominantly used by the global geospatial information management community.
3. It would be also called *entities* or *features*.
4. See the book *Geographical Information Systems: Principles and Applications* from Paul A. Longley, Michael F. Goodchild, David J. Maguire, and David W. Rhind.
5. SQL is an International Organization for Standardization (ISO) standard ISO/IEC 9075, a standard database query language adopted by virtually all mainstream databases.
6. *The Handbook of Geographic Information Science,* edited by John P. Wilson.
7. The relational model for database management uses a structure and language following some basic logic rules and was first described by Edgar F. Codd in 1969.
8. See pages 3–36 in the book *The Entity-Relationship Model: Toward a Unified View of Data* by Peter P. S. Chen.
9. See "What is a geodatabase?" in ArcGIS Desktop Help at https://desktop.arcgis.com/en/arcmap/latest/manage-data/geodatabases/what-is-a-geodatabase.htm.
10. The scale is the most important parameter that must always be present on a map: it is the ratio of the distance on a map to the corresponding distance on the ground. For example, on a 1:100,000 scale map, 1 cm on the map equals 1 km on the ground. Also, 1:1,000 or 1:5,000 is considered a large scale while 1:1,000,000 or less is considered a small scale. But this is often confusing or interpreted incorrectly, most likely because large scales are used to represent small areas of earth, while small scales represent large areas.
11. We will not go into the principles of satellite remote sensing and GPS because the concepts are easily found online and in many books, including the UN's *Handbook on Geospatial Infrastructure in Support of Census Activities* and several books from Esri Press, including *The ArcGIS Imagery Book*, *Imagery and GIS*, and *Essential Earth Imaging for GIS*.

12. An orthophoto is an aerial photograph that is usually of very high resolution and which has been geometrically corrected. It combines the detail of an aerial photograph with the geometric accuracy of a topographic map. It is also called an orthoimage.

13. Examples include the Landsat initiative that makes data open and accessible or the new Sentinel 2 data. See chapter 5 on imagery for more information.

14. The definitions in this book follow the guidelines of the UN's *Principles and Recommendations for the 2020 Round of Censuses*. See pages 94–95 of *Principles and Recommendations for Population and Housing Censuses* (UNSD, 2015).

15. See Timothy Trainor's "Advantages and Disadvantages of Grid-based, Population and Administrative Geography Approaches" from the second meeting of the UN-EG-ISGI in Lisbon, Portugal, in 2015.

16. See Timothy Trainor's "Common Geographic Boundaries: Small Area Geographies, Administrative, and Grid-based Geographies—One or Many?" from the US Census Bureau in 2014.

17. See "Production and Dissemination of Grid Data Since the 1970 Census in Finland." 2010 CES - ECE/CES/2010/11. Available at http://ggim.un.org/meetings/2010-Paris/documents/Production%20and%20dissemination%20of%20grid%20data-Finland-e.pdf.

18. See note by the US Census Bureau in *Combining Variable Spatial Data with Grids to Improve Data Visualization*. ECE/CES/2010/12. Available at http://ggim.un.org/meetings/2010-Paris/documents/US%20Paper-e.pdf.

19. As stated earlier, the UN-GGIM Committee of Experts established an Expert Group to carry out the work on developing a statistical-geospatial framework as a global standard for the integration of statistical and geospatial information.

20. For example, Japan started with a population/administrative approach and then moved to a grid-based approach.

21. See "In-Depth Review of Developing Geospatial Information Services Based on Official Statistics," Note by the United Kingdom Office for National Statistics. ECE/CES/2016/7. Available at https://www.unece.org/fileadmin/DAM/stats/documents/ece/ces/2016/mtg/CES_7-In-Depth_Review_Geospatial_adv_copy.pdf.

22. See *South Africa Dwelling Frame*. Available at https://undataforum.org/WorldDataForum/wp-content/uploads/2017/01/TA2.03_Laldaparsad.SouthAfricaSLaldaparsad_UNWDF_Jan2017-ver1.2.pdf.

23. See the Poland Central Statistical Office's "The Polish Modern Census: Incorporating Geospatial Technology and Data with Administrative Information." Available at http://ggim.un.org/meetings/2014-Global_Forum/documents/PL%20J.Dygaszewicz%20GGIM%20NY%202014.pdf.

24. Other countries are increasing using the register-based approach like Australia and the Gulf countries.

25. See the UN's *Principles and Recommendations* rev.3. Available at https://unstats.un.org/unsd/publication/seriesM/Series_M67Rev3en.pdf.

26. See Netherlands paper: *Cartography, Google and Neighbourhood Statistics* presented at the Conference of European Statisticians (CES), 2010. ECE/CES/2010/16. Available at https://www.unece.org/fileadmin/DAM/stats/documents/ece/ces/2010/16.e.pdf.

27. Enumeration area—the operational unit for data collection during the census that comprises the lowest level of the geographic hierarchy of administrative and statistical units. (Cf. *Principles and Recommendations* definition.)

28. For more details, see the UN *Handbook on Geospatial Infrastructure in Support of Census Activities*.

29. See Philippine Statistics Authority's "2015 Census of Population." Available at http://rsso05.psa.gov.ph/content/2015-census-population.

30. Where geocoding requires a database of properly formed address, a database of streets, and a set of rules for matching the addresses to the streets.

31. See the UNSC'S *Final report for the Expert Group on the Integration of Statistical and Geospatial Information, May 2015*. Available at https://unstats.un.org/unsd/demographic/standmeth/handbooks/series_f103en.pdf.

Chapter 5
Imagery

Introduction

As mentioned in chapter 4, up-to-date imagery has proven to be a critical source of information to support NSOs as they plan and execute their national census efforts. This chapter will explore in detail the key use cases of imagery for national census programs. Imagery, if used practically, can save incalculable work time and allow the NSO to focus on areas of significant change or growth. Imagery and remotely sensed data can also be used to cover dangerous or inaccessible areas, saving countless hours of fieldwork if done properly. Characteristics of population that can be analyzed using satellite imagery include counts of dwellings, measurements of settlement areas, measurements of areas that have had significant land-use change (e.g., agriculture and forestry), and residential increases.

In this chapter, our primary focus will be on satellite images, but aerial imagery should also be considered. Satellite images are obtained from space-based systems and are collected by governments and businesses around the world. Aerial photography traditionally was captured using cameras on low-flying planes, but today can also be obtained by using UAVs or drones.

Key imagery use cases for national census programs

Imagery has key applications that benefit the national census program, including the following:

- Imagery basemaps—Provide highly updated context for planners and enumerators. Assists in locating census targets and delineating appropriate EAs.
- Change detection—Comparing imagery from different times lets enumeration planners focus their mapping and feature collection efforts based on areas that have had the most change since the last census.

Figure 5.1. This area in Las Vegas, Nevada, highlights urban change detection between two dates using National Agriculture Imagery Program (NAIP) imagery. The green thematic layer was created from a change detection process and is overlaid on an older image to show where change occurred.

- Updating basemap and feature layers—Use recent (high-resolution) imagery to ensure that roads, utilities, buildings, and other infrastructure layers are up-to-date for accurate canvassing strategies.
- Agriculture and natural resource assessment—Use imagery to map the extent of specific farms, agricultural areas, and other natural resources for inventory purposes.
- Visualization—Imagery provides an unadulterated view of the land whereas maps can have misrepresentations and omissions. Tools to visualize imagery empower apps on mobile devices used for enumeration.

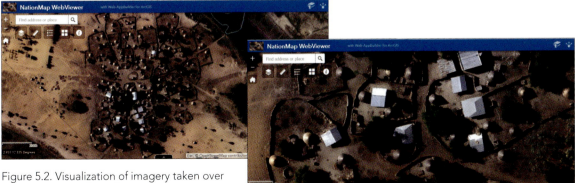

Figure 5.2. Visualization of imagery taken over Niger. Courtesy of Woolpert.

Support for key enumeration business processes

Imagery can be used at all phases of the statistical business process model. This table provides a general usage model for imagery during each phase of the enumeration process.

Phase	Application	Technique
Planning Pre-Enumeration	• Create accurate enumeration basemaps • Identify areas of change from last census • Update infrastructure feature layers • Extract building footprints • Update the extents of EAs	• Ortho mapping • Image analytics • Image analysis • Image analytics • Image analysis
Enumeration	• Imagery basemaps on mobile devices • Imagery visualization tools for devices • Agricultural analysis and assessments • Land resources analysis and assessments	• Imagery management • Imagery apps and widgets • Image analytics • Image analytics
Dissemination Post-Enumeration	• Imagery-based story maps and reports • Updated basemaps • Derived agricultural products (e.g., yields) • Derived land resource products	• Imagery management • Imagery management • GIS analytics • GIS analytics

Figure 5.3. Support for key enumeration processes.

Image-processing techniques that support the enumeration process

The various techniques listed in the preceding table are used to create the numerous information products that support the statistical business process model. Esri provides software tools to support all these techniques. These tools are a seamless part of the ArcGIS platform. The following provides a short description of each technique and the relevance of the resulting information product to the enumeration processes:

- Ortho mapping—This process is used to make imagery as geospatially accurate as a map. It is the most critical process used in the creation of any type of imagery product for the census effort, particularly for making basemaps and performing change analysis. The ArcGIS platform provides ortho-mapping capabilities for all types of imagery, including satellite, aerial, and drones. Because the ortho-mapping process requires some specialized skills (depending on the source), many organizations require that the imagery vendor provide imagery already orthorectified and map-accurate.

- Imagery management—Operating a nationwide imagery program capable of supporting a census effort requires a robust image management capability because imagery files can readily exceed multiple terabytes of storage. Two key functions of imagery management include cataloging and serving of imagery content. Cataloging is used to ensure the efficient discovery of all imagery holdings for both manual and automated processes. Image serving ensures the efficient delivery of imagery content to end-user applications typically via web services. ArcGIS® Image Server is ideal for managing and serving imagery and readily scales to meet any amount of imagery data.

- Image analysis—This manual process is performed by an image-processing specialist to extract information from imagery. It is used to update GIS feature layers such as roads, building centers, and other infrastructure features that are key to an EA. Workflows typically include some form of visual change detection so that existing feature layers can be updated from the most recent image covering the interest area. ArcGIS® Pro provides a variety of tools to aid with the manual analysis and extraction features from the imagery. This functionality even includes a new stereo viewer for working in 3D. While manual extraction can be time consuming, it is often much more accurate than using automated ways to extract features from imagery, especially for constructed features in urbanized areas.

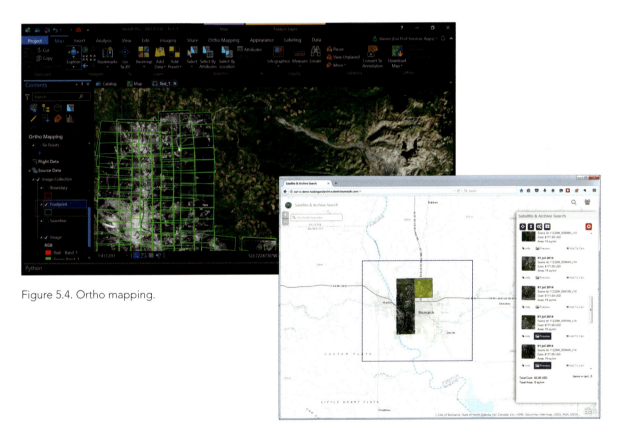

Figure 5.4. Ortho mapping.

Figure 5.5. Imagery management.

Figure 5.6. Impervious surface image analysis from Louisville, Kentucky.[1]

- Image analytics—This process includes highly automated methods of extracting information from imagery. Proven image analytical capabilities include automatically mapping land cover, identifying areas of greatest change, and evaluating agricultural health. With high-resolution elevation data, ArcGIS now includes analytics for the automated extraction of building footprints. While there are currently no "easy buttons" when it comes to feature extraction, new AI techniques are showing promise and may become available by 2020. Image analytics will continue to improve the ability to rapidly extract the key geospatial information needed to perform a modern national census.

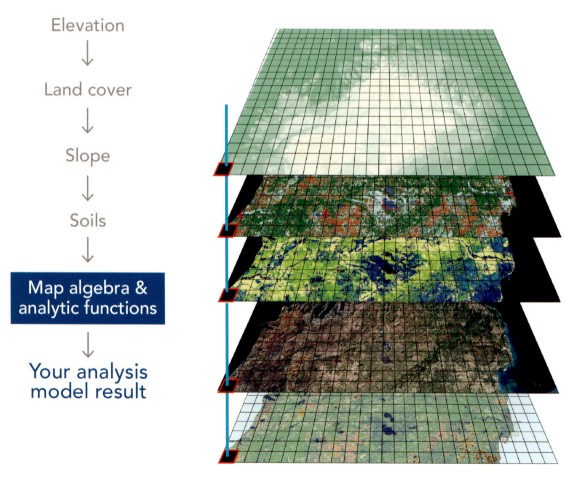

Elevation
↓
Land cover
↓
Slope
↓
Soils
↓
Map algebra & analytic functions
↓
Your analysis model result

Figure 5.7. Rasters facilitate analysis.

Figure 5.8. Image analytics example. A trained dataset showing various samples used to extract different roof types in Mozambique.

- Imagery apps—These apps include imagery-specific widgets that enable enumeration and apps on mobile devices that take advantage of imagery. These JavaScript widgets contain functionality such as automated contrast and brightness tools, image sharpening, swipe comparisons, and image measurements. Web AppBuilder for ArcGIS® can be used to build enumeration apps.
- GIS analytics—With ArcGIS, all imagery-derived products can be used in advanced GIS statistical analysis because accessing and processing images are integrated into the ArcGIS platform.

Imagery characteristics important for NSOs

Different sources of imagery have different characteristics suitable for NSOs. Because the acquisition of imagery can be expensive and difficult to maintain, careful consideration must be given before deciding the proper mix of imagery. Key characteristics that must be considered include image resolution, accuracy, spectral resolution, spectral fidelity, and obliquity. Elevation data is also important and should also be factored in the decision.

- Resolution—Image resolution is undoubtedly the most critical characteristic of imagery for national census programs. It provides enumerators the ability to visually identify all the various structures that may potentially house people or businesses and the infrastructure that supports them. In general terms, urban areas need a resolution of at least 30 cm while rural areas should have a minimum of 50 cm. Once resolution is worse than 50 cm, it becomes difficult to properly distinguish the key geospatial features needed to help guide enumeration. The two exceptions for this premise are imagery that is used to identify generalized areas of change and basic land cover/use. In both cases, where specific structures do not have to be identified, a medium resolution from 1 m to 30 m may be adequate.

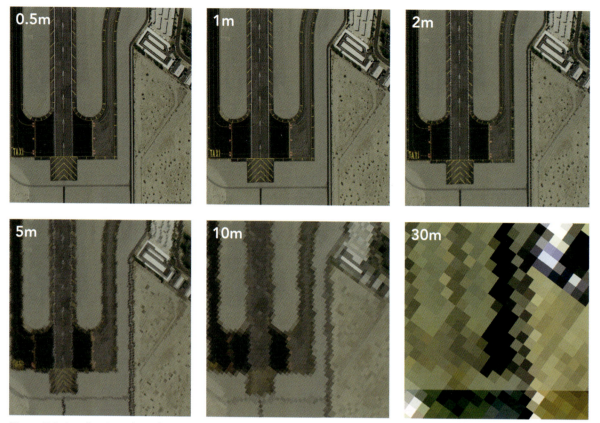

Figure 5.9. A collection of Landsat, NAIP, and aerial imagery over the airport runway in Palm Springs, California. The images vary in spatial resolution from 0.5 m to 30 m. The runway markings are easier to identify in the higher-resolution images. As resolution decreases, the features become pixelated.

- Accuracy—All imagery must be orthorectified and should be accurate to within one-half pixel of resolution. For instance, 30-cm imagery should be accurate to 15 cm. The ability to quickly collect accurate imagery is improving, so updating GIS layers from inaccurate imagery will quickly become obsolete and unusable.

- Spectral resolution—The concept refers to the number of bands each image has. True color images contain three spectral bands: red, blue, and green. Many aerial collection systems add a fourth near-infrared (NIR) band to help with vegetation analysis. In practice, the more spectral bands, the better automated feature extraction (analytics) can work. For enumeration work, three-band true-color imagery will work, but the fourth NIR band is a good choice if not overpriced. (Aerial collectors will typically acquire the NIR band regardless, so strongly negotiating a reduced price for this band is recommended.) For extracting land cover and performing change detection, more bands (even if they have less resolution) is preferred.

- Spectral fidelity—The concept refers to the color quality of the imagery. Sources with good spectral fidelity are better for building seamless mosaics for basemaps and automated feature extraction. Remember that atmospheric effects can have a huge impact on spectral fidelity, so it is often difficult to build quality basemaps from satellite imagery.

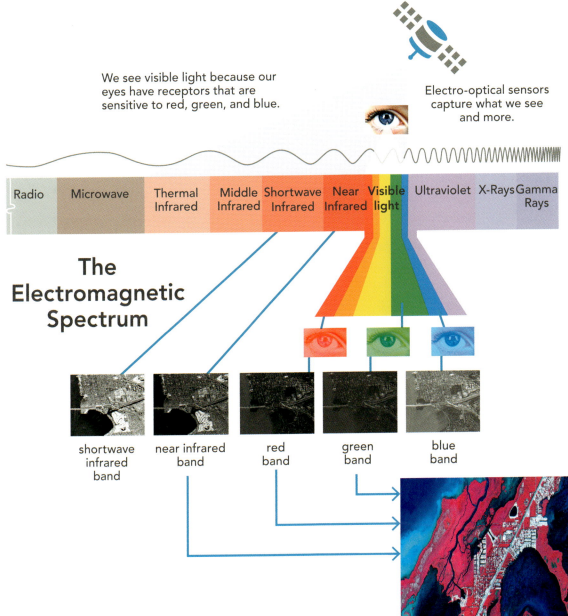

We see visible light because our eyes have receptors that are sensitive to red, green, and blue.

Electro-optical sensors capture what we see and more.

| Radio | Microwave | Thermal Infrared | Middle Infrared | Shortwave Infrared | Near Infrared | Visible light | Ultraviolet | X-Rays | Gamma Rays |

The Electromagnetic Spectrum

shortwave infrared band

near infrared band

red band

green band

blue band

Figure 5.10. Spectral resolution and the electromagnetic spectrum.

- Obliquity—Most images for basemaps are taken as nearly vertical as possible (in other words, the camera is pointing straight down). However, the trend is growing toward oblique imagery taken from the side. For enumeration purposes, this method allows users to see things not apparent in vertical imagery, such as building sides for counting the number of floors in an apartment building. The downside to obliquity is that it does not make good basemaps and cannot be used for analytics. Users should also be aware that high-resolution satellite imagery is also often oblique, and because collection angles vary from image to image, this obliquity is not uniform and results in significant distortions in urban areas.

- Elevation data—High-resolution elevation data is a key source of geospatial information. Once difficult to collect, new lidar sensors and elevation extraction techniques have made this source more prevalent. For enumeration purposes, it is currently most useful for the automated extraction of building footprints.

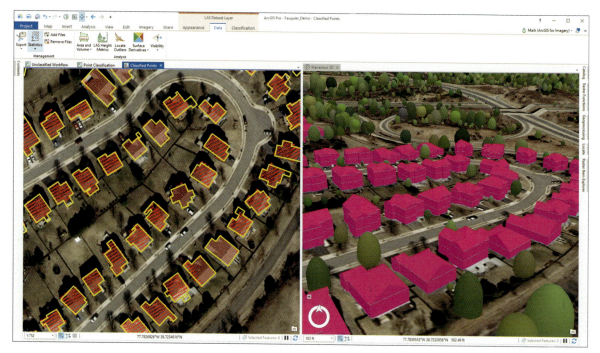

Figure 5.11. Building footprints extracted using lidar data. Fauquier County, Virginia, from US Geological Survey 3DEP program.[2]

Sources of imagery content for national imagery programs

The following is a portfolio of imagery programs provided by Esri or its content partners. Each program listed has been optimized to work with the ArcGIS platform with minimal implementation efforts.

- Esri imagery basemap—The Esri imagery basemap web service has been compiled by Esri from different sources of satellite and aerial imagery. It provides moderate- to high-resolution imagery data covering the entire globe. In many parts of the world, including most of Africa and the Middle East, the service has recently been updated with DigitalGlobe® satellite imagery collected from 2016 to 2017 with an average resolution of 50 cm. Efforts have been made to color balance the imagery so the basemap is as seamless as possible at all resolutions. The service is free to all ArcGIS users. If web services are not suitable for the application, the imagery can also be acquired on an Esri solution known as the data appliance. The imagery itself is served as a tile cache, meaning that it is not suitable for analytics. But Esri does provide relevant metadata, such as source and acquisition dates, for all the imagery in the archive. The imagery and metadata can be accessed via this link: https://services.arcgisonline.com/ArcGIS/rest/services/World_Imagery/MapServer

- Woolpert national imagery map—Woolpert is an Esri business partner that specializes in the collection of high-resolution aerial imagery and elevation (lidar) data. It has recently implemented a collection program to cover key countries throughout Africa and the Middle East. Its products include four-band 15 cm imagery over urban areas and four-band 25 cm imagery over rural areas. Its imagery is of high-color fidelity, so it is ideal for seamless imagery basemaps and can be used in automated extraction processes. Woolpert's collection activities have recently begun, so all its imagery will be extremely up-to-date for the 2020 census time frame.

- MDA/DigitalGlobe Imagery + Analytics (I+A)—I+A is a joint program of Esri and DigitalGlobe to provide high-resolution satellite imagery for basemapping and analytics. I+A expands DigitalGlobe's Geospatial Big Data Platform (GBDX) program with image-processing functionality and ready access to its imagery archive via an ArcGIS image server interface. Access to I+A imagery is provided on an annual subscription basis and is updated on a fragmentary basis depending on cloud cover and the collection rate of its satellites. Its absolute best resolution is 30 cm but actual images can range

Figure 5.12. Esri imagery basemap.

Figure 5.13. Woolpert nation map. High-resolution aerial imagery from Niger.

5.14. Image of Paris, true color 30 cm pan-sharpened. Courtesy of DigitalGlobe.

from 30 to 60 cm depending on the look angle of the satellite. Imagery fidelity varies depending on atmospheric effects and different collection dates and time.

- Copernicus—Copernicus is the European Union's Earth Observation Program for which the Sentinel satellites are developed to meet its specific needs. Sentinel-2 provides high-resolution imagery for land services, including imagery of vegetation, soil and water cover, inland waterways, and coastal areas. Esri enhanced ArcGIS technology to simplify the use of free global imagery from Sentinel-2. ArcGIS supports the visualization, interpretation, and analysis of Sentinel imagery, which is valuable in applications of agriculture statistics and forestry statistics as well as land and environmental monitoring.

- Light detection and ranging (lidar)—This relatively new remote-sensing technology allows us to collect very dense point samples of features in 3D. Lidar technology has evolved to become a common source of geographic data in GIS. Lidar data is typically stored in LAS files. Each lidar point can have additional attributes such as intensity, class code, and RGB color values, which can be used in ArcGIS. ArcGIS reads LAS files natively, providing immediate access to lidar data without the need for data conversion or import. LAS attributes can be used to filter content and symbolize points in 2D and 3D. Lidar can be used for feature extraction, validating existing GIS data, and measuring heights and distances between points.

- Landsat—The US Department of the Interior has made Landsat information available for the whole world for free—over eight terabytes of multispectral imagery collected over the last thirty years that describes how the planet has changed. Esri has developed a website called Change Matters (http://changematters.esri.com/compare) that provides fast access to this huge reservoir of data. It is made accessible through image services in ArcGIS. This is not just an image in a browser; it allows you to perform a query about a particular geography, and the server will process it into a continuous mosaic that can be analyzed dynamically. The earth is constantly changing; this new collection allows users to measure change over time and help them understand the changes using a web browser.

Figure 5.15. Image from Sentinel-2/Copernicus[3] of a Hawaiian volcano.

Figure 5.16. Lidar image showing points being used to extract a building—Goettweig Abbey, Austria. Courtesy of RIEGL®.

Figure 5.17. Landsat data on display in the Change Matters web app. Data courtesy of USGS Landsat.[4]

Many other imagery providers are available. Depending on your needs and geographic area, the options will vary. Often, the NMA maintains a national imagery program for the country. If the NMA does not have imagery available, the NSO may need to consider other ways to compile image services capable of supporting its imagery needs. This area may be considered for contract or managed services. Specialists familiar with all types of satellite, aerial, and drone imagery can build seamless tile cache basemaps or true imagery services for analytics. Common sources of imagery for managed services include aerial and satellite imagery already owned or being collected by the NSO, Landsat satellite imagery, and Sentinel-2 satellite imagery from the European Space Agency (ESA). By outsourcing the compilation and management of the imagery service to experts, valuable time and critical personnel in the statistical organization are freed for the actual tasks of building the imagery-derived information products needed to support a national census.

Implementation

An NSO conducting a national census using imagery may need a dedicated platform that combines imagery with GIS. Starting with ArcGIS version 10.5, a new image server has been added to complement ArcGIS Enterprise. This image server allows organizations to separately scale their imagery program to best meet the data loads and services they want to provide. A new image catalog app facilitates imagery cataloging and management. Recent additions for ArcGIS Desktop and ArcGIS Pro include the ortho-mapping workflow, the extraction of 3D features from stereo imagery, and automated feature extraction and change detection. As drones become more prevalent, Drone2Map® for ArcGIS provides a robust processing capability for these emerging sources of overhead imagery. All these capabilities can run on in-house systems or in the cloud. Organizations can start with a basic desktop single-server approach and then expand their capabilities as their imagery needs grow. ArcGIS now provides all the imagery capabilities needed by NSOs for national census and inventory programs. Furthermore, through Esri content providers, numerous sources of imagery content are available that meet the needs of the national program.

In summary, the many advantages of satellite remotely sensed data and aerial imagery include the following:

- Imagery can allow for the mapping of inaccessible areas.
- Imagery can be used in basemap updates and to identify new settlements.
- Imagery can be used as a validation in field data collection and verification.
- Up-to-date coverage can be obtained at relatively low costs with lower spatial resolution.
- Imagery can be applied to multiple surveys and census, and once acquired can be applied to other areas and applications.
- Aerial imagery typically shows a large amount of detail and thus allows for visual analysis.

Satellite earth observations (EO), in addition to their use for the census, can support measuring and monitoring the global indicator framework for the SDGs. In fact, the Group on Earth Observations (GEO) has an initiative[5] to organize and realize the potential of EOs and geospatial data to advance the 2030 agenda and enable societal benefits through achievement of the SDGs. Additional information on GIS and the SDGs will be provided in chapter 9.

Recommendations

For NSOs wanting an enterprise imagery management system, the following are recommended guidelines for system configuration and imagery content:

- System configuration—NSOs can start small with their imagery programs but must be smart enough in their configuration strategy to allow growth. The first step in modernizing an imagery approach is to move away from separate imagery files to a web services approach supported by the new ArcGIS Image Server. A file management system will not scale. On the other hand, Image Server can work with millions of image files to automatically find the correct image pixels needed for the basemap being visualized or the analytical process being run. A baseline configuration includes ArcGIS Desktop with ArcGIS Pro, the new Image Analyst extension for ArcGIS Pro, ArcGIS Enterprise, and ArcGIS Image Server. This system can reside on premises, in the cloud, or be a hybrid of both.
- Imagery content—For NSOs, it is recommended that high-resolution four-band aerial imagery be used for basemapping and manual feature extraction such as the imagery being provided by the Woolpert National Imagery Map Program. For change detection, land cover extraction, agricultural assessments, and other analytics, Esri recommends Sentinel-2 satellite imagery from ESA's Copernicus program. A possible alternative to both these sources is DigitalGlobe satellite imagery, especially if the new competitive pricing of Access + Analytics can beat out the aerial sources. For smaller high-density areas and areas with rapid change, NSOs should consider implementing a drone program.

See the online ancillaries at esri.com/Census2020 for a list of imagery providers.

Case study: Portugal

To prepare for the 2021 census, Instituto Nacional de Estatística Portugal (INE) initiated a work plan for creating the geospatial components of Portugal's census operation. The plan is built on the agency's location-based strategies established two decades previously, when INE first included GIS in its 2001 census. The agency realized that any data that links people, business, and the economy to a particular place offers a more complete understanding of social and economic issues. From then on, INE has been committed to making geospatial data an integral part of its work.

Today, geospatial data is present in most phases of INE's statistical production processes. The country's goal is that through the census, every statistical unit, person, household, dwelling, building, and business register will be geocoded.

In 2006, INE developed a spatial data infrastructure (SDI) that adds a geospatial component to all phases of statistical production. The SDI is more than a sequence of mapping operations and census data dissemination. It is a continuous digital transformation program that makes it possible for INE to evolve its operations, meet changing demands for information, and stay current with society's technology expectations.

To understand Portugal's census program is to understand the European Union's (EU) census program. INE follows recommendations and standards set by the EU's statistical office, Eurostat. Agencies that follow the EU's General Guidelines of Statistical Activity have highly credible and authoritative data, thereby giving researchers confidence in the data for analysis. Furthermore, EU standards make it possible for Portugal to compare its statistics with those of other member states. Portuguese economists, for instance, can compare unemployment, housing, and other economic indicators with those of France.

When it comes to geo-enabling statistical production in Europe, two EU initiatives set the course. One is Eurostat's GEOSTAT, which defines the procedures for processing official statistics, including using generic statistical models that integrate geospatial data. The other is the European spatial data infrastructure (INSPIRE), a directive that state members follow to build the European network for sharing geospatial information. To make European data compatible, INSPIRE defined data standards for thirty-four spatial data themes such as transportation, utilities, and population. Each country builds these into their data models.

In Portugal, INE works with the strategic body responsible for implementing the INSPIRE directive throughout the country. INE mainly works on developing INSPIRE's metadata and services. It has also built data themes for Portugal that are similar to INSPIRE's data themes.

Although EU initiatives prescribe the approach for developing geospatial data, it is Portugal's Census 2021 that drives the nation's integration of statistical and geospatial information. For instance, Portugal is updating procedures and work processes that respond more efficiently to the challenges of organizing fieldwork and data processing. INE also developed social survey processes for data sampling. The agency uses GIS to manage procedures and automate work processes that simplify tasks.

INE's geoinformation group manages the Buildings Geographic Database (BGE), which contains point-based data for all residential building units. INE uses this georeferenced data to generate tailor-made statistical products at different scales, such as a 1 km^2 grid map that includes a range of census attributes.

GIS is used to check the quality of three data types. The EAs are blocks having three-level structure (sections, subsections, and localities), which are integrated with official administrative boundaries. The Road Segments Network is street-line coverage at national and local levels. Data is edited with geometric and alphanumeric data submitted by municipalities. This is used for the delineation of the agency's geographic information referencing base (BGRI). Finally, GIS is used to check the aforementioned BGE building locations data. The agency's quality-control process increases the accuracy and consistency of every building's x,y coordinates and address.

All of Portugal's municipalities share their building permit information and completed-construction work data with INE via a web GIS platform. To check the data, the geoinformation group follows SDI quality-control procedures, which are predominantly GIS-based quality routines. To identify topological and attribute errors, the group uses ArcGIS software to check the data against orthoimagery and boundary data provided by Portugal's cadastral agency. They then make edits accordingly.

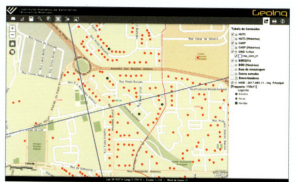

Figure 5.18. BGE buildings location data.

The entire GIS is a hybrid system that includes ArcGIS and Oracle® as well as some open-source software. In addition, INE developed web mapping applications to help with data sampling, collection, and dissemination procedures. For the 2021 census data collection, INE has been developing web mapping applications that make relevant spatial data available to all enumerators and data collection managers.

Figure 5.19. GeoINQ GIS web app.

Portugal is relying on GIS to help it efficiently execute the Portuguese 2021 Census and ensure the availability of quality information. However, the country's plans for its GIS extend years beyond the upcoming census. INE will use GIS to transition to a future census that will be based on administrative registers. In doing so, INE looks forward to decreasing the statistical burden on citizens, improving the frequency of outputs, and reducing collection costs associated with census operations.

Notes

1. Data: 2012 6-inch imagery. Courtesy of Louisville/Jefferson County Information Consortium (LOJIC).
2. See 3DEP Elevation Program from USGS at https://www.usgs.gov/core-science-systems/ngp/3dep/data-tools. Downloadable data can be found at https://viewer.nationalmap.gov/basic/.
3. See http://www.esa.int/Our_Activities/Observing_the_Earth/Copernicus/Sentinel-2 and https://scihub.copernicus.eu; also available via USGS Earth Explorer at https://earthexplorer.usgs.gov.
4. See https://landsat.usgs.gov.
5. See the GEO document *Earth Observations and Geospatial Information: Supporting Official Statistics in Monitoring and Achieving the 2030 Agenda*. Available at www.earthobservations.org/documents/publications/201704_geo_unggim_4pager.pdf.

Chapter 6
Planning your work with GIS

The ubiquitous use and application of geospatial information technologies have been recognized as beneficial at all stages of a population and housing census process. GIS can be used to create efficiencies in the preparation, enumeration, processing, and dissemination phases of the census. This chapter will go in depth on how to use GIS in pre-enumeration work as well as the use of imagery for the EA delineation and validation process. You will also learn how GIS can be used in the field and examine other application areas that contribute to the efficiency and improvement of census work.

EA delineation process

The EA delineation process requires sufficient resources, including multiple sources of data, and is underpinned by two principles: (1) balancing—an EA should be small enough to be within reach of an enumerator and all households in that EA can be covered within the allocated number of days, but it should also be large enough to ensure data privacy; and (2) consistency and updating—ensuring that boundary datasets are consistent with administrative units and, to the extent possible, with other relevant geographic units, and their updates are consistent with previous census boundaries.

In chapter 4, you learned that an early decision must be made about the required criteria for the design of EAs and guidelines determined for some basic parameters, in terms of the types of EAs to be delineated; the size of the EAs to be delineated by type; the demarcation rules pertaining to EA boundary selection requirement; and the appropriate EA geocoding scheme creation. Once all the relevant EA parameters have been determined, actual EA delineation can commence.

The fundamental information that needs to be known at the outset of the EA delineation process is the estimated number of persons living in an area and their geographic distribution. Traditionally, cartographic field work would have been carried out to count the housing units and obtain the estimated number by multiplying the number of the households associated to the housing units by an average household size (a reliable estimate of the average number of persons per household—i.e., known from a survey or the previous census). Rough estimates of population could be also obtained through extrapolation from previous census results, official governmental sources, or increasingly by means of aerial photography or satellite imagery. The use of geospatial information technologies—GIS, GPS, and remote-sensing imagery—in support of the EA demarcation has affected the traditional way of demarcation. The noticeable impact is the decrease of the costly fieldwork needed to field verify and validate. The use of imagery in office can also reduce the total time needed to conduct this important work.

The delineation process, using GIS and other geospatial information technologies, would be generally carried out in three main steps outlined as follows:[1]

- An initial office demarcation phase is a preliminary step involving the preparation of fieldwork maps, map services, and materials to be used during fieldwork. It can include the demarcation of EAs through on-screen (heads-up) digitizing; superimposing the vector data such as administrative boundaries, roads, rivers, place names; and other point-based features (dwellings/buildings, landmarks) on top of the satellite/aerial imagery as a backdrop. An unverified dataset of demarcated EAs is created, maps would be produced, and map services would be established, as well as mobile map packages for offline use in the field using mobile devices prepared or printed as needed. It can also include feature extraction using remotely sensed imagery to help create a more up-to-date and accurate basemap and to analyze EAs in the office.

- The second step is fieldwork, specifically field verification: it entails the process by which the data and maps prepared and created in the GIS unit are verified and updated in the field. The existing data on the map is verified and updated, any new data is captured, and any suggestions or changes are brought to the EAs and captured on the map. Today, this can be done via a mobile device (tablet or smartphone), which helps streamline the quality assurance process and allows for more transparency overall in the process. This can use configurable apps in the field, which will also allow for faster work and more accurate updates. Point-based data such as dwellings, landmarks, or other points of interest are also verified and captured by GPS, and any changes are also captured.
- The third step is about quality assurance checks of the data captured in the field as well as the

creation of the EAs and SAs to be used for the enumeration. Once all the fieldwork for an EA has been completed, the updated information is verified, and the database will then be up-to-date and ready for optimization. The changes to the EAs can be confirmed once all the updated data has been submitted. This process is much different from the process in the past, when manual edits were made to paper maps that then had to be digitized and combined to create a new database. By using digital and mobile technologies and apps in this process, the EA updates are streamlined.

Once complete, the database can be used to create map services, serve out layers of data to online mobile devices, or create offline mobile map packages (see figure 6.1) for use in the field during enumeration and for operations management. If paper maps are still required, EA maps and all other maps associated with the management of the actual census will be created and printed, in accordance with cartographic standards (size, color, quality of paper, self-explanatory symbols not requiring special complex training instructions for the enumerators, etc.).

In the following section, we will elaborate on the type of maps and data sources required for the demarcation process, the format required for the integration of this data into a GIS, the imagery used to support the demarcation, and the fieldwork needed for the updates of the EAs created in the office.

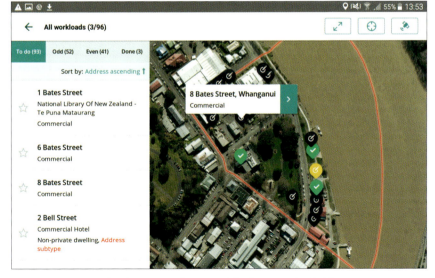

Figure 6.1. New Zealand maps used on a mobile device in the field.

Maps and sources required

A GIS-based census database has at its core the smallest statistical unit for data collection, involving some specific data sources. We will look at the sources of the data required to construct the census data collection units, in this case the EAs, to be captured into the database. Until recently, maps constituted the main sources of data for the delineation of EAs, but emerging data sources, such as imagery data, are increasingly used to support the delineation of the EA process.

NSOs need to proceed with a comprehensive inventory of all the existing maps in the country, in analog or digital formats, covering the country in various scales, to identify those maps that are suitable to respond to the requirements of enumeration demarcation. However, in many cases, the available maps may not fully provide all the data needed, corrections may be required, or there may be a total lack of maps suitable for EAs delineation. This requires some work in the field or additional searches for various data sources.

It is generally recognized that the principal types of maps and imagery required for census-mapping operations, including EAs demarcation, are as follows: small-scale maps (national map overview); topographic maps; city and cadastral maps; maps of administrative units at all levels of civil division; thematic maps showing population distribution for previous census dates, or any features that may be useful for census mapping; sketch maps; and relevant high-resolution satellite images and digital aerial photos. These various types of maps and layers can be created in one continuous and multiscale geodatabase that can serve out the appropriate operational layers needed for the end user and information product needed.

More specifically, the categories of maps and their scales needed for an accurate census may include the following:

- Rural and urban basemaps covering the whole country, at small scale (generally from 1:250,000 to 1:1 million, depending on the size of the country, and even to 1:5 million for very large countries), showing the major administrative area boundaries; the location of major features, including large settlements and places, important transportation networks, and water bodies; and important points of reference and other landmarks.
- Administrative maps (1:50,000 to 1:500,000) and maps of local government areas (1:25,000 to 1:50,000).
- Topographic maps generally produced by NMAs at large and medium scale (1:25,000 to 1:50,000), which show elevation contours and other major topographic features. In some countries, topographic maps are available at smaller scale (1:100,000 to 1:250,000).
- Large-scale basemaps at town and city levels (1:25,000 scale or larger) showing land parcels; details about important features such as transportation networks, parks, and water features; points of interest such as schools, hospitals, and police stations; and important city buildings and landmarks.
- In addition to these basemaps, NSOs need administrative maps at all levels of civil divisions as well as thematic data showing population distribution from the previous census or any features that may be useful for census-mapping purposes.

| 1:3,500,000 | 1:2,500,000 | 1:1,500,000 | 1:750,000 | 1:180,000 | 1:75,00 |
| Country | Region | Department | Arrondissement | Canton | Commune |

Figure 6.2. Basemaps at various scales.

Up-to-date base data is critical to the success of any census activity. For example, new built-up areas and other improvised settlements often may be missing, as may be geographical names of localities, places, and features. As stated earlier, this will require some additional work using imagery or other digital sources and fieldwork.

Other data that can benefit the demarcation process includes aerial maps, orthophoto maps, and satellite image maps, which can be available at suitable scales. In this case, these maps can provide necessary information, particularly at the local government, cities, and towns levels, and form the respective basemaps on which the development of the database system for census management is founded. Moreover, we are experiencing in the current digital environment the increasing use of remote-sensing images to generate the needed maps, even in large scales, since demarcation of administrative boundaries is faster with digital remotely sensed imagery.

It is worth reiterating that, since the data captured from the various types of maps and imagery will be incorporated into the GIS-based census database, the metadata about the maps should be well documented to be part of the data dictionary.

Figure 6.3. An example of Esri imagery and an orthophoto map. *Left*, red relief image map of landslide from the 2016 Kumamoto earthquake, Minami Aso, Kumamoto, Japan. *Right*, orthophoto of the same location.

This includes the geographic referencing information and other cartographic parameters (e.g., map scale, projection and geographic datum, map compilation date, compiling agency, legend, etc.) that should be appropriate for use by a GIS.

Worth reiterating is that, usually, few if any NSOs would have or be custodian of all these various maps. An institutional collaboration may be required for their acquisition. Generally, NSOs must contact various agencies, such as the national geospatial information authority or mapping agency; cadastral agency; the military mapping services; province, district, and municipal governments; various government or private organizations involved with geospatial data; geological or hydrological survey; environmental protection authority; transport authority; utility and communication sector companies; and other donor organizations. The use of data from these different sources is made easier particularly if map services are published and shared from other agencies. These map services can be readily consumed by the NSO and used to verify existing EAs and make modifications.

Conversion of existing data (analog/digital)

Once the inventory of the existing data, maps, map services, and other data sources required for the census-mapping operations is carried out, you will need to determine how to integrate these varied sources into your geodatabase. Typically, you will find data at varying scales and in multiple formats. Some data conversion and data integration may be needed to make all this data usable in your GIS.

In fact, data conversion may include the conversion of hard-copy maps to digital maps through digitizing and scanning, editing, and building topology. Since the structure of EAs is more appropriate to vector-based GIS, the conventional method to

Figure 6.4. Heads-up digitizing, Palo, Philippines.

trace all required point and line features visible on a map used to be manual digitizing.[2] However, manual digitizing is very labor-intensive and requires a lot of patience from the operator. Scanning is another option, but too many errors could be generated in this process. The method that combines scanning and (on-screen) digitizing, called *heads-up digitizing*, gained popularity in the last census round. With this method, a scanned map image is displayed on the screen of the computer (which can be superimposed on a satellite or aerial image providing reference information as a background) and, through heads-up digitizing,[3] can be easily converted into vector format. However, with the increasing development and affordability of imagery, the trend is more on using imagery and doing feature extraction, for example, to create EAs. We will elaborate further on this in the following sections.

Simply digitizing the features on the map in vector format is not sufficient. The datasets captured through digitizing do not relate to each other (recall that this is referred to in GIS parlance as *spaghetti*, and performing data conversion includes cleaning and correcting omissions and building the topology. Objects with topology know their locations in absolute space and know what they are in relation to other objects (their nearest neighbors). (See chapter 4.)

Once the topology is built, we proceed with data integration, which includes georeferencing, projection, coding, and additional attribute information. The map coordinates, which are initially recorded in units used by the digitizer or scanner, need to be converted to the real-world coordinates corresponding to the source map's cartographic projection. Some systems allow the determination of the projection prior to digitizing. In this case, the coordinates are converted on the fly during the digitizing process with the same results. The final

step is to attach consistent codes to the digitized features and to add additional attributes.

Although the sequence of steps for data conversion and data integration may vary, the required procedures are similar in each case, and the method of heads-up digitizing is increasingly used to delineate the EAs, as stated earlier.

Use of imagery in updating EAs

As stated in chapter 5, remote-sensing imagery, which includes aerial photography and satellite imagery, is increasingly used for the pre-enumeration operations of a census, either as additional data sources to the existing maps (or basemaps) or as a geographic base for producing and updating EAs when the maps are outdated or not available. It is generally recognized that image basemaps are a suitable basis for the demarcation and production of census EAs and SA maps. We will elaborate on the characteristics of both aerial photography and satellite imagery and how their use is beneficial to the updating of EAs. It is worth investigating a sharing mechanism of the costs of imagery with other national agencies or partners, especially in the context of the NSDI.

Like satellite imagery, aerial photographs provide a view of the earth from above. Using specialized cameras aboard low-flying planes or drones, aerial photographs provide a large amount of detail of an area on the ground that can be interpreted visually. Aerial photos using digital cameras can offer high resolution, extending scope to small urban areas, especially dense informal settlements where more detailed imagery is needed. Sometimes, additional processing is required to produce orthophoto maps that combine the geometric accuracy of a topographic map with the large detail of an aerial photograph. The NSO should work to acquire imagery that has been preprocessed by the supplier so that it is rectified and georeferenced (with a known scale and coordinates), thus reducing the amount of work required to prepare the data for census work. Also, if the NSO is going to use aerial imagery, the organization will require certain skills to work with imagery.

Ortho-mapping tools can be used to process a range of 2D imagery into terrain and ortho-rectified image products. These tools, which are included with ArcGIS Pro, provide a familiar experience for practiced imagery users. For example, you can use ortho-mapping tools to create digital terrain models and orthophotos within your GIS or to increase the accuracy of imagery managed in mosaic datasets. Drone2Map for ArcGIS also offers streamlined workflows that quickly convert drone images into usable products. In addition to 2D imagery, Drone2Map also supports 3D workflows. Drone2Map is a stand-alone product that doesn't require ArcGIS Desktop, and may be more approachable for a GIS user with less imagery experience. These new tools exemplify

the trend to develop user-friendly imagery with minimal processing by end users.

Orthophoto maps also support dwelling unit counts and population estimation if a reliable estimate of the average number of persons per household is available. Orthophotos have an additional advantage: when they are created, they are correctly georeferenced. This means that the resulting EAs will also be registered in a proper map projection with known parameters. In the past, the acquisition of aerial photographs for large areas of a country may have been expensive compared with high-resolution satellite imagery. Today, costs for aerial imagery continue to decrease.

In the past, aerial photography has played a major role in census, though it was primarily used in urban areas. Today, aerial imagery can be used in both urban and rural areas across a country.

The use of satellite imagery is also changing as improvements in resolution, capture frequency, and costs make it a more viable approach. For some time, the most popular method for applying satellite imagery in support of the EA delineation

Figure 6.5. An example of aerial imagery taken over Niger, West Africa. Courtesy of Woolpert.

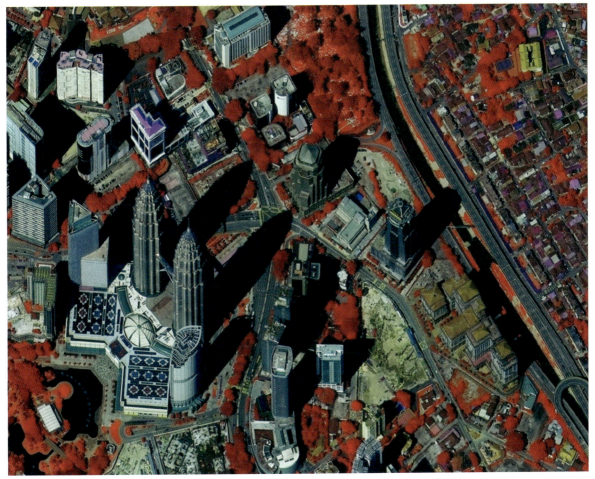

Figure 6.6. Example of a high-resolution satellite image of Kuala Lumpur, Malaysia. Courtesy of DigitalGlobe.

process was the change-detection approach, which involved performing change detection in the office first and then investigating in the field only areas with important changes. However, satellite imagery is extending its application with the increase of spatial resolution to the submeter level, offering a wide range of panchromatic and multispectral imagery (e.g., WorldView-3 from DigitalGlobe provides commercially available panchromatic imagery of 0.31 m resolution and eight-band multispectral imagery with 1.24 m resolution).[4]

High-resolution images can cover large areas, particularly areas that are otherwise inaccessible. Satellite imagery providers also typically have no restriction in acquisition. High-resolution satellite images show a level of geographic detail that is almost equivalent to digital orthophoto maps created from air photos, sufficient for EA delineation. Satellite image-processing technology using computer algorithms can be used to estimate population density from the layout of streets and buildings, and even help define different types of neighborhoods (e.g., upper-middle-class neighborhoods indicated by larger houses, mixed-used buildings, and gridded streets).[5] For example, neat street grids and large structures often indicate wealthier areas, whereas clusters of disorganized lines can be used to identify slums and informal settlements.[6] However, to be fully suitable for census-mapping operations, particularly the need to identify housing units to help delineate EAs, the satellite imagery should meet some criteria.

We can outline four main criteria for selection of satellite imagery (even these criteria can vary depending on the country's situation): (1) resolution: less than 1 m is acceptable, but ideally 30 to 50 cm for urban and not greater than 2.5 m for rural; (2) currency: preferably less than one year; (3) cloud coverage: 20 percent, the maximum allowable interference; and (4) cost: reasonable, relative to the whole cost of the census operations. This multicriteria selection could speed up the decision-making process of procuring the imagery and render it more understandable to other people that may not be familiar with the technical aspects.

The demarcation process involves overlaying imagery with administrative boundaries and then demarcating the EAs within local government units and editing the demarcation after field verification. The use of color image maps makes it easier to interpret the features and greatly enhances pre-enumeration mapping in terms of accuracy and overall quality of the delineation of EAs. For example, high-resolution satellite and photogrammetry imagery was used by Gambia, Namibia, Seychelles, and South Africa. EA boundaries had to be corrected to fit the corresponding features on the imagery and the collected data from the field.[7] The process also implies minimal training of census enumerators and supervisors in the use and interpretation of EA and SA maps. The information product created at the end of EA demarcation would be an EA map and would likely include a satellite imagery background, administrative boundaries, EA boundaries, and annotations for each EA.

Satellite and aerial imagery represent the bulk of data sources being used to augment conventional maps; in some cases, this imagery may be the only relevant current data source. The use of imagery can have a substantial impact on the intensive and costly operations of traditional fieldwork: while the use of satellite and aerial imagery to support the delineation and/or updates of the EA boundaries requires more work at the office, it can significantly decrease the amount of work and time (and therefore costs) needed in the field for verification. The decreased fieldwork activities also allow the NSO to focus on validating the updated information and

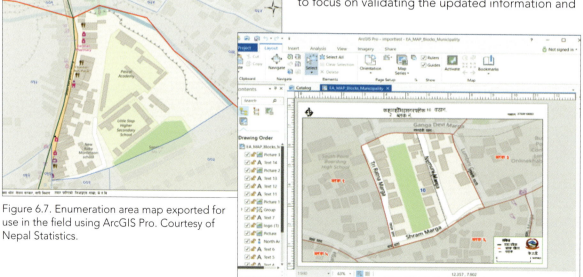

Figure 6.7. Enumeration area map exported for use in the field using ArcGIS Pro. Courtesy of Nepal Statistics.

on critical areas—e.g., new settlements, new built areas, and boundary changes—that can further affect and increase overall accuracy of the census. Since fieldwork can be relatively expensive and time consuming, a good compromise must be found between office work and fieldwork.

Today, huge imagery archives exist, and a range of recently launched modern satellites ensure the swift acquisition of new imagery. The emergence of miniature satellites (small satellites with a weight less than 5 kg) is attracting the attention and interest of users, and expectations are high about a dramatic increase in imagery supply and a massive use of imagery in the near future, cementing it as an essential data source.[i] Modern imagery from satellites and airborne digital aerial photography systems provides a realistic, cost-effective, and current image basemap of a country. As stated earlier, costs continue to decrease, and some global initiatives are even offering free and open EO data, such as the ESA's Copernicus program (Sentinel 2), USGS Landsat Imagery, or the Radiant Earth Project. [ii] In addition, users of Esri technology get access to ArcGIS Living Atlas of the World, the foremost collection of geographic information from around the globe. The atlas includes imagery, maps, apps, tools, and data layers to support your work. One of the newest apps, the Wayback app, provides access to an unprecedented amount of imagery. Wayback imagery is a digital archive of the World Imagery

Figure 6.8. Esri World Imagery of Buenos Aires, Argentina. Courtesy of Clarity.

basemap, enabling users to access more than eighty different versions of World Imagery captured over the past five years. Each record in the archive represents a version of World Imagery as it existed on the date it was published. This data provides current satellite and high-resolution aerial imagery for the world.

Cloud storage and processing capabilities are making it simpler to handle and apply EO satellite datasets, which can be large and complex. Space agencies and data providers are prioritizing efforts to further remove the burden on potential users by making more data "analysis ready" (analysis-ready data, or ARD).

The future for imagery is bright—including the prospects for countries to get access to the EO data required. Usage is expected to grow exponentially over the next decade—in particular among developing countries.

In summary, the use of satellite imagery with GPS and GIS for census mapping is highly recommended, particularly for the following previously discussed and additional reasons:

1. With the help of satellite imagery, NSO census geographers can monitor and detect change by observing, for instance, new-built areas since the previous census or areas that are now vacant, abandoned, or destroyed in a disaster.

2. Time series analysis (multiple observations over the same area) can reveal significant changes such as land cover. These changes are frequently associated with changes in population, so this allows the NSO to identify the critical areas most in need of updating through fieldwork and distinguish those areas from others with no change or requiring minimal updating.[iii]

3. Overlaying EA boundaries of the previous census atop a recent satellite image with an appropriate resolution allows population settlements to be quickly located and priority areas identified.

4. Combining both high- and low-resolution imagery to achieve full coverage can result in a cost-effective way to produce a basemap at a national level. Recent experiences in some countries have shown that 2.5 m pixel resolution satellite images provide a cost-effective coverage at the national level. Higher-resolution satellite images, where pixel sizes measure between 0.5 and 2 m, with existing maps are generally sufficient for delineating EAs in urban areas. For example, it has been reported that this imagery basemap solution was used with satisfaction in recent censuses in some African countries.[8]

5. NSO census geographers can use high-resolution satellite images to capture the dwelling units to build a registry of housing units. GPS-enabled tablets or smartphones could further be used to locate, geocode, and capture attributes that define every dwelling unit in the country. (However, to distinguish housing units from the other types of nonresidential structures, field verification is still necessary.[9]

6. Satellite imagery can be used for an agriculture census and then extended to a more demanding population and housing census. Satellite imagery allows users to identify and stratify the land by intensity of land use and land cover characteristics and therefore help in the construction of area sampling frames for surveys.[10]

7. Analyzing satellite imagery with computer algorithms enables estimation of residential population and can also be used to define the type of neighborhoods. Classification

techniques for mining satellite imagery can label households according to family size, which can then be used to collect census data. The current state of image classification technology can complement the creation and maintenance of geospatial data. These imaging techniques reinforce the overall advantage from using satellite imagery: the bulk of work is carried out in the office, limiting fieldwork (generally the costliest component in a census-mapping project) to merely field verification (see the country example of Malawi).

Example: Census Malawi, 2018[11]

Background
- Due to the shortfalls experienced in the census-mapping exercise in 2008, the NSO of Malawi decided to use satellite imagery as the main tool for 2018 census mapping. The NSO also decided to use computer-assisted personal interviewing (CAPI) for the main census, thereby abandoning the use of pen, paper, and scanning.

Satellite imagery
- The Regional Centre for Mapping of Resources for Development (RCMRD) from Nairobi, Kenya, provided the satellite imagery and the technical assistance required to do the mapping.
- RCMRD provided satellite imagery of the following resolutions:
  - Ultra-urban   0.5 m
  - Regular urban   2.5 m
  - Rural (excluding protected areas)   2.5 m

Training and pilot
- RCMRD trained a pool of twenty mappers from the NSO.
- The officers were trained to capture dwelling frame (DF) and demarcate the EA boundaries using ArcGIS software.
- Piloting was performed in four districts to test the new tool.
- Once the NSO became confident that it was working, it was rolled out to the rest of the country.
- All the demarcation is being done in the GIS lab; fieldwork only involves verification.

Modus operandi
- The plan is to have between 200 and 300 households per EA.
- Structures are used as proxies for households.
- The mappers use dots by clicking each structure that is deemed a household.
- Once the structure has been clicked, it is marked red and counted, and coordinate points are registered automatically.

Example (continued)

- Using features such as rivers, roads, etc., the mapper draws the boundary, keeping in mind that an EA should have between 200 and 300 households.
- The small number of households per EA enables the enumerator to collect information from all households within the specific census period.
- The number of EAs will increase drastically. The current estimate is that they will reach 25,000, up from 13,000 in 2008.
- Budgetary implications require recruiting more enumerators, procuring more tablets, and other costs.

Field verification

- After mapping in the lab, the mappers take the maps to the field to do field verification.
- They carry with them handheld GPSs, which they use to verify the boundaries drawn in the lab.
- The exercise is also used to verify if the marked structures are indeed households.
- Back at the office, the results are compared with what was drawn.
- Any deviations are rectified and corrected.

Advantages and disadvantages of satellite imagery

- Mapping using satellite imagery is fast and less tedious. While the 2008 census mapping took four years to complete, the 2018 census mapping will take less than one year.
- Boundaries using satellite imagery are more accurate because the mapper sees where the features are physically located. In many instances where the 2008 maps were superimposed on the satellite imagery, they were completely off the feature they were following.
- Since the main census will be conducted using CAPI (which has a GPS provision), it is easy to monitor that each household has been visited by the enumerator.
- Satellite imagery is very expensive. RCMRD alone charged NSO USD$1.1 million for the images and technical assistance. With CAPI, the main census is going to cost an additional USD$10 million.

Fieldwork and EAs

As stated earlier, the EA demarcation process is generally carried out in three steps: preparatory work, fieldwork, and quality assurance work. What distinguishes this process, when we use GIS and remotely sensed data at the preparatory phase, is that the office work involves the preparation of the provisional EA maps and material to be used during fieldwork and thus limits the work in the field to verification and validation (as opposed to primarily a manual data collection activity).

In the preparation phase in the office, satellite imagery and aerial photographs may be used to estimate small population-size areas and delineate the EAs (e.g., in a rural environment where buildings are generally scattered) with only one or two stories. In urban areas, the point-based features like dwellings and landmarks can be identified and captured through remote-sensing analysis using GIS. Building footprints can also be extracted if appropriate data is available. This data is then used to update the basemap and EA boundary files and is prepared for use in field validation.

Field verification entails the process by which the information that is captured and created using GIS and remote-sensing imagery is verified and updated in the field. Fieldwork activities for dwelling counts are required for a reliable delineation of EAs. During fieldwork, the existing data and maps prepared in the office are used as visual reference and to verify and capture any new data, including geocodes or x,y coordinates. The use of GPS can support fieldwork activities, allowing for further verification of point-based features and more. Field verification can include the EA data, point-based features such as dwellings or landmarks, and topographical features such as roads and water bodies. During fieldwork, the EA boundary, size, and shape will be verified against the set criteria (see chapter 4). The field-workers can suggest changes for the EA boundaries using digital map-based applications on a smartphone or tablet or via annotation on the map. Attributes can also be captured by the digital map-based applications.

In addition to the capture of the point-based features, GPS may also track linear features and thus be useful for mapping boundaries. The use of GPS in fieldwork is beneficial because the collected data can be read directly into GIS databases, avoiding intermediate data entry or data conversion. In other words, it allows for the linking of records of the EA database to corresponding points on the map.

To do the field verification needed, apps such as Collector for ArcGIS® can be used on a smartphone or tablet to collect and update information in the field (whether connected or disconnected). Configurable apps today allow NSOs to capture the data that is needed in their organization, easily include images or other attachments, and share work.

By simply using a geodatabase, adding the correct field types, and configuring them to meet the requirements of the data collection form,

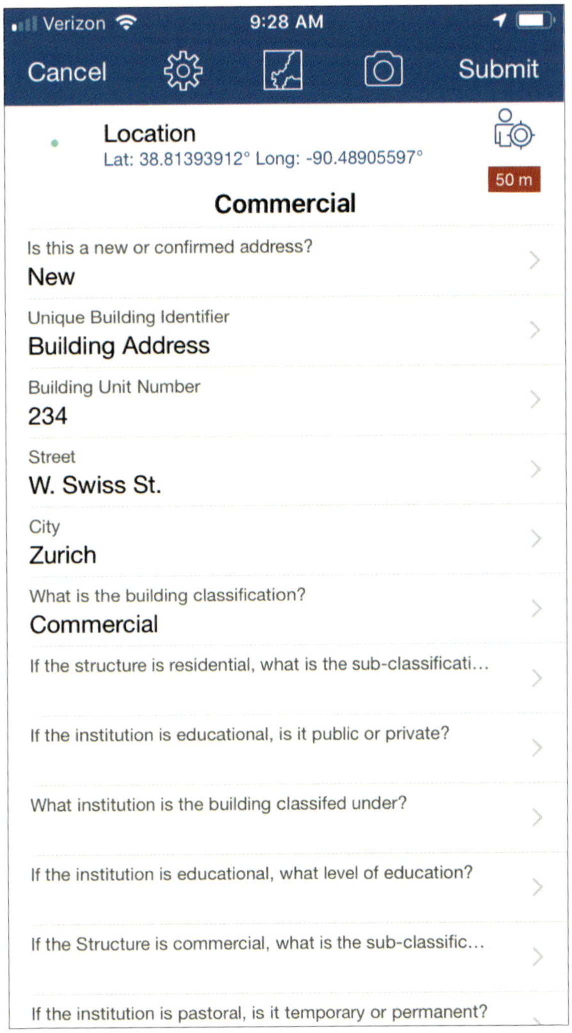

Figure 6.9. Form used for field data collection on Collector for ArcGIS.

field-workers can be ready to conduct field data collection and verification using digital or mobile GIS.

Once the information model has been configured, building an information product in ArcGIS and publishing a feature service to your organization is needed. This service will be used as a layer in a map and by the mobile workforce to collect information in the field. Once the map is ready to be used and shared, the app that will be used should be selected.

Figure 6.10. Publishing a service for use in apps.

Field-workers often work in areas without a data connection. In these cases, they can download the map to make it available when a connection cannot be made. Downloading or copying basemaps directly to a device and reusing them can also be done easily. An offline map can still be worked on, including collecting and editing data, similar to an online map. Consider the amount of data that will be downloaded to each device and the process to retrieve the data once the updates have been made. This workflow should be carefully analyzed to make sure that it is simple, compact, and easy for the field-workers to follow.

Collector for ArcGIS can be used to collect attribute data and capture or edit features. By using the editing function in this app, field-workers can be provided with the ability to edit and suggest changes to existing EAs, plot the location of new buildings, or capture points of interest not showing on the existing basemap.

Apps like Collector for ArcGIS also allow data syncing as needed. Sync allows sending and receiving updates for offline maps. When connectivity is regained, updates can be checked or sent for other people to see.

Collector for ArcGIS can be configured to work as needed in the field. For example, in most EA validation work, field-workers only push edits to the server when they sync and not pull edits made by others while they are offline. This reduces the amount of data transferred, making it faster to share changes and saving data transfer costs on cellular networks.

If the edits being made by others are important to see (for example, for supervisors), push-only synchronization can be disabled so that all edits submitted can be seen.

All data collected using these configurable field applications can then be submitted for final verification or QA and QC checks.

Example of CARICOM, Small Island nations[12]

The concept of using GPS technology comprehensively to overcome the lack of location information was an option during the preparation of the census for Caribbean Community (CARICOM) countries. They used GPS to create an independent database containing the location of all households. This largely involved recording GPS locations (*waypoints*) at the doorstep of each house (e.g., Dominica). For example, the census-mapping office of Suriname has georeferenced many building locations and maintains a comprehensive building database of these locations that is consistently updated. Using standard-grade GPS devices, the census-mapping personnel visit areas not previously captured using GPS. Only recently have they used imagery to compare their results of the GPS exercise with available georeferenced imagery.

Data quality and metadata

Like with any data production process, geospatial data is subject to quality and consistency issues.[13] Data quality is crucial regarding the development of a GIS database at the EA level, requiring the use of technology and data conversion and integration from multiple sources, which will be used at the national level for the census and beyond. In past censuses, it was recognized that EA maps were inaccurate or incomplete. This had a direct impact on the coverage and quality of the census and other survey results. This led to the recognition that the quality of geospatial data, including maps that are used in the census operations, has a major influence on the quality and reliability of census data.

What separates geospatial data from statistical data within an NSO is that there is often pre-existing geographic data available outside the office, including commercial data. Hence, the quality of this data must be analyzed to assess reliability and accuracy prior to inclusion into the geographic data infrastructure of the NSO to support the census. The International Cartographic Association's Commission on Spatial Data Quality has identified seven dimensions of geospatial data quality: positional accuracy, attribute accuracy, completeness, logical consistency, lineage, semantic accuracy, and temporal accuracy. Some of these elements must be imbedded in the metadata that accompanies the transfer of a digital spatial data file or is available in a separate metadata catalog. In the following section, we will elaborate on some of the main aspects of data quality, including data accuracy, quality assurance/quality control, interoperability, and metadata. New tools such as ArcGIS® Data Reviewer help to automate these processes (see chapter 8 for more detail).

Accuracy

The accuracy of geospatial data is the degree to which digital data values within a GIS correctly represent a real-world or true value.[14] The accuracy of digital data in a GIS concerns the descriptive or attribute data and geographic data of geographic features, such as EAs or other features on a map. However, we will focus only on geographic data accuracy because the attributes of descriptive data accuracy are no different from the conventional census data accuracy ones, well known and addressed at any NSO.

Geospatial data accuracy, as generally recognized,[15] refers to both positional accuracy and logical accuracy. Positional accuracy is critical because GIS is used primarily to integrate data from different sources (in different scales and formats). To align all of them, the coordinates of the features in the GIS database should be accurate in relation to their true ground positions and thus should overlay geographically without deviation. For example, the analysis of the positional accuracy of digitized features (points, lines, and polygons) superimposed on the satellite or aerial photos planned by the NSO to be used for EA delineation should overlay correctly and not show a shift between the two datasets: the vector-based features and the raster dataset.

Positional accuracy is of primary importance not only for the needed adjustments of the geospatial data available at the NSO but especially for the fieldwork verification planned for the map-updating activities. In this regard, positional errors can be associated with the use of a GPS in the fieldwork owing to the device itself and the conditions under which the measurements are undertaken. NSOs should ensure that the measurements undertaken with GPS devices are within acceptable positional accuracy[16] and sufficient degree of precision to capture point-based feature coordinates.

Logical accuracy refers to spatial data inconsistencies such as incorrect line intersections, duplicate lines or boundaries, or gaps in lines. These errors are commonly referred to as spatial or topological errors. These types of errors occur during the process of digitizing data. The sources of these errors can be scanning algorithms, digitizing processes, and human errors in manual digitizing. Data conversion and integration are error prone. Checking the resulting data for both positional accuracy and logical consistency should therefore follow a rigorous procedure to avoid the propagation of these errors within the GIS; this is part of quality assurance, which is discussed in the next section.

Quality control/quality assurance

Recommendations stated earlier for data quality and accuracy need to be implemented. Good practices[iv] have shown that NSOs stand to gain if they devise a set of procedures and a process to follow throughout the census to measure the quality of each stage of the census. The extent to which data is protected against errors (quality assurance) but also a control mechanism trying to detect errors and fix and reduce most errors (quality control) are both necessary. In *Principles and Recommendations*, the UN has recommended that each country have a quality assurance and improvement system that should be developed as part of the overall census program and integrated with other census plans, schedules, and procedures.[17]

We have stressed that geospatial information and technology should be used at every stage of the census. At the pre-enumeration stage, the building of the database at the EA level is a foundational building block for the subsequent geospatial information–based census activities. A quality assurance program should put the census people undertaking the process in a good position to identify problems and suggest improvements,

Figure 6.11. An example of positional accuracy. This web app shows aerial photography from Nearmap over Naperville, Illinois, with a water network overlaid on the imagery.

including geospatial data issues. The quality assurance process therefore relies on established, documented procedures, systems to monitor outcomes, and active encouragement by management to involve staff in identifying and resolving quality issues. The human factor is crucial, and managers play a key role in achieving quality. NSOs should establish a culture of focusing on quality, give staff responsibilities to allow staff to achieve, ensure staff understand the philosophy of quality, and provide the opportunity for staff to actively contribute.

The quality assurance program generally aims to improve the process of quality rather than just identifying and fixing errors. It recognizes the existence of errors in the process and gives staff a responsibility in improving the process. Still, setting a quality control mechanism for finding and fixing errors, to the extent possible, is of utmost importance for the acceptance of geospatial data and the building of confidence in its use for the census. A quality control mechanism relies on the ability to review, audit, and find all errors, whether at the digitization and scanning of maps, their integration with other data sources, or the use of geospatial technology in fieldwork. The noticeable tendency is to use "quality control" and "quality assurance" interchangeably, but there are subtle differences. Quality control is a reactive process that focuses on identifying defects and errors, while quality assurance is a proactive approach whose purpose is prevention.[18]

Data conversion and integration are prone to error, and thus a rigorous procedure for checking the resulting data for both positional accuracy and logical consistency should be part of the data control process. Similar procedures should be implemented to ensure the quality of derived output products, such as cross-tabulations or GIS overlays. In addition to the final checking and acceptance of data conversion, quality control will be conducted at the key stages of fieldwork and data collection to ensure the quality of the data collected (see more details in chapter 8).

GPS and imagery also serve as a powerful quality-control mechanism of enumerator work because they provide near-real-time feedback. Using GPS has a significant advantage because coordinates (x,y or latitude–longitude) captured could easily and quickly be plotted over the high-resolution geo-referenced image on which all housing or dwelling units are visible, offering a unique quality control opportunity. Furthermore, the integration of GPS with the EA map on a handheld device allows the tracking of the census enumerators in the field during enumeration and controls whether they covered all households in their areas (see more details in chapter 8). It also allows us to rapidly find out which of the housing units have not been recorded and thus most probably have not been counted.

Interoperability/metadata standards

Quality assurance and quality control also include the development of metadata[19] standards and the systems and services that allow data to be accessed and shared—what is known as *interoperability*.[v] Metadata is descriptive data that includes the data lineage and all relevant information that provide context, contents, and meaning for its use. This includes the (1) source of the data ("who"); (2) contents and definitions ("what"); (3) date of compilation and collection ("when"); (4) geographic reference and coverage of the data ("where"); (5) method of compilation and conversion, such as manual digitizing, on-screen digitizing, scanning and automatic vectorization, image interpretation and classification, and computations ("how"); and (6) method of data collection, field surveys, GPS, remote-sensing imagery, etc., and the reasons for the data collection and its uses ("how" and "why").[20]

Documenting geospatial data, as it encompasses various datasets from different providers, is vital to avoid loss of data source and data quality owing to a lack of information about each specific dataset. Metadata has the advantage to benefit the primary data provider by maintaining the value of the data and ensuring its continued use over a significant number of years. By developing metadata, it helps to sustain knowledge management in the organization.

Metadata is crucial for the management and maintenance of a digital GIS database because its use spans all the stages of the census and beyond, and metadata can be helpful with version control. During the process of database construction, relevant data is recorded in a standardized way, and metadata base (data dictionary) is associated with it. In this regard, metadata goes beyond the map legend,[vi] which is one representation of metadata, to encompass all the types of descriptive information applied to a digital geospatial data file. With the digital approach and the use of GIS for geospatial data management, it is easier to incorporate metadata in a digital database and automate its processing. Commercial GIS software is now facilitating a close link between geospatial data and its associated metadata. For example, Esri software includes templates with its ArcGIS technology.

These templates allow GIS data providers and users to easily access information about their data. In this regard, metadata benefits are being increasingly recognized by data providers and users alike. Some NSOs have started to incorporate metadata collection within the overall census data management process.

Ideally, metadata structures and definitions should be referenced to a standard because standards developed through a consultative process provide a basis to operate systems and services for the access, exchange, and distribution of data. In this regard, in 2012, a global consultation on the inventory of issues to be tackled by the UN-GGIM during its first years has identified standards as one of the key issues to be addressed by the committee. It was found that, in many countries, no shortage of geospatial data is being collected, but rather there is a lack of interoperability between the different sources of data, reducing its use and sharing by multiple users. What was particularly noted is that, while international standards in support of geospatial and location-based information have been in development since the early 1990s,[22] many countries are still slow to adopt and implement the existing internationally agreed-on standards.

Figure 6.12. Cape Verde improvements in data quality.[21] *Left*, a map of employment statistics available as part of the Instituto Nacional de Estatística (INE) portal (*right*) open to the public.

Furthermore, the UN-EG-ISGI, created in 2013, has included in its mandate the following focus area: "Encourage the use of existing, and development of new data and metadata standards as well as other standards to enhance the interface of location-based datasets from multiple sources." It has addressed interoperability and metadata standards and notably stressed that standardization is a key aspect in enhancing the integration process of statistical and geospatial information into daily decision-making at all levels of society.

Some geospatial metadata standards that have been developed by international standards organizations, such as the International Organization for Standardization Technical Committee (ISO/TC) 211 and the OGC, and used by many NMAs and regional organizations such as in Europe[vii] can be adapted to the requirements of statistical purposes. On the other hand, the statistical community has developed statistical metadata standards, the most known of them being the SDMX.[23] Therefore, the UN-EG-ISGI has recommended, as a future area of standardization, working on a statistical-geospatial metadata interoperability in integrating, for example, SDMX and the DDI[24] with ISO-19115. Other areas were suggested, such as ISO standardized representation of boundaries to which statistical data is linked—the development of an ISO standard for the second administrative-level boundaries (http://www.unsalb.org/) dataset developed by the UN Geographic Information Working Group (UNGIWG) was proposed. Metadata should be an integral part of statistical collection and dissemination processes. In this section, we focused more on its role at data collection and in the development of the geospatial database; we will elaborate on the role of metadata in census data dissemination in chapter 9.

Ensuring compatibility with previous censuses

Undertaking a population and housing census provides a picture at a specified time of the size and characteristics of the population of a country and where its inhabitants live. Since the census is conducted periodically, analyzing the changes of these population and housing characteristics over time increases the understanding of the dynamics of socioeconomic and demographic structures and helps create more accurate, timely, and unbiased information for better decision-making. It is important for census data to be comparable and compatible with previous censuses and with other data produced by the NSO and the wider community.

Changes in geographic boundaries do occur over time and pose challenges for the EAs to remain compatible between censuses, thus compromising any comparability of census data. Interpolation and other statistical techniques reconcile information for incompatible area units but are sophisticated and difficult to handle by many NSOs and other census data users.[25] This is one of the reasons why there are recommendations for the applicability of a grid system or other systems of enumeration at a smaller geographic unit than the EA that can create stability and independence of political or administrative boundary changes and sustain a comparability of statistical data over time. However, to mitigate the impact of changes and ensure compatibility with a previous census, the principle that NSOs need to follow in designing their census geography is to try to preserve boundaries from the previous census or keep at least one geographic unit on a lower level (as stated earlier) stable in terms of its boundary, which should not be changed, altered, or retraced, even if political or administrative boundaries are changed.

With respect to the preservation of boundaries and when changes are made owing to an increase of population size or any relevant reason to reduce the size of the existing EA, it is recommended to split in two or subdivide the existing EA rather to change its boundaries.[viii] When adjacent EAs must be merged, we should merge the totality of the EAs and not part of them to make the new census data compatible with the information from a previous enumeration. If boundaries are to be changed, outside of splitting or merging units of the existing EAs, more complicated methods of adjustment are necessary and should be documented. The NSO should therefore maintain a master list of EAs and administrative units and their respective codes and commit any changes made to the master list to the GIS and census databases.

One component of the census geography that can accommodate the boundary changes is the geocoding scheme, which should be designed to allow the inclusion of additional geographic units (i.e., when splitting a unit into two). If possible, efforts should be made to ensure that census geocoding is consistent with existing coding systems like local administrative units; this would ensure comparability of information at least at a certain level.

Moreover, a fundamental component that can facilitate change analysis is the compilation of a table of correspondence (concordance) to record the changes and data reassignments and that can be provided to census data users. The table would consist of compatibility or equivalency files and would list the codes of each EA in the current census and the corresponding code in a previous enumeration. This process ensures that if units have been split or aggregated, the split or aggregate would be indicated in these files. Besides the monitoring of the changes to be brought to the geographic base, other considerations relate to standards and classifications. Indeed, to provide

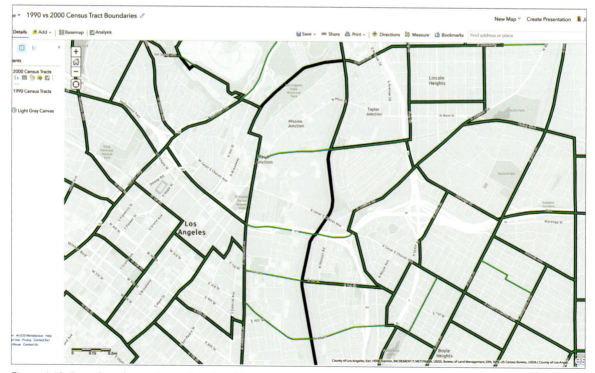

Figure 6.13. Boundary change in Los Angeles, CA—comparing 1990 with 2000 tract boundaries. The black boundaries are 1990, and the green boundaries are 2000. In the map, the two boundaries overlap (black and green lines), the 1990 boundaries were dropped (black lines only), and new 2000 boundaries were drawn (green lines only).

comparability between censuses, it is advisable to use the existing metadata standards and revise the classifications, concord them with the previous ones, and add footnotes to the concordance table to indicate them.

Cloud considerations in census activities

Cloud computing is probably the most used buzzword in the IT community today.[26] Cloud providers charge for cloud-computing services based on usage, like home utilities such as water or electricity. Cloud computing is becoming increasingly popular for data storage, analysis, and dissemination, and organizations and end users are turning to cloud-computing services for the following reasons:

- Cost benefits—the up-front costs are reduced on IT resources and operational expenses, including the traditional need for IT administrators to manage computer resources.
- Speed—organizations acquire and operate necessary resources delivered in almost real time, instead of much time needed to plan, acquire, and set up their own resources.
- Global scale—the delivery of a scalable amount of IT resources in terms of computing power, storage, and bandwidth commensurate with demand at the right time and the right geographic location.
- Productivity—the IT teams of the organizations, spared from spending time on IT resources management, can focus on achieving their more important core businesses.
- Performance and reliability—allowing users and organizations to store and process data either in a privately owned cloud or on a third-party server in a well-maintained, secure data center. The data center is regularly upgraded to the latest computing hardware, thus making data-accessing mechanisms more efficient and reliable.[27]

The three main types of cloud-computing services are infrastructure as a service (IaaS), platform as a service (PaaS), and software as a service (SaaS).

- IaaS is the most basic category of cloud-computing services, allowing consumers to rent the IT infrastructure (servers, processing, storage, networks, operating systems, and other computing resources) from a cloud provider on demand and typically on a subscription basis. Examples of IaaS include Amazon® Web Services (AWS), Microsoft® Azure, and Google® Compute Engine.
- PaaS provides consumers with cloud-computing services that supply an on-demand environment for developing, testing, delivering, and managing software applications, including web or mobile apps. Examples of PaaS include AWS, AWS Elastic Beanstalk, Google® App Engine, and Heroku®.
- SaaS provides consumers with software applications over the Internet, usually with a web browser on a phone, tablet, or PC, while the cloud provider hosts and manages the software application and underlying infrastructure and handles any maintenance.[28] Examples of SaaS include Salesforce®, ArcGIS, NetSuite®, and SAP Concur®.

Similarly, there are three different ways to deploy cloud-computing resources: public cloud, private cloud, and hybrid approaches.

- Public cloud is a deployment model in which the cloud infrastructure is provisioned for open use by the public (Microsoft Azure is an example of a public cloud). With a public cloud, all computing resources (hardware, software, and other supporting infrastructure) is owned, managed, and operated by a third-party cloud service provider. This model is based on a multitenant architecture, enabling users to pay only for the resources and workloads they use.

- Private cloud refers to the model in which the cloud infrastructure is provisioned for exclusive use by a single business or organization. Private cloud services are delivered from the organization's on-site data center to its internal users. This model offers the versatility and convenience of the cloud, but it's based on a single-tenant architecture in which the maintenance and direct control are undertaken at the local private data center.

- Hybrid cloud is a combination of both public and private cloud infrastructures that remain distinct but bound together by standardized technology that enables data and application interoperability.[29]

ArcGIS is available for deployment via public clouds such as AWS or Microsoft Azure, and can be deployed to a private cloud depending on user needs. A hybrid approach is also possible by combining ArcGIS Online capabilities with enterprise GIS systems that are public or private. ArcGIS Online is an Esri SaaS offering.

Esri entered the SaaS arena early on. The Geography Network represented the first work in offering content through the web in 2000, followed by ArcWeb Services in 2002. This early work proved the value of web service delivery and helped to form the foundation for the future. In 2009, with the launch of ArcGIS Online, Esri began to steadily offer more and more content and capabilities in the cloud, paving the way for today's robust SaaS offering.

Today, there are more than six million users of ArcGIS Online, and more than eighteen million items (maps, apps, and layers). More than one billion map requests are made every day, and that number continues to grow by more than 20 percent year over year. More than thirty thousand new items are added every twenty-four hours, with more than three thousand new subscribers every day.

While traditional GIS was in the past installed on a desktop or on a server at the NSO, cloud deployments of GIS offer the flexibility of the cloud environment for data storing, computing, visualization, and sharing. In fact, the functionality in online platforms continues to expand; today not only includes great mapping and visualization but analysis, 3D

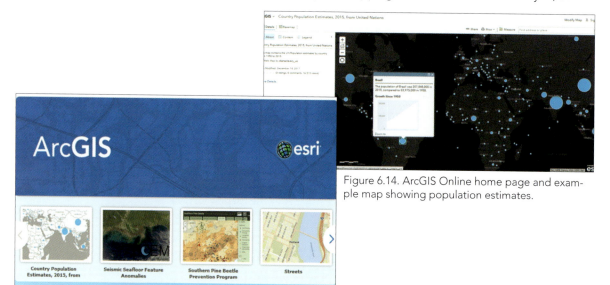

Figure 6.14. ArcGIS Online home page and example map showing population estimates.

mapping, new smart-mapping tools, configurable apps, and more.

ArcGIS Online is an online, collaborative web GIS that allows usage, creation, and sharing of maps, scenes, apps, layers, analytics, and data. Access is also provided to Living Atlas of the World, apps, and Esri's secure cloud, where items can be added and web layers can be published. Because ArcGIS Online is an integral part of the ArcGIS system, it can be used to extend the capabilities of ArcGIS® Desktop, ArcGIS® Enterprise, ArcGIS® web APIs, and ArcGIS® Runtime SDKs.

Also available today is the ability to deploy ArcGIS in AWS or Microsoft Azure. In AWS, customers can deploy ArcGIS themselves by bringing their own license and using Esri's ArcGIS Amazon machine images. Esri provides AWS cloud formation templates to set up ArcGIS on AWS. ArcGIS Enterprise on Microsoft Azure allows deployment of an ArcGIS Server site, ArcGIS Enterprise, and ArcGIS Desktop clients on Microsoft Azure virtual machines.

With respect to census operations, since GIS SaaS is online without any on-premises deployment, it may be desirable for both the operational phase and the dissemination phase of the census. NSOs may wish to consider an enterprise GIS that can be deployed in the cloud because it offers many benefits to the census operations in terms of better human resources management and cost effectiveness. Esri also offers ArcGIS Enterprise behind the firewall, which provides similar capabilities as ArcGIS Online and includes Portal for ArcGIS®, with similar functionalities of a portal website with Map and Scene Viewer, a content repository, and APIs for developers.

Creating map services and mobile map packages in support of census operations

A map service allows maps to be made available to various users. After a map is made in a desktop app, it can be published as a service to a server site. Internet or intranet users can then use the map service to access maps, features, and attribute data available in web, desktop, online, mobile, and other client applications. One common use of a map service is to show business POIs or demographic or thematic data on top of basemap tiles from ArcGIS Online, Bing™ Maps, or Google Maps.

Map services are designed to work in many web and intranet scenarios. The same map service may be used in ArcMap by one user, a web app by another user, ArcGIS Online by another user, and a mobile app by still another user. The following are some common reasons for setting up a map service:

- To serve dynamic maps
- To serve dynamic layers
- To serve cached maps
- To serve features
- To serve network analysis functions
- To serve images, features, or raster maps through OGC specifications

Most map services are exposed through Simple Object Access Protocol (SOAP) and Representational State Transfer (REST) interfaces.

Dynamic maps are drawn at the time they are requested by a user. While not as fast as cached maps, they may be appropriate for highly focused intranet applications and applications that require real-time display of data.

Cached map services (those that use a set of pre-created images) are the fastest way to serve maps on the web. In this way, ArcGIS Online, Google Maps, Bing Maps, and many other services expose their maps. Although users view static pictures of a map, these pictures can be supplemented with a cached map service with find, identify, and query tasks to reach the underlying data. The cache can also be updated regularly if data changes.

Map services can also play a key role in streamlining work in all phases of the census. Map services such as the above can be used throughout the census business process, serving basemaps to desktop users doing planning, for use in operational dashboards by field managers, and to executives needing to see a current status of the project. These same services can also be used in the dissemination phase to help publish results securely.

Map services don't need to display images and can be set up to return a set of features to work within an application. These features can be retrieved through tasks added to the application. For example, one might want to query a map service and display the resulting features as graphics in the map. This query could be phrased as follows: "Give me all the features with 'London' in the name" or "Give me all the features longer than 100 kilometers."

The OGC has published specifications for exposing map images (WMS), vector features (WFS), raster datasets (WCS), and web map tiles (WMTS) on the web. Some organizations require their geographic data and maps to be available in this way. Map services can be configured to return images or data conforming to OGC specifications.

Careful consideration should be used with user requirements while deciding which map services may be needed. Field validation and field data collection as well as operations management can all benefit from using these services.

In addition to map services, a GIS-based census should also include consideration of the use of

offline maps or mobile map packages (.mmpk file). As we discussed earlier, these packages allow NSOs to serve map data to a mobile device, where it can be accessed even in offline mode. Apps allow users to explore maps, collect information, edit asset data, find places, and route to new locations while disconnected from the Internet, and data edits can by synced with other users when a connection is re-established.

The following capabilities can be added to an off-line map:

- View basemaps: For basemaps, tiled layers or compressed mobile basemap layers can be used. Tiled layers consist of either raster tiles or vector tiles. Raster tiled layers (sometimes referred to in ArcGIS platform documentation as *tiled layers*) are pixel-based images of the basemap with cartography prerendered at multiple scales. Using less data than raster tiled layers, vector tiled layers deliver cartography that often looks better on high-resolution devices because they are rendered quickly on the fly using the display's native resolution.

- Edit operational data (also known as *feature data* or *vector data*): This editing includes querying and editing the location, shape, attributes, related tables, and attachments of features.

- Sync edits: When online again, one can upload edits made on the device or pull down only the updated features that others have edited, if data is service based.

- Performing fast searches for locations (geocode and reverse geocode) and routes.

There are different ways to serve maps and map layers to users. The NSO should carefully consider which workflow will best match its needs:

- Preplanned workflow: Author and generate an off-line map ahead of time so that your field-workers can simply download and take it into the field.

- On-demand workflow: Allow users to define a map's area of interest, generate the off-line map content, and download it to their device, as required.
- Individual layers off-line: Allow users to take individual layers off-line and use these to construct a map within their app.

The preplanned workflow is appropriate for organizations when the map area is prepared in advance of the field-worker entering the field. For example, a census area manager may have a team assigned to collect survey data. The manager can prepare a set of map areas prior to the week's work so that the team simply downloads the map areas at the beginning of the week. The team members will be able to take the map off-line to locate the household or business and collect the data. They can synchronize their changes back to the agency database when connectivity is restored.

The preplanned workflow is probably the best choice for creating EA maps to serve to mobile devices, when the work will be assigned for a given area and used by enumerators.

Use of GIS for optimizing the site placement of field offices

In many countries, particularly those with a large geographic area, field offices need to conduct census operations at regional and local levels. A statistical network of field offices covering the country's territory needs local staff experienced in collecting and producing statistics. Generally, decentralizing census-mapping activities is beneficial: a regional or local office can carry the fieldwork more rapidly due to the proximity of the region being "mapped" and eventually "remapped," and more efficiently due to

the knowledge of the geography of the region and any recent changes to it; and it is easier for local staff, acquainted with the administrative structure, to develop and maintain a continuous working relationship with the local authorities. An additional benefit when the decentralization process is facilitated by geospatial and communication technologies is that both a digital geospatial infrastructure and an expertise at the local level are created, which will generally benefit the region. However, decentralization is not totally implemented without difficulties because census-mapping activities may face some issues at the local level, particularly in training, the division of tasks, and the coordination between central and regional census offices.

NSOs may have already some components of the census infrastructure available, but they may need to set up new field offices. They would face the following question: where to place these new regional and local field offices? This is a typical site location selection problem. The site selection is generally based on a set of potential sites to be evaluated against numerous relevant criteria. The required criteria would be relevant for establishing a census infrastructure allowing for the optimal allocation of resources for adequately undertaking and managing the census.

Site selection is based on what is called *suitability analysis*, a type of spatial analysis provided by a GIS to determine the most suitable location or site for a facility (such as a new factory, hospital, school, or field office) from a set of candidates by meeting specific criteria. When performing site selection analysis, we must initially define the site candidates and then select a set of relevant criteria to which it can be assigned some weight, and the GIS software functionality can evaluate and rate the best or most suitable sites. It is possible for the decision makers to adjust the weights, which reflect their preference.

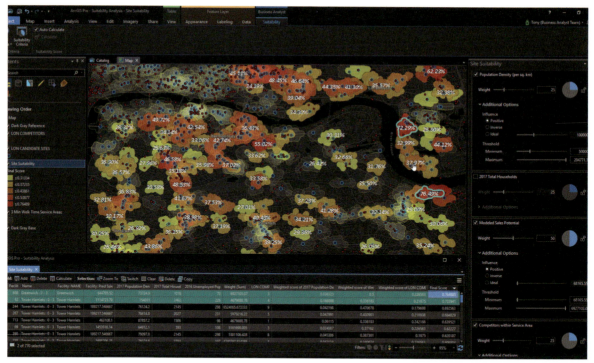

Figure 6.15. Example of site suitability analysis.

Site selection analysis can be performed with the use of vector data (a set of point location sites or polygon areas), but raster data, suitable for overlay functionality, is more widely used for site selection, particularly for weighted site selection.[30]

The criteria for the selection of sites for field offices vary depending on the conditions of the country. But they generally revolve around the following items: density and distribution of the population in the region with a certain threshold, appropriate location for a field office (for example, not in an industrial park or a residential zone), proximity to workforce, minimum space requirement for a workplace, required amenities (e.g., parking lot), location accessibility (e.g., not far from a major road or intersection), site location near an available telecom, connectivity and network coverage, etc.[ix]

Use of GIS for optimizing capital and asset distribution

The adage "You can't manage something if you don't know where it is located" applies well to infrastructure assets because they occupy a location. Managing assets[31] for organizations such as public works, municipalities, and utilities is a capital asset business that requires an efficient management system such as a GIS. These organizations know, for example, that assets such as roads, poles, water, wastewater networks, and other waste facilities are interconnected and in proximity with other assets and features, even if their locations are dispersed.

Census operations involve the use and management of many assets—physical assets, such as tablets and smartphones, as well as human resources and field offices.

GIS platforms not only serve as a system of record but also allow insight and transparency into the movement and optimization of assets. GIS systems allow for the tracking of the movement of people and things via sensors, GPS, and other new technologies such as RFID. GIS systems provide powerful analytic tools to perform spatial queries and analyze interconnectivity, proximity, and other complex spatial relationships. The geospatial database is inherently "location-aware," providing far more power for managing assets than traditional non-location–aware database systems, including the ability for 3D modeling.[32]

The value GIS brings to improving efficiencies and maximizing productivity and cost savings has been proven in many areas,[33] such as fleet management, delivery, routing and logistics for services and transportation, and other location-based services. Moreover, its cost effectiveness is increasingly recognized by utilities and other infrastructure-related organizations, at least for tracking the location of the facilities to be maintained and helping to reduce the time and resources expended to proceed with their maintenance and repair responses. This can save an organization a great amount of time and resources. This same type of analysis can be used, for example, by census organizations to optimize workers in the field, providing both time and cost savings.

The concept of asset management using GIS can be applied to the census infrastructure of a country and benefit the NSO. GIS offers a platform to monitor the census workflows between the central census office and the field offices in different sites in the regions and contributes to the management of the overall census. For example, workers in the field can use mobile devices or laptops to view online GIS maps in real time and confirm to the regional or central office that they are at the correct location or look up details about infrastructure before starting.

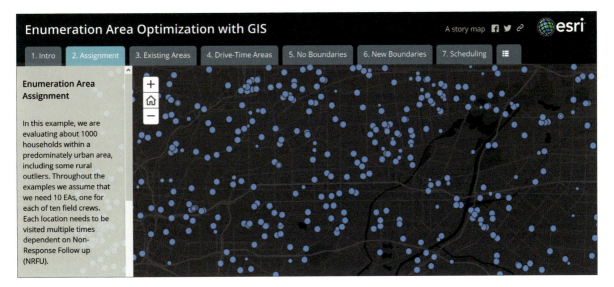

Figure 6.16. EA optimization plan, showing points to be assigned.

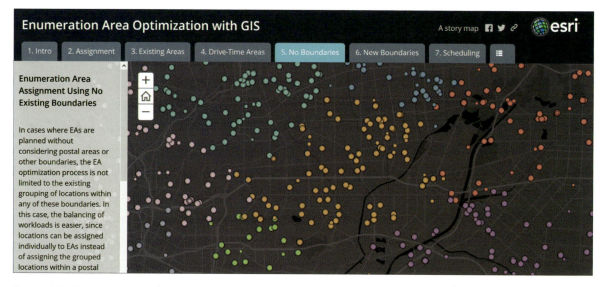

Enumeration Area Optimization with GIS   A story map 🄵 🐦 𝒫   🌐 **esri**

| 1. Intro | 2. Assignment | 3. Existing Areas | 4. Drive-Time Areas | 5. No Boundaries | 6. New Boundaries | 7. Scheduling | ☰ |

Enumeration Area Assignment Using No Existing Boundaries

In cases where EAs are planned without considering postal areas or other boundaries, the EA optimization process is not limited to the existing grouping of locations within any of these boundaries. In this case, the balancing of workloads is easier, since locations can be assigned individually to EAs instead of assigning the grouped locations within a postal

Figure 6.17. EA optimization plan, showing clustering.

EA optimization

EA optimization can be conducted once all EAs have been validated and updated with field information. This process can be done using spatial analysis tools as well as data for the natural and built environment to make intelligent and efficient areas. Optimization should take into consideration existing EAs and try to minimize changes to boundaries where possible while looking for efficiencies in time and costs savings. For example, it may be necessary to split existing EAs owing to growth in housing, the addition of a new bridge across a waterway, or other changes in the built environment.

GIS can also be used to inject response rates or difficulties found during the last census in the delineation process (for example, to delineate smaller EAs in areas more difficult to enumerate during the last census). Similarly, EAs may have been drawn

arbitrarily in the past, not taking into consideration natural features, such as rivers, that might pose a natural barrier to access.

There are two main objectives for EA planning, which may compete with one another: the first objective is to minimize travel and keep locations as tightly grouped as possible, while the second is to balance the capacity among the territories so that field personnel have similar workloads. EAs are typically defined based on target numbers, such as total number of households or total population. We also need to include estimates for total on-site time based on household size (total time of interview expected).

When EAs are based on existing boundaries, the individual areas will be summarized for each EA, and the new EA outline will follow the input boundaries. If EAs were built without using existing areas, boundary areas could still be built for each territory using GIS. These boundaries can later be used to quickly assign new locations to these EAs. In such cases, new locations would simply be assigned to the EA in which they are located.

A final operation in the EA map design is to add labels and map symbols, which should follow cartographic standards and be self-explanatory. Annotations on the map must be clearly legible to make it easier to use and avoid any need for complex training instructions for the enumerators. We should avoid drawing too many features on a map because features require too much text information. Labeling can be performed by GIS[34] or mapping software. As we create these map products for use in the field, it is useful to remember that the use of EA maps is an essential part of the enumerators' work.

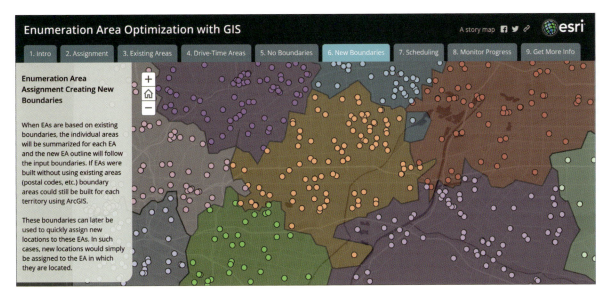

Figure 6.18. Optimization plan showing new derived boundaries.

Case study: Republic of the Philippines

The Philippine Statistics Authority (PSA) is a young organization, having been formed in 2013 from the merger of four separate agencies. With PSA's creation, the policy is to affect the "necessary and proper changes in the organizational and functional structures of the Philippine Statistical System (PSS), to promote efficiency and effectiveness in the delivery of statistical services." In line with this, the Philippines is also committed to achieving the SDGs. The PSA is responsible for acquiring and managing SDG data for the country. It was in the context of 1) the policy in its creation and 2) its designation as the official repository of SDG indicators in the Philippines that PSA agreed to a location value assessment (LVA) seminar facilitated by Esri and Geodata Systems Technologies Inc. in August 2016. The results of this LVA provided PSA with a road map for implementing GIS inside of PSA and identified areas of high priority and value to the organization.

PSA administrators believe that GIS technology has a critical and integrative role to play in national statistics projects. They found that ArcGIS makes building and scaling up platforms vastly simpler and cheaper than other solutions. They also noted that it allows nearly frictionless participation that strengthens network effects and enhances a user's ability to capture, analyze, and exchange huge amounts of data. This functionality increases the value of census data to the entire nation.

The UN noted the Philippines modernization efforts and chose PSA to participate in an SDG research exercise called the Federated System for the SDGs. As a member of the UN, the Philippines is expected to own the mission and establish national frameworks for sustainability. The country is required to set its own goals and incorporate them into its national planning processes, policies, and strategies.

In partnership with Esri, the UN Statistics Department provided a modern platform for collaboration among data producers and data users. The platform facilitates interoperability across a wide range of data and information sources, including those outside the traditional boundaries of the national and global official statistical systems.

Dr. Lisa Bersales presented the work of the Philippines on integration of statistics and geospatial information efforts during the initial UN research project meetings in Redlands, California. She also presented what the PSA is doing toward SDG monitoring. Dr. Bersales identified two activities that the PSA is pursuing as the way forward: "1) PSA is now on the planning stage to pre-test ArcGIS solution for its possible use in the 2020 Census of Population and Housing, i.e., planning, pre-enumeration activities, data collection, post-data collection processing, and data dissemination, and 2) PSA shall also work closely with a newly created ministry, the Department of ICT, on integrating geospatial and statistical information." This jump-started the use of ArcGIS not just for SDG monitoring but for the pilot activity to adopt the technology in the 2020 Census of Population and Households.

During the census pilot project, PSA tested two data collection mobile apps. One was Collector for ArcGIS® for geotagging buildings nationwide. The other was Survey123 for ArcGIS® for gathering census data. The field apps improved the accuracy and completion of data and speeds data processing.

Another GIS strategy was to host the Philippines SDG-related spatial content on ArcGIS Hub® technology. This portal improves timeliness, data quality, and accessibility to user-friendly products and services. Hub incorporates open-data formats and includes geospatial dimensions in data presentation.

PSA adopted the open-data approach to ensure interoperability with other data management systems and tools. Others can download published datasets to their own GIS and map it.

By modernizing its census and survey operations, PSA is fulfilling its vision of becoming a solid, responsive, and world-class authority on quality statistics and civil registration.

Figure 6.19. Philippine Statistics Authority SDG hub.

References

i. Companies like Skybox Imaging and Planet Labs have the first of these small satellites already active, with plans for more. For example, as of November 2017, Planet Labs has a constellation of more than 175 miniature satellites, called Dove, and is manufacturing twenty of them per week. It also provides 95 percent cloud-free imagery of earth's land mass, at 3–5 m optical resolution, each week.

ii. According to .Earth, earlier in 2017, "Bill and Melinda Gates joined forces with Pierre Omidyar, founder of eBay, to fund the 'Radiant Earth' project, which is a new repository and archive of the world's satellite, aerial and drone imagery. The effort aims to combine and analyze Earth data and imagery, and offer it for free to 'governments, NGOs, companies, developers, and entrepreneurs to build open source ecosystems that accelerate the use of earth imagery technology and commercial adoption.' "

iii. For example, the US Census Bureau is doing in-office canvassing using interactive review and a block assessment, research, and classification application, which was developed in-house. "This will allow us to focus field work, our most expensive efforts, in only the areas where it's absolutely necessary, where we can't find information through technology," said Dierdre Bishop, chief of the bureau's geography division, to the Federal News Network. The article, continues: "The application works by comparing satellite imagery from 2009 with 'very recent' current imagery, Bishop said. An analyst looks at a particular block and can label it stable or unchanged. If they do see a change, they can drop a pin, which triggers a review by a more experienced analyst using additional resources to look at what has changed between the two images." See "Statistical Agencies Looking to C-suite, New Digital Tools to Address Biggest Challenges." Available at https://federalnewsradio.com/technology/2017/02/statistical-agencies-looking-c-suite-new-digital-tools-address-biggest-challenges/.

iv. "Following good data quality assurance practices does not guarantee that the data are correct, but it does reduce the likelihood of errors. Completing a data quality assessment is a way of measuring the extent to which the data are protected against errors, and sharing that assessment with data users gives them confidence in the quality of the data" (Statistics Canada). Available at https://www.statcan.gc.ca/eng/data-quality-toolkit/.

v. "Interoperability is the capability of a product or a computer system to function with other existing products or systems without restrictions and independently of their own physical architecture and operating systems. Interoperability can be achieved through the use of Internet open standards. The mission of the World Wide Web Consortium W3C . . . is to provide guidance and to contribute to the Web evolution by developing protocoles, standards and guidelines supporting interoperability" (St. Lawrence Global Observatory). Available at https://slgo.ca/en/scientist-portal/data-management/definitions.

vi. We have already mentioned in chapter 4 that a map legend is one representation of metadata, containing information about the publisher of the map, the publication date, the type of map, a description of the map, spatial references, the map's scale and its accuracy, etc.

vii. As an example, the European Location Framework (ELF), a technical infrastructure delivering authoritative, interoperable, cross-border geospatial reference data for analyzing and understanding information connected to places and features, relies on the following geospatial metadata standards:

- INSPIRE metadata—datasets and services
- ISO 19115-1:2014—Geographic information—Metadata—Part 1: Fundamentals
- ISO 19115-2:2008—Geographic information—Metadata—Part 2: Extensions for Imagery and Gridded Data (under revision)
- ISO 19115-3—Geographic information—Metadata—Part 3: XML Schema Implementation of Metadata Fundamentals
- DCAT AP—describing public-sector datasets in Europe
- DCAT—interoperability between data catalogs

viii. Example of Canada: "For the 2006 Census, their focus was on business process reengineering of the overall census collection process and mapping. Eighty-two percent of their block remained constant; 15 percent blocks were split or collapsed together. However, they didn't want to do many changes on the geographic structure of the data to improve the quality of other areas."

ix. Another approach involving quantitative and qualitative criteria for site location, known as *multicriteria analysis*, has gained prominence in the evaluation of projects, where group decisions and the opinions of the participants concerned by the project are taken into account. Jacek Malczewski in *GIS and Multicriteria Decision Analysis* (April 1999) defines this concept well. The integration of GIS with multicriteria analysis constitutes what is called a *spatial decision support system*. See *SIG et analyse multicritère* from Amor Laaribi. Available at https://www.amazon.com/analyse-multicrite%CC%80re-French-Amor-Laaribi/dp/2746201224.

Notes

1. This approach has been applied in some developing countries such as Seychelles, Lesotho, and Namibia. See *Demarcation of Census Enumeration Areas for the 2016 Population and Housing Census in Lesotho*, Hennie Loots, Geomatics Indaba Proceedings 2015—Stream 1. Available at http://www.ee.co.za/wp-content/uploads/2015/08/Hennie-Loots.pdf.

2. Manual digitizing involves tracing the points, lines, and polygons of the visible features of a source map using a pointing device (called a *digitization cursor*) and a digitizing tablet (also known as a *digitizer*).

3. Heads-up digitizing involves using a scanned map or image on the computer screen and tracing the points, lines, and polygons on the screen. This method of digitizing is commonly named heads-up digitizing because the operator's attention is on the screen and not down on a digitizing tablet.

4. See the online ancillaries at esri.com/Census2020: *Characteristics of the main commercial earth observation satellites*.

5. See the article "Satellite images reveal gaps in global population data: Algorithms help to produce precise maps of where people in developing countries live and work" from Jeff Tollefson. Available at https://www.nature.com/news/satellite-images-reveal-gaps-in-global-population-data-1.21957.

6. See "Satellite images reveal gaps."

7. See "Use of Geospatial Tools During Census Enumeration: Leveraging the Enabling Capabilities of Geospatial Information Technologies in All Stages of Statistical Processes" from the UNECA presentation at United Nations Regional Workshop on the 2020 World Program. Available at https://unstats.un.org/unsd/demographic-social/meetings/2017/dar-es-salaam--regional-workshop-on-2020-census.

8. As reported by many recent African country presentations and the article "Demarcation of Census Enumeration Areas for the 2016 Population and Housing Census in Lesotho." Available at http://www.ee.co.za/wp-content/uploads/2015/08/Hennie-Loots.pdf.

9. See the South Africa presentations "Use of Geospatial Tools During Census Enumeration" and "Planning for the Adoption of Electronic Data Collection Technologies" at the United Nations Regional Workshop on the 2020 World Program on Population and Housing Censuses: International Standards and Contemporary Technologies. Available at https://unstats.un.org/unsd/demographic-social/meetings/2017/lusaka--regional-workshop-on-2020-census.

10. See more details in *Chapter 5. Cartographic Preparation* from the Food and Agriculture Organization of the United Nations. Available at http://www.fao.org/economic/the-statistics-division-ess/world-census-of-agriculture/conducting-of-agricultural-censuses-and-surveys/chapter-5-cartographic-preparation/en/.

11. See the presentation "Census Mapping Using Satellite Imagery in Malawi" at the United Nations Regional Workshop on the 2020 World Program on Population and Housing Censuses: International Standards and Contemporary Technologies (with few adaptations). Available at https://unstats.un.org/unsd/demographic-social/meetings/2017/lusaka--regional-workshop-on-2020-census.

12. See CARICOM's *GIS and Census Mapping Training Manual*. Available at http://www.caricomstats.org/helpdesk/documentarycentre/Dom4/GIS_Census_Map_Training_Manual.pdf.

13. Data quality, in general, refers to the degree to which GIS data accurately represents the real world, the suitability of the data for a certain purpose, and the degree to which the data meets a specific accuracy standard. (See *A Data Quality Dictionary*, GeoWorld, vol. 13).

14. Data accuracy is the extent to which a measured or estimated value approaches its true value. Accurate GIS data truly represents the real world within specified tolerances, especially with respect to spatial GIS data (see *A Data Quality Dictionary*).

15. See the UN's *Handbook on Geospatial Infrastructure in Support of Census Activities*. Available at https://unstats.un.org/unsd/demographic/standmeth/handbooks/series_f103en.pdf.

16. High positional accuracy is no longer costly. Many would argue that the democratization of GPS is here.

17. See the UN's *Principles and Recommendations for Population and Housing Censuses*, rev. 3, paragraphs 2.169–2.170. Available at https://unstats.un.org/unsd/demographic-social/Standards-and-Methods/files/Principles_and_Recommendations/Population-and-Housing-Censuses/Series_M67rev3-E.pdf.

18. See the National Birth Defects Prevention Network's *Guidelines for Conducting Birth Defects Surveillance*. Available at https://www.nbdpn.org/docs/NBDPN_Guidelines2012.pdf.

19. Metadata is most simply described as data about data or "data that defines and describes other data" (ISO definition).

20. For more details, see *Developing Spatial Data Infrastructures: The SDI Cookbook*. Available at http://gsdiassociation.org/images/publications/cookbooks/SDI_Cookbook_GSDI_2004_ver2.pdf.

21. Clodomir Pereira, the team leader of INE's cartography and GIS department, explained that the greatest benefit of using GIS during the 2010 census was improved data accuracy. The full article is available at https://www.esri.com/esri-news/arcnews/fall15articles/simplifying-the-census-in-cape-verde.

22. This is mainly through the work of the ISO Technical Committee 211 on geographic information/geomatics, the OGC, and other organizations such as the International Hydrographic Organization (IHO) and the Unicode Consortium.

23. ISO 17369:2013 Statistical Data and Metadata eXchange (SDMX). In 2008, the UNSC recognized and supported the SDMX standards and guidelines as "the preferred standard for the exchange and sharing of data and metadata," and ISO/TC 154 has accepted the SDMX Technical Specification (TS) (version 2.1) for approval as international standard ISO 17369.

24. Like SDMX, the DDI has become a well-established international metadata standard, designed to describe socioeconomic surveys, censuses, and other microdata collection activities.

25. Many studies have discussed this issue but with limited practical solutions for the NSOs.

26. Simply put, cloud computing means storing and accessing data and programs over the Internet instead of a local server or a personal computer; the cloud is a metaphor for the Internet. See details at https://www.pcmag.com/article2/0,2817,2372163,00.asp.

27. See the Microsoft Azure online article *What Is Cloud Computing: A Beginner's Guide*. Available at https://azure.microsoft.com/en-us/overview/what-is-cloud-computing.

28. See *The NIST Definition of Cloud Computing*. Available at http://nvlpubs.nist.gov/nistpubs/Legacy/SP/nistspecialpublication800-145.pdf.

29. See *What Is Cloud Computing: A Beginner's Guide*.

30. Weighted site selection analysis allows users to rank raster cells and assign a relative importance value to each layer (Esri). Available at https://doc.arcgis.com/en/community-analyst/help/suitability-analysis.htm.

31. Asset management is generally defined as "managing infrastructure capital assets to minimize the total cost of owning, operating, and maintaining assets at acceptable levels of service."

32. Details available at http://www.cityworks.com/products/what-is-cityworks/asset-management/.

33. See the 2012 Esri Press book *Measuring Up: The Business Case for GIS*, which demonstrates the real business value of implementing GIS in costs and staff hours saved.

34. ArcGIS offers labeling management tools. In ArcGIS, labeling refers specifically to the process of automatically generating and placing descriptive text for map features. A label is a piece of text on the map that is dynamically placed and whose text string is derived from one or more feature attributes. See http://desktop.arcgis.com/en/arcmap/10.3/map/working-with-text/essential-labeling-concepts.htm.

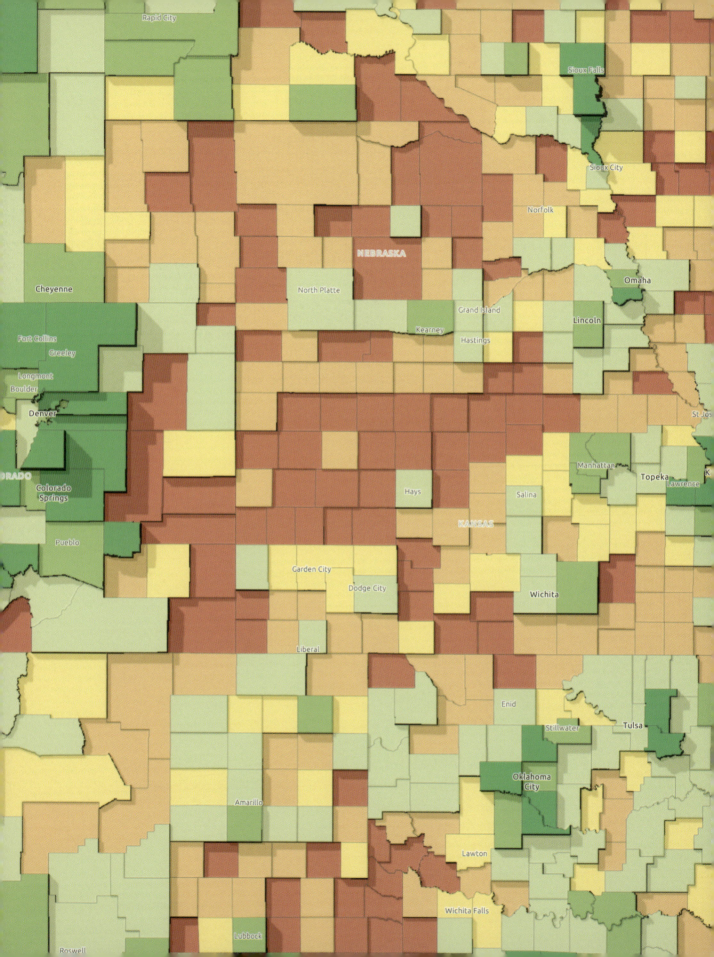

Chapter 7

Use of geospatial tools during enumeration

Fieldwork benefits of using GIS/GPS and imagery

In previous chapters, we highlighted the use of remotely sensed data, GPS, and GIS in basemap creation and the delineation of EAs and how they affect the work at the pre-enumeration stage. This chapter will focus on the combination of the various geospatial tools during the fieldwork of the enumeration phase, including how to rely on the geospatial database to provide the enumerators with the mapping tools they need to conduct the actual enumeration operation. We will specifically highlight the use of the handheld electronic devices for data collection, workforce management, and how geospatial technologies contribute efficiently to the organizational operations and management of the census enumeration.[1]

Field data verification and quality checks

GIS is used during the pre-enumeration stage (including fieldwork) to build the most complete and accurate delineation of administrative and EA units, and produce the best possible quality EA maps for use during enumeration. As discussed in previous chapters, the digitally created EA map is the result of the integration of data from existing maps (or basemaps) and/or from imagery, complemented by data captured from the field. All this data is structured and organized in the geospatial database. While the EA data is generally accurate, it must mesh with other data (e.g., topographic, built environment, transportation) and then be integrated into the database. This requires final quality checks and verification.

For example, some country experiences have shown that, in the lapse of time between the initiation of GIS-based census work and the time of production of EA maps, some changes to administrative boundaries may have occurred, new buildings may have been built, or some other buildings may have been destroyed. Even when there are instructions to freeze any changes in the last year before conducting the census, there will inevitably be last-minute changes. This means a final verification is required, including consultations with local administrators about any recent changes in their regions.

To do the field verification needed, apps such as Collector for ArcGIS can again be used to collect and update information in the field (whether connected or disconnected). Collector for ArcGIS can be used to collect attribute data as well as capture or edit features. By leveraging the editing function, field-workers can be provided with the ability to edit and suggest changes, plot location of new buildings, or capture POIs not showing on the existing basemap.

Updating EA maps

Once the field data verification and quality checks have been carried out, the focus should be on editing and correcting the content of the EA maps as a final step for their design and distribution. Tools such as version control should be used throughout this process to ensure data quality. ArcGIS allows you to set the access level of a version to protect it from being edited or viewed by users other than the version owner or those allowed to edit. It also provides tools that allow for the reconciliation of versions after field-workers have synchronized edits made to versioned data.

For example, a field-worker using Collector for ArcGIS may be tasked to confirm edits from EA maps. The worker goes to the field and collects new data or edits existing features. Once back in the office, the worker synchronizes edits made in the field.

Supervisors or others given permission to accept changes (such as editors) can then conduct QA review. Editors can reconcile with the default geodatabase version and post edits to the default version. (This process can be automated, as well.)

EA map production, map services, and map packages

At this stage, after the completion of the updates and corrections of the EAs and quality assurance checks for all the maps, office work proceeds with the final enumeration map production and printing. The traditional paper-based approach requires a massive production of hard-copy maps in different scales that meet the needs of the enumerators, field supervisors, regional managers, and other staff involved in the census enumeration. Experiences from countries have shown that at least one map must be produced for every EA in the country, with two copies to be printed: one copy to be used by the enumerator and the other by the field supervisor for training and reference purposes.[2]

However, the use of geospatial technology in the enumeration process in a CAPI mode is distinguished from the traditional paper-based approach in terms of the reduction in hard-copy map production. In a digital census, once all map data has been verified and EA boundaries signed off, the creation of maps, map services, and printed maps can begin. Digital maps offer better functionality for the enumerator and supervisors—having a detailed basemap available online or offline, in color, and with well-presented features. Digital basemaps also make knowing the location of features and POIs easier and more readily understood compared with hard-copy maps.

All EA maps—whether digital or paper—should be simple, clear, and easy for the enumerator and field supervisor to use. EA maps typically contain the following:

- Basemap with streets and roads, buildings, major water bodies, topographic and other hydrologic features, and map annotations
- EA boundaries
- POIs for orientation with symbols (e.g., church, school, hospital)

Many countries may not be fully digital in their data collection. For those that use multimode methods (paper-and-pencil interviewing [PAPI] and CAPI), they must create both printed maps for PAPI and map services and map packages for CAPI.

Printing maps involves considering such decisions as color or black and white, map size, map scale, the need for inset maps, the use of QR codes or bar codes, and the creation of digital map files in easy-to-print formats as backups for the field and regional offices (including .pdf).

If countries use CAPI, they must rely on map services and mobile map packages more so than printed maps. Today, geospatial technology allows field-workers to use maps and imagery as basemaps in a web GIS approach, allowing the field-worker to collect data and transmit it back to the regional or central office in near real time. For example, mobile apps such as Survey123 for ArcGIS® can be configured to enable a user to download map areas where connectivity is available, show the user's GPS location, and, with a simple tap on the feature (dwelling or housing unit), add information about the location and accurately capture statistical data about a household, completing the electronic questionnaire related to that household. The enumerator then transmits the data collected online, feeding it directly into the GIS, or saves it until he or she is back within connectivity range for sending to the central office.

As mentioned previously, maps can be used in both online and off-line modes. By creating mobile map packages and downloading these to the device when connected, users simply continue their work in the same manner whether connected or not. The collected data should be uploaded as soon as possible once back in range because progress reports are based on data gathered at the central server. We will elaborate further on the use of handheld devices in the next section.

During enumeration, the EAs may still need additional updates and corrections that must be brought to the master database. Traditionally, the census cartographic staff would collect the paper EA maps after the census and incorporate the edits into the master database; this task can be tedious and sometimes affect the time of the census results. But with the digital approach of the enumeration, this operation can be automated if an app is used with field edits captured for QA. Updates captured in this manner can be verified and then submitted to the database in a more streamlined fashion.

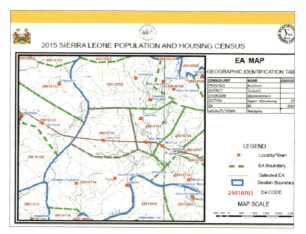

Figure 7.1. Example of an EA map of Sierra Leone. *Source*: United Nations Regional Workshop on the 2020 World Program on Population and Housing Censuses: International Standards and Contemporary Technologies, Dar es Salaam, Tanzania, 2017.

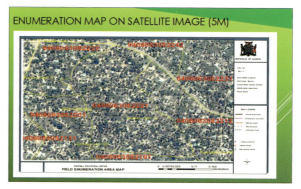

Figure 7.2. Example of an EA map overlaid on satellite imagery of the Republic of Zambia. *Source*: United Nations.

Figure 7.3. Example of an EA map from a device in the field. *Source*: Central Agency for Public Mobilization and Statistics (CAPMAS), Egypt.

Field data collection

Mobile devices and apps

Traditional paper-based methods of census data collection have proven to be tedious, time-consuming, costly, and often prone to errors. To overcome these problems, CAPI methods are increasingly replacing pen-and-paper methods (such as PAPI) as a viable alternative for census data collection. The technological developments in mobile computing, storage, higher connectivity, and network coverage have made the CAPI approach possible for many. Increasingly powerful handheld devices are now an affordable and realistic option, so the CAPI approach is more commonly used. Realizing the advantages of directly entering digital data into a computer software application at the point of data collection using mobile technology for data collection and statistical production, the UN has recommended its use in the 2020 Round of Censuses[3] in recognition of its importance and usefulness for many countries.[4]

Handheld electronic devices have been used by NSOs for many years for the collection of statistical data, initially for surveys and increasingly for census operations. Basically, a handheld electronic device allows for census data to be captured and stored electronically. The contents of the census (questionnaire) form are stored on the handheld device so that the questions appear sequentially on the screen. The enumerator then enters the answers in different ways: with a selection from the offered list of answers or from a classification in hierarchical order presented in the form of a drop-down list; or by entering a variable via a free-form text field, attachment of a photo, or even a scan of a bar code.

In operational terms, the app will not allow the enumerator to skip a question or move from an incomplete answer to another question unless the former has been completed. This ensures that all questions are completed and avoids the lack of answers due to forgetfulness or mistake by the enumerator, which occurs frequently with the traditional paper method.

In addition, building automatic skips and logic into the questionnaire allows the enumerator to avoid covering unnecessary items and ensure increased accuracy. Further, the electronic questionnaire can be designed so that the enumerator conducts minimal data entry as some administrative data can be used to prepopulate fields in the census forms in the office, significantly reducing time needed to complete the form, reducing data errors, and improving accuracy.[5]

Moreover, data is recorded against predetermined validation rules, and procedures for instant data verification are programmed into the app so that a warning is activated if any data is inconsistent with the format or with other responses already entered in the app. The fact that the app warns the operator when there is an error means that the data can be immediately verified and evaluated by the enumerator, allowing him or her to look for more accurate data while still on location at the time of the interview with the household. In addition, the app cannot accept codes or answers beyond the logical and acceptable norms, thereby decreasing data recognition errors and improving the quality of the data. Another useful feature allows the provision of on-screen help for the enumerators. A help system can make it easier for the enumerators to access definitions or other items needing clarification during the interview. Unlike in a paper manual, the help feature in an electronic questionnaire is more flexible because it can be linked to each question or a term that often needs clarification.

As mentioned in chapter 6, another feature that can provide substantial aid to the CAPI enumeration process is to upload the EA maps onto the device. This allows the enumerators to visualize the EA maps, helping them in their field orientation to find the correct housing units within their assigned EAs. Use of the EA maps and the electronic questionnaires filled out by enumerators, along with GPS points collected on the device, allow the NSO to verify the collected data and confirm whether the EAs were fully covered. Ideally, once the data is transmitted to the central data center, the data including geocodes would be synced with the GIS census database, providing information about the progress of the census coverage.

This highlights another benefit of using handheld devices and configurable apps in the field: being able to report on enumerated units (cumulative) in real time. By using real-time data and operational dashboards, census operations managers can observe, measure, and monitor the progress of the work as well as the remaining time needed for enumeration of each separate enumeration unit. Regularly uploading the data from a handheld device and transmitting it in near real time to the server can also minimize the need to re-enumerate an area if the device suddenly is lost or begins malfunctioning.

Esri's CAPI tool: Survey123 for ArcGIS

Census survey questions are one of the most powerful ways of gathering information for making decisions and taking action. Survey123 for ArcGIS is a simple and intuitive form-centric data-gathering solution that makes creating, sharing, and analyzing surveys possible with the ArcGIS platform.

A versatile data-gathering tool, Survey123 for ArcGIS makes collecting data in the field straightforward. After a survey is configured in Survey123, downloading and using it in the Survey123 field app is a matter of a few steps. Data captured in Survey123 for ArcGIS is immediately available in the ArcGIS platform. This data can be used to optimize field operations, understand data or data gaps (areas with missing or under-reported data) to communicate and make adjustments in the collection, and communicate and share work with others. Survey123 allows data capture anytime and anywhere because it works across devices as a native app and in a browser (online and off-line). The user-friendly intuitive interface also means that training field staff is made simpler.

Figure 7.4. Survey123 for ArcGIS on a handheld device.

In summary, what distinguishes the handheld digital approach from the paper-based one is its integrated data collection process, in which data collection, entering, coding, and editing are carried out simultaneously and automatically. The process is also more efficient and cost-effective overall in the census process when taking into consideration the true total cost of ownership of paper methods. Several country experiences have shown that this method of capturing and processing census data is faster, leading to timely availability of census information results.[6] Generally, when using handheld devices, NSOs will significantly automate the whole process of data collection by having a centralized data center (often with regional data centers and even possibly local ones for some large countries) where the data collected and transmitted by each handheld device would be compiled automatically. The data center would also enable the supervisors of the census collection process to make real-time checks into the data collected to verify that the data collected is relevant and correct.

In response to many African countries that expressed their interest in the use of mobile technology for data collection, UNECA has developed guidelines on the use of mobile devices for census data collection and dissemination. The guidelines outlined the main features for selecting a desirable mobile device in terms of hardware and software (see the table) and detailed the key criteria for selecting a mobile device.

Feature	Description
Affordability: price of the device	• License/subscription cost or purchase fees • Maintenance fees • Annual/monthly renewal fees
Interface	• User interfaces, color, resolution, keyboard, screen
Battery life and management	• Length of battery life
OS support and updates	• What type of operating system is used? (Android®, iOS®) • How often is the OS updated with bug releases and features?
Customizability	• Can the device be customized, including shortcuts, color schemes, keyboards, etc.?
Storage/memory	• Storage capacity
Peripheral (or APP) support	• The ecosystem of peripherals or apps (GPS, camera, etc.)
Multiple-language support	• Local language support
Interoperability and connectivity	• Exchange of data directly or through a network • Cellular mode • Wi-Fi mode • Bluetooth capable
Security	• Hardware security (manual lock) • Supports data encryption • Biometrics

Figure 7.5. Mobile device considerations for data collection (originally from Economic Commission for Africa [ECA] and adapted for current requirements).

Technology is constantly evolving, and computer technology is becoming more portable and more powerful, making the tablet computer affordable and suitable for data collection in the field. Tablets, being computers, do what other personal computers do but lack some I/O capabilities that others have. Tablet computers vary in size, ranging from around 5 inches to 12 inches depending on the model[7] and are available in a variety of forms: the main slate tablets don't come with a physical keyboard, while the hybrid tablets come with a detachable keyboard or an integrated one (convertible).

While available connectivity varies by model, most tablets include Wi-Fi connectivity, and many can also access the Internet over-the-air using a service provider subscription. A tablet's touch interface makes some common tasks more intuitive, and the device provides easy web browsing and navigation in many applications. Tablet computers, like standard computers, are powered by different operating systems. Three operating systems prevail currently in the tablet world: Android (Google®), iOS (Apple®) and Windows® (Microsoft®),[8] though the Amazon Fire Tablet® (with custom Android OS) is also gaining traction.

The compact design of tablet PCs makes them suitable for fieldwork; they are easy to use, lightweight, and portable.

Smartphones are also making a big impact in field data collection. With rapid changes in technology, smartphones today can do many things that would have required a personal computer just a few years ago.

A smartphone is a handheld personal computer with a mobile operating system and an integrated mobile broadband cellular network connection for voice, short message service (SMS), and Internet data communication. Most if not all smartphones also support Wi-Fi. Smartphones are typically

Figure 7.6. Dell® Rugged device.

pocket-sized, as opposed to tablet computers, which are much larger. For fieldwork, smartphones and tablets each have their own advantages and disadvantages. Both can capture, store, and transmit data, but they have distinct differences in price, features, and functionality.

One of the most important options that contributed to the adoption of handheld electronic devices for census data collection is the built-in GPS receiver. A GPS receiver integrated into the handheld device allows enumerators to understand their current location and capture the geographic location of where census data is being collected. GPS data also allows local supervisors and/or those at the NSO to track the enumerators and check whether the capture of the data was performed at the right place in the household, avoiding false data entry. In addition, captured GPS locations can be used as a reference point for other post-enumeration activities. Since many handheld devices are designed as consumer items, the built-in GPS receiver may vary greatly in locational accuracy (1 to 5+ m) to capture the latitude and longitude of each housing unit or building. Therefore, NSOs should inquire about the accuracy and proceed with field tests in both urban and rural areas.[9] If greater locational accuracy is needed, you can pair with third-party external

GPS receivers that connect to the smartphone via Bluetooth.

No matter what type of device is chosen, security must be a consideration. If a device is lost or stolen, procedures need to be in place to make sure that data privacy is secured.

Figure 7.7. Bad Elf® GNSS Surveyor, which offers submeter accuracy.

No single type of security will ensure the prevention of data tampering or theft. Multiple levels of security should be considered, including hardware security, application-level security, data encryption, and data transfer security protocols. For more information on mobile security and GIS, see the Esri white paper on mobile security (*ArcGIS Secure Mobile Implementation Patterns*) in the online ancillaries at esri.com/Census2020.

The benefits of using handheld devices lie in their ability to provide consistency and validity checks during the interview of the households, facilitating the control of the enumerators' work—for example, by checking that the coordinates captured by the GPS correspond to the assigned EA and transmitting the data collected in real time or near real time to the data center. Paradata from the device can also be used to validate, using date and time stamps for the start and stop of a survey—for example, as a key indicator of accuracy and to help prevent fraudulent entry.

Even though the benefits of mobile data collection are many and are leading to its adoption by numerous countries[10] with many more planning for its adoption in the ongoing 2020 Round

of Censuses, its use will present some challenges that the NSO may be unfamiliar with and should consider, including the following:

1. Consideration should be given to the configuration and use of the devices. Planning for the use of mobile devices should be considered in all parts of the business process, testing will need to be conducted, training plans will need to include device training, and the loading of data and applications should also be understood and planned for.

2. When designing the digital questionnaire, consider the mode or modes of use. In a multimode survey, a digital version may vary slightly from a paper version, which doesn't allow for skips in the same manner.

3. This approach also requires the consideration of the field operations and support necessary during enumeration, including provisioning and field support and connectivity for the devices. The mobile data collection process is an integrated approach that requires the following:

   a. Device—A device manufacturer is required to provide the devices as per specifications, or an agreement with a connectivity provider on a hardware lease program.

   b. Connectivity—A wireless carrier or connectivity provider is needed to provide service for the device so that the data can be transferred seamlessly to the data center.

   c. Applications—Consider the applications that are needed on the device beyond just the basic data collection applications. Email, calendar, or other productivity applications, navigation applications, and security applications all need to be understood.

d. Capacity building—An important component requiring the enumerators to be trained on using the survey app and forms on the device, the entire process of data collection, the basics of the device, and troubleshooting.

4. The use of the device in the field requires that the battery life and the practicalities of charging the device be tested and checked because failure in the field would also cause support issues (e.g., if the battery lasts less than needed, a portable charger, solar charger, or some type of battery extender may be required).

5. Testing the download process and data transmission speeds should be conducted. This testing may identify parts of the system that require scaling to accommodate any expected peak or heavy loads. This should also include the testing of security protocols.

6. If the unit is lost or stolen, precautions should be in place to transfer data from the device and remotely wipe the device.

Case study: Jordan

In 2015, Jordon took a geospatial digital approach to its census, and the outcomes were astounding. The kingdom's Department of Statistics (DOS) reduced a two-year-long process to just two months, improving data accuracy, speeding the delivery of vital data to stakeholders, and safeguarding millions of records of sensitive personal information.

Every ten years, the DOS gathers census data to formulate and improve diverse national programs such as economic development, agriculture, and healthcare. The government welcomed the modernization of its census processes and hoped that doing so would produce accurate and up-to-date statistical data and information. Census data is an important and essential tool for making evidence-based decisions and intelligent planning. Furthermore, the 2015 census project represented a major step forward in Jordan's digital transformation that would move it closer to its vision of becoming a regional technology hub.

The DOS was faced with the challenge of running a census at a national level for the first time and using a digital system to do it. By the time the DOS completed the Population and Housing Census 2015, it had collected census data for 9.5 million citizens. More than twenty thousand surveyors had participated in the largest statistical project in the kingdom's history.

How did they do it? In the digital world, all projects begin with data. The DOS needed good data to set the data groundwork for a well-run enumeration operation. In cooperation with governmental agencies and local private companies, the department procured aerial images and created a current and accurate basemap. Using GIS, it digitized census blocks and created data layers that delineated collection areas on a map.

The department acquired more than twenty-three thousand high-spec HP tablets that enumerators would use to capture survey data. Staff prepared the tablets with aerial imagery, census blocks, building points, routes, and the survey form. They also synchronized the tablets with the operation's server and added census applications to them.

The census application's rules-based workflow ensured that the correct questions were asked, no questions would be missed, and correct data was collected. Survey data was not stored on the tablets but synced back to the server. The application communicated with a central server in Amman via the tablet's 3G communications. Thus, the system could cross-check the validity of information in real time during the survey.

In previous censuses, fraud was a concern, including the altering of data before it was reported. To address the problem, administrators devised another workflow for data security. Once surveyors left their assigned areas, the application suspended access to the system by the surveyor. Furthermore, automated processes controlled the amount of data feeds emitted by surveyors and stored data in an Oracle® DBMS geodatabase. The method secured data against corruption and manipulation. DOS administrators reported that the digital solution inspired more trust from citizens because it was modern and that they perceived it to be less susceptible to inaccurate reporting.

The DOS usually outsources census field survey labor and hired twenty thousand surveyors and two thousand field managers for the 2015 operation. Because the department had deployed easy-to-use mobile apps, workers needed only a little training before going into the field. Assigning work areas to so many people is a geospatial problem, so, again, GIS proved useful. It defined surveyors and assigned them to designated census blocks, thereby avoiding survey duplication and wasted effort. Other time savers were apps that showed surveyors their assigned work areas along with routes that would help them collect the data in sequence.

The ArcGIS platform made managing data collection a smooth process. It provided census operations managers with tools to control and monitor human resources, material, and time. The approach produced better data quality and turned it around faster than ever before.

Jordan's census project was further marked by its extensive use of GIS throughout all phases, including operations planning, fieldwork management and monitoring, and data proliferation throughout the kingdom. It also provided an online infrastructure for spatial data dissemination and analysis that included tools for analyzing data about the population's economic, social, and demographic characteristics.

The ArcGIS platform, the project's cornerstone software, integrated with Microsoft® Windows 10 and the HP® tablet to enable mobile capabilities. The platform also processed data and disseminated key statistics. The DOS completed its operations in record time and was publishing 2015 census results about three months after the fieldwork had been completed, compared with the 2004 census results that took one and a half years to publish.

Most importantly, e-census data provides analysts and decision makers with a simple, intuitive means to get answers to their inquiries.

Internet

Like with mobile technology, the use of the Internet for census data collection is growing. Considerations for using GIS technology in Internet self-reporting should also be given.

The big difference between mobile data capture and Internet self-reporting is that the Internet-based data collection directly involves the household and requires household members to fill out the census questionnaire online, eliminating the enumerator as an intermediary. The self-response method requires that the household respondent have the necessary equipment and reliable Internet connectivity, with a sufficient level of computer literacy.

Similar to mobile data collection, the online Internet questionnaire or computer-aided web interview (CAWI) is not a simple replication of the paper form. Adjustments are likely to be made to accommodate the respondent with an easy-to-access user-friendly interface. GIS functionality can be included in the web-based form by way of a map presented to users, allowing them to indicate their place of residence. This information can be captured and stored along with the form providing the location component of the survey for validation against preassigned codes or other information.

CAWI data collection relies on self-enumeration and, like other modes, must ensure that every household and individual is counted once and only once. A key factor in managing data collection requires the provision of each respondent with a unique code. This code may be linked to a geographic location (e.g., the "census-assigned unique address identifier" to be used at the 2020 US census). Also, since the CAWI-collected data must be incorporated into the database with other modes of collected data (CAPI/PAPI), census data collection methodology requires careful thought

as does the management of the other streams of data, when the census is multimodal.[10]

Field operations management

Field enumeration operations are often a huge undertaking with a large workforce that can range from hundreds of people to hundreds of thousands of people, depending on the size of the country, the methodology for data collection, and the time frame for its execution. Field operations management presents a big challenge in several areas, including logistics, the movement of assets, the movement of employees and data in the field, employee safety, and data security. One of the benefits of using new technologies (including GIS) is the capability they provide the NSO to streamline and automate field operations and thus improve their management and the quality of the census itself. Field operations require efficient communication among possibly thousands of field-workers, field supervisors, and census managers, as well as the constant monitoring of a large variety of logistical items and materials, most of which must be distributed to field offices in all regions of the country and then recollected. Achieving productivity in the field depends particularly on the NSO's ability to share information that's accurate and up-to-date.

The key concern is the flow of timely information to and from the field. Mobile technology provides the real-time bidirectional flow of information between census managers in the back office and enumerators in the field. Bidirectional workflows allow the census managers to be informed of the progress of the data collection operations while providing the enumerators with updates, including which households need follow-up. Furthermore, with GPS-enabled handheld devices, census managers can locate and track the location of the enu-

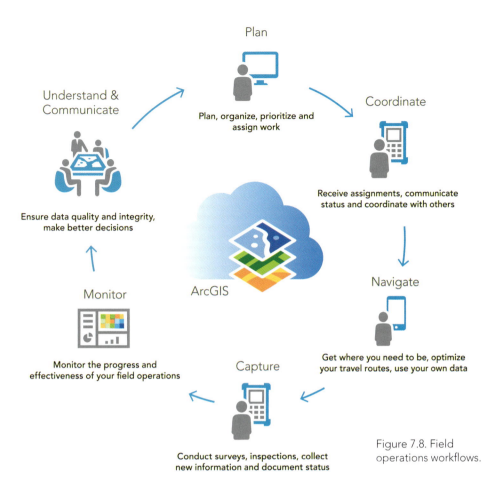

Plan

Plan, organize, prioritize and assign work

Coordinate

Receive assignments, communicate status and coordinate with others

Understand & Communicate

Ensure data quality and integrity, make better decisions

Navigate

Get where you need to be, optimize your travel routes, use your own data

Monitor

Monitor the progress and effectiveness of your field operations

ArcGIS

Capture

Conduct surveys, inspections, collect new information and document status

Figure 7.8. Field operations workflows.

merator (in real time or near real time) or identify areas of gaps where enumeration is falling behind or not meeting quality standards. This triggers urgent attention to be given to the affected EAs for appropriate decisions to remedy the situation. In this manner, GIS systems provide for better engagement and needed transparency across all levels of management and field-workers.

Operational dashboards can also be used to provide a view of geographic information that helps you monitor events or activities. Dashboards are designed to display multiple visualizations that work together on a single screen. They offer a comprehensive and engaging view of data to provide key insight for at-a-glance decision-making.

From a dynamic dashboard, supervisors can view the activities and key performance indicators most vital to meeting objectives.

Optimizing workloads

Another management activity is the assignment of workloads to the enumerators. GIS-based analysis of the EAs helps optimize the workload assignment. Since the master EA database or plan is centralized and available on the same system, the GIS manager and the staff in charge of the census organization have a complete view of the distribution of the EAs and supervisory maps in the field. The geographic database helps in the assignment

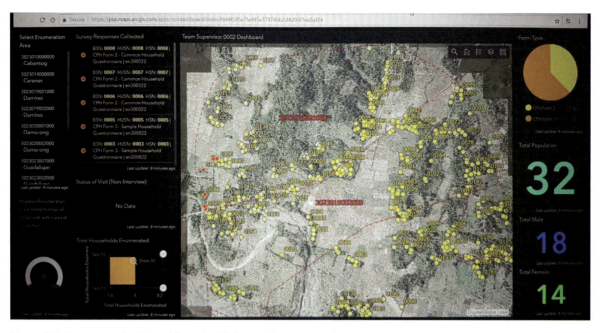

Figure 7.9. Supervisor dashboard from the Philippine Statistics Authority.

of administrative units to operational areas and, as we saw earlier, in the location of field offices.

For each field office, the map compiled from EA maps for use by the supervisors allows the manager to know exactly who is assigned to which tasks combined with the list of tasks to be executed. It also, importantly, allows the field manager to estimate the optimal workforce needed and to optimize the workloads and potential travel needed to cover the area the field office oversees. This includes the optimal scheduling of fieldwork (see figure 7.10). Optimization is essential to avoid field teams having to drive unnecessary distances between operational areas; avoiding duplication of effort where the same operational area is allocated to two teams or multiple enumerators (e.g., gated community with limited time constraints); allocating and delivering the right number of handheld devices and appropriate logistical material to the teams of enumerators; and obtaining status reports from the field and office.

In addition to the provision of digital maps for use in the field, GIS allows us to use apps such as Workforce for ArcGIS® that help efficiently manage field operations. Sometimes, the unexpected can happen: a trained enumerator may get sick or quit, and reassignments must be made. Workforce for ArcGIS enables a common view of the workload in the field and the office. It enables managers to assign tasks and make sure the count stays on track. By using a web-based app in the office, managers can create and assign work to mobile workers, who use the mobile app to receive and work through their list of new assignments.

Optimizing routes

Once the assignment of the workloads has been made and fieldwork is ready to begin, the teams of enumerators need to know where to go and ideally the best route to take. GIS provides tools for solving complex routing problems and can be used to

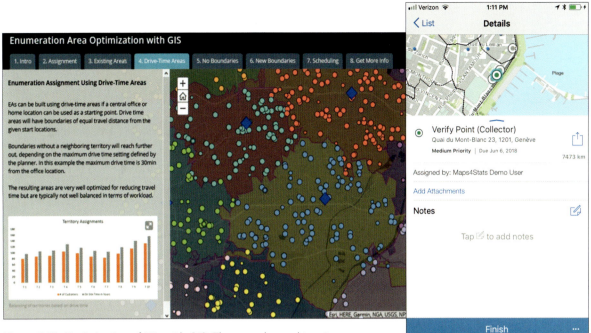

Figure 7.10. Optimization of EAs with GIS. The map shows drive-time calculations from the central office location.

Figure 7.11. Workforce for ArcGIS app on a mobile device.

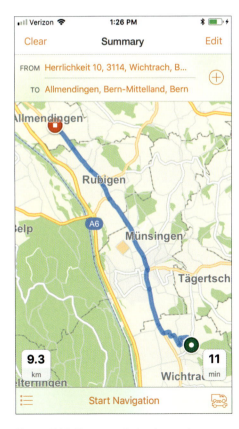

Figure 7.12. Route optimization and navigation.

create suggested routes for the workers. These tools allow us to solve for variations in schedule, such as days of the week, time of day, or even the skill set in workers (e.g., language skills). Once the routes are generated, they can be shared with workers via the mobile device. If a navigable dataset is not available for the area, workers can simply use built-in maps on the device as a visual guide along with GPS coordinates of the locations (households) to be enumerated.

Optimizing routes to enumeration sites in urban areas will usually not be a problem because the road network is generally well-defined. Optimization can be difficult in rural and remote areas where the road networks are less demarcated and perhaps data is not available for routing.

GIS-based mobile apps are increasingly available to cope with specific navigation or routing problems. For example, Navigator for ArcGIS®, a mobile app that gets the field workforce where it needs to be, works in online and off-line mode on any device. Navigator for ArcGIS even allows field crews to navigate vehicles on their organization's custom data and street network. Crews can also search by asset ID or location and easily plan their day by creating a work list of all their stops.

Monitoring the progress of census operations

Mobile technology has the advantage of being able to feed in real time (or near real time) data collected from each device to the central database. This data can also be used to monitor the progress of the enumeration and identify which households the enumerators may need to revisit. As explained earlier in the chapter, workload assignments and the navigation and optimization of routes happens on the same system, so the GIS manager not only knows exactly who is doing what at any moment but also more importantly can monitor the overall status and progress of each stage of the census operations. GIS dashboards can display supervisory maps combined with work assignments and schedules and can track the progress of completed work.

Monitoring the progress of census operations, from supervisors through the regional census of-

fices and on to the central office, allows managers to assess where operations are running smoothly and where problems may be encountered. With the traditional approach, these assessments are compiled in tabular form and would take time to provide a clear idea of the progress and to review and proceed with any follow-up. But with the use of geospatial and mobile technologies, census managers can be informed of the progress of the collection operations as the enumerators deliver and collect completed census forms. The assessments of the situation and the progress can then be visualized geographically through a dashboard. This allows census managers to review the situation in near real time, identify areas where the enumeration is not progressing as expected, and provide the enumerators and their supervisors with appropriate updates and instructions on the households to be followed up.[12]

Figure 7.13. Operational dashboard, CAPMAS Egypt.

Project management oversight and identifying trouble spots

Project management oversight is generally conducted and based on management standards, policies, processes, and methods to ensure that a project has been carried out on time, within scope, and on budget. The oversight ensures that the risks threatening the project have been identified and mitigated. This model of management oversight applies to the census field operations. As we have seen earlier, the use of GIS and mobile technology supports the management of field operations, including the optimization of workloads, routes and navigation, and monitoring of the enumeration progress. Streamlined field management using automation and technological tools has the advantage of rapidly producing performance metrics associated with field operations, which can then be used to measure whether tasks have been carried out on time, the rate of coverage is within expectations, and the cost estimates are within the budget allocated.

The geographic approach to these field operations with the use of GIS- and GPS-enabled handheld devices also has an important risk management advantage in terms of the identification of trouble spots and the solution brought to mitigate their effects, including adequate and timely feedback to enumerators so that they can update their own collection control information and arrangements of visits by office personnel to field locations. Since the handheld devices are integrated into the central census database, alerts may be sent to the field staff or supervisors—for example, when the monitoring system detects that "coverage is lower than expected."[13]

Based on good practices from the 2010 Round of Censuses and recent country experiences, studies, and reviews, there is general recognition that the use of geospatial information technology offers integrated systems for field management that have a positive impact on the management of the field operations, including the reduction of costs and improvements in the quality of the data collected, provided that some arrangements are taken into consideration. As stated previously, those arrangements include the early planning of their use, the existence of reliable telecommunication and connectivity infrastructures, testing, and trainings. GIS can provide both operational dashboards to see the status of the project and survey dashboards to see the status of the work. Supervisors can use these dashboards to spot-check data collection activities and to ensure the survey sample size is being met as expected.

Location-based apps used during the enumeration process can create improved workflows to replace repetitive and outdated stand-alone fieldwork processes; make data available across the NSO so that operations run more smoothly; and monitor field activities accurately to improve reliability, consistency, and create transparency.

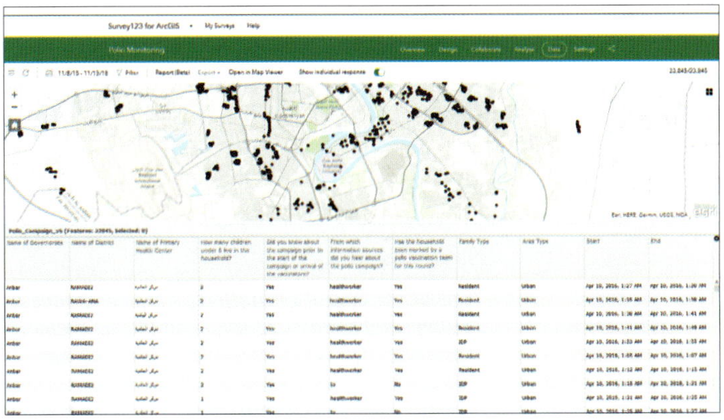

Figure 7.14. Survey123 for ArcGIS dashboard.

US Census: Mobilizing field operations

[The Former Chief Geospatial Scientist Tim] Trainor thinks the Census Bureau will save the most money by infusing its field operations with more GIS and mobile technology.

Although the census has a 65–67 percent response rate, which is exceptionally high, the Census Bureau still has to get the rest. And nonrespondents live across the United States, so this ends up being a huge field operation that must be completed in a short amount of time.

In the past, this has required hiring hundreds of thousands of temporary staff to go door-to-door to find the people who didn't fill out the census and convince them to do so. All these employees had supervisors as well to introduce them to their assignments and oversee each portion of the larger operation.

"We used mobile technology in 2010, but it was basically to ensure that we had complete coverage and to give folks an idea of where they were," said Trainor. "There was no navigation capability."

For the 2020 census, however, the Census Bureau is looking to expand its use of mobile technology and incorporate navigation and workload management into it.

"When we hire [these temporary staff members], we geocode them to their location . . . to give them assignments close to where they live so we don't have people traveling [farther] than they need to," said Trainor. "It's also an opportunity for us to manage whether or not we have enough people in a given area to do the work, which has always been one of our greatest concerns."

The Census Bureau also wants to use mobile technology to provide field employees with short, portable training segments.

"We're very good at making manuals, and we've made hundreds of pages of training manuals that some people read and others don't," said Trainor. "But we're moving away from that and trying to make it as easy as possible for people to understand . . . how to do their jobs"—ideally allowing them to refer back to their training materials while they're out in the field by using their mobile devices.

This will let the Census Bureau significantly reduce its field infrastructure and supervisory setup.

"This time around, we'll have six regional census centers and approximately 300 local census offices," estimated Trainor.

That's a 50 percent cutback in regional management and a 40 percent reduction in on-the-ground labor.

A more seamless census

The US Census Bureau is hoping that its increased use of GIS and other technologies will lead to a safe and easy 2020 Census and bring expenses down to 2010 levels.

"We're estimating we'll be in the neighborhood of a $5 billion savings," said Trainor.

Not only that, but by digitizing many operations and using GIS more pervasively throughout the census cycle, the Census Bureau anticipates a more efficient, seamless enumeration on census day, April 1, 2020. States across the country will certainly appreciate this, since they only have a few months after the first part of the census data is released in early 2021 to redistrict their jurisdictions for elections later that year.

Extract from *ArcNews* "2020 [US] census embraces digital transformation." Fall 2016. Available at http://www.esri.com/esri-news/arcnews/fall16articles/2020-census-embraces-digital-transformation.

Case study: Arab Republic of Egypt

The Egypt 2017 national census for population, housing, and facilities is the country's first census completed electronically. The transformation from a paper to a digital census system enables Egyptians to see census data in a geographic context. Moreover, the modernization of the process introduces technology that is a gateway to information at a greater depth and scale than ever before.

Understanding the country's data strengthens the Egyptian government's ability to monitor social trends and mitigate disaster. Egypt's statistical office—the Central Agency for Public Mobilization and Statistics (CAPMAS)—implemented an enterprise GIS platform so that government, industry, and the private sector can easily access and analyze data. The central technology for disseminating census data is the CAPMAS geospatial portal Egy-GeoInfo, which gives officials and citizens alike access to the nation's statistics.

Project planning

To plan the project, CAPMAS worked with the H.E. minister of planning and the World Food Programme (WFP) to evaluate the system's business goals and anticipate user requirements. The partners worked with a team of economists and statisticians to determine how people could use geospatial national statistics for investment, economic development, building policies, and so forth. They also took into consideration the Sustainable Development Goals (SDGs) for Egypt 2030.

CAPMAS, which was responsible for executing the plan, called on Esri to provide the GIS platform and technical direction. WFP offered technical support and its international knowledge of best practices to guide the system's design. The partners carefully considered all aspects of census activities and determined if and how GIS could support them.

Data planning

The 2017 census plan included bringing all statistical data into a geospatial database. The team implemented a new geospatial database repository for organizing geospatial and nongeospatial data. It also added big-data management capabilities to the system. The 2017 census geodatabase now manages one-half billion records.

The team knew that data is more valuable if it can be harmonized with other data. Therefore, the team specified that data be open so that it can be used by other organizations and systems. The metadata would include time and GPS location. They also devised a strategy for keeping data updated.

Enumeration planning

To train surveyors, CAPMAS developed agile-training activities for everyone from top management to enumerators. It also developed a faster training course to get new recruits up to speed if they joined the enumeration after it started. Training was included in the census budget.

The 2017 e-census covers more than ninety million capita over approximately one million square kilometers. Administrators used GIS to monitor forty thousand enumerators and synchronize forty thousand tablets. CAPMAS created high-quality maps for surveying activities and made live updates to them reflecting field data collection. The system updated digital maps for all urban and rural areas in Egypt.

Dissemination planning

CAPMAS set goals for census data distribution. The dissemination mechanism had to be built on a decision support system. The system needed to be easy to use and easy to update. Also, the data needed to be anonymous. The ArcGIS platform's portal technology met these requirements, and CAPMAS used it to build the Egyptian Geospatial Information Portal, or Egy-GeoInfo.

Egy-GeoInfo (geoportal.capmas.gov.eg) provides transparency to census data by allowing citizens to see all census and other statistics produced by the national official statistical system. The secure system aggregates data to the village level but does not disclose statistical information at the address level. People needing the most updated statistics, from high-level decision makers to common Egyptian citizens, can use it. In addition, Egy-GeoInfo provides the evidence-based regional info-structure to monitor and evaluate Egypt Vision 2030 activities for meeting the country's SDGs.

The portal accesses cross-discipline information that expands the system's research capabilities. In addition, geoanalytic tools help users manage much of their own research. For instance, they can see clusters of unemployment, trends for home ownership, and education levels by area. They can also see population growth over time and analyze changes in population patterns and location. Because the data is on the ArcGIS platform, decision-makers can combine different statistics, such as income levels and education, to research sales and investment potential.

From planning to execution to dissemination, Egypt completed the digital census project in four years. It now has the foundation to complete other statistic projects that will move the country toward meeting its sustainability goals. Egy-GeoInfo is an award-winning technology and has been highlighted at the UN GIS conference. It also received a smart government award for the best Arab smart application.

References

- A. E. Anderson and A.J. Tancreto. 2011. "Issues, Challenges and Experiences of the Internet as a Data Collection Mode at the US Census Bureau." Paper presented at the International Statistical Institute (ISI), Dublin, Ireland.

- UN Department of Economic and Social Affairs Statistics Division. 2009. *Census Data Capture Methodology: Technical Report.*

- UN. 2009. *Handbook on Geospatial Infrastructure in Support of Census Activities.*

- UN Statistics Division. 2010. *Report on the Results of a Survey on Census Methods Used by Countries in the 2010 Census Round.*

- Zelia Bianchini. 2011. "The 2010 Brazilian Population Census: Innovations and Impacts in Data Collection." Paper presented at the 58th World Congress of the International Statistical Institute (ISI), Dublin, Ireland.

Notes

1. According to the UNSD's *Report on the Results of a Survey on Census Methods Used by Countries in the 2010 Census Round of Censuses*, 102 of the 138 countries, representing about 74 percent of the responding countries, reported employing GIS/GPS technology. This report is available at http://unstats.un.org/unsd/census2010.htm.

2. See the UNSD's *Handbook on the Management of Population and Housing Censuses*, rev. 2. Available at https://unstats.un.org/unsd/publication/seriesF/Series_F83Rev2en.pdf.

3. The UN has recognized the following:

   a. Availability of wide range of geospatial technological tools for use in census mapping

   b. Enablers for NSOs to collect more accurate and timely information about their populations

   c. Use and application of geospatial technologies are very beneficial to improve quality of census activities at all stages of census

   d. Satellite images

   e. Aerial photography

   f. GPS

   g. Georeferenced address registry

   h. GIS for enumeration maps and for dissemination

   i. Adoption of GIS should be a major strategic decision

   j. A census GIS database is an important infrastructure to manage, analyze, and disseminate census data

   k. Geospatial analysis must become a core competence in any census office

   l. Statistical offices should develop GIS applications with population data and other georeferenced data from other sources for more advanced forms of spatial analysis

   m. Use of interactive tools

   n. Mapping functionality

4. See *Principles and Recommendations*, rev. 3. ST/ESA/STAT/SER.M/67/Rev.3. Available at https://unstats.un.org/unsd/demographic-social/Standards-and-Methods/files/Principles_and_Recommendations/Population-and-Housing-Censuses/Series_M67rev3-E.pdf.
5. See the UNSD's *Census Data Capture Methodology Technical Report*. Available at https://unstats.un.org/unsd/demographic-social/census/documents/CensusDataCaptureMethodology.pdf.
6. For example, Egypt used mobile devices for its 2017 census data collection, improving the timeliness of census releases—releasing data in a few short weeks instead of more than one year for previous censuses. *Source*: CAPMAS presentation at Esri UC 2018 "MRamadan Geo-SoOSs-2."
7. Those tablets suitable for census data collection range from 7 to 10 inches, which allows for the optimized size, weight, and brightness and holding with one hand, all of which are suitable for fieldwork.
8. Just a few words about pricing: Tablet prices are changing rapidly, ranging in 2017 from dozens of dollars to hundreds of dollars, depending on the type of the tablet.
9. See the US Census Bureau's "New Technologies in Census Geographic Listing." Available at https://www.census.gov/content/dam/Census/library/working-papers/2015/demo/new-tech-census-geo.pdf.
10. Ranging from large countries such as Australia, Brazil, Canada, and Egypt to small countries such as UAE and Cape Verde.
11. There were three streams in the case of Singapore, where computer-assisted telephone interviewing (CATI) was another alternative.
12. See *Conference of European Statisticians Recommendations for the 2020 Censuses of Population and Housing*, ECE/CES/41–2020 Census Recommendations. Available at https://www.unece.org/publications/2020recomm.html.
13. See the UNSD's *Handbook on the Management of Population and Housing Censuses*, rev. 2. Available at https://unstats.un.org/unsd/publication/seriesF/Series_F83Rev2en.pdf.

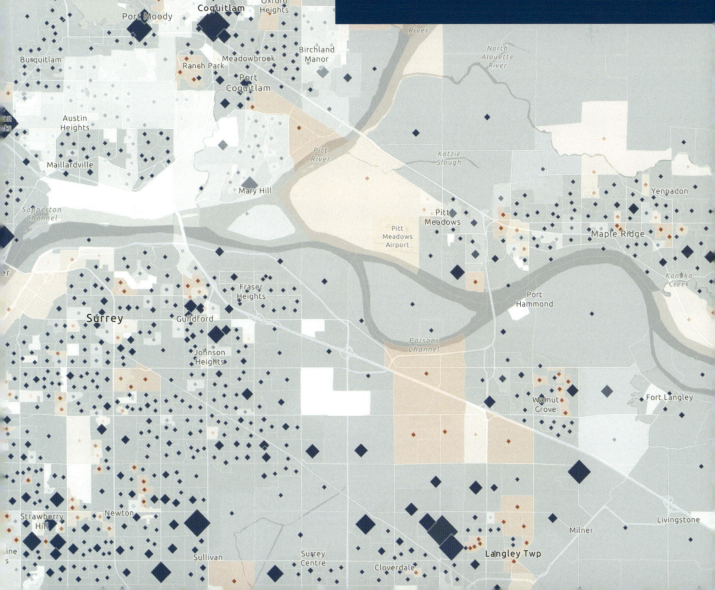

Chapter 8
Post-enumeration—processing

This chapter elaborates on some post-enumeration data operations, including the updating and verification of the changes that are made to the master GIS census database, EA-based or boundary aggregations, database archiving and maintenance, and open data systems. These operations contribute to the quality assurance of data prior to its dissemination, and even beyond dissemination, to facilitate such activities as post-census evaluation, sampling frame, surveys, and particularly future censuses.

Updating and verifying changes to the database

In chapter 6, we discussed updating and correcting EA maps during the pre-enumeration fieldwork process. You also learned that EA updating must continue to be carried out during enumeration, particularly when the fieldwork was begun a long time before enumeration began. Even when EA maps are created after an extensive fieldwork update and verification, errors may still be found due to simple human errors, omissions, buildings that have been destroyed, or new developments between the fieldwork and the actual enumeration. This requires enumerators to make and report updates and corrections of the EA maps either manually or electronically through "ground-truthing."

When enumeration was done with paper maps, the census geographers at the office would gather a massive number of the EA maps after the enumeration operation, manually capture the correct data, and update the GIS census database for post-enumeration and intercensus activities. With the advent and use of handheld devices equipped with GPS, point-based data (dwellings or housing units, landmarks, addresses, etc.) is relatively easy to collect and validate, including its integration into the database. Even polygon editing is made easier

with the use of GIS on mobile devices, particularly with the use of mobile map packages with imagery or basemap data and layers that can be edited interactively in the field. The edits and new points collected during enumeration, however, still need to be incorporated into the master database. There should be an established workflow of incorporating edits and verifying changes to the master geospatial census database.[1]

Usually, additional data-cleaning operations, coding activities, and other imputation operations are performed on the full set of data after the enumeration period, enabling the source database to produce all dissemination products. These procedures contribute to the quality assurance of data prior to its dissemination. Once data collection and processing operations are complete, it is essential to correct major errors to avoid any significant problems, and make sure that the final statistical data is quality assured, where possible, prior to its publication.[2]

Updating and verifying changes to the database after the field enumeration operation is advantageous to having the most accurate database of EAs post-enumeration. Curated data facilitates post-census evaluation and sampling frame and will be used in all future survey work. The automation of data collection has had a positive impact on the speed at which the work can proceed with updates and quality checks for database consistency. A mobile digital data collection also speeds the release of census results and helps ensure a faster delivery of results than a paper-based data collection.

For these purposes, ArcGIS Data Reviewer is a beneficial tool. Data Reviewer is designed to improve data quality by providing a complete system for automating and simplifying data quality management.

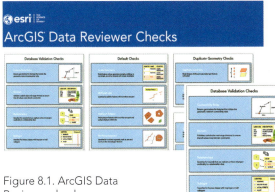

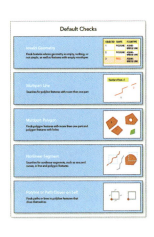

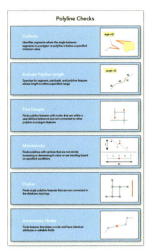

Figure 8.1. ArcGIS Data Reviewer checks.

Data Reviewer provides tools that support both the automated and visual analysis of data to improve data quality control across multiple platforms. Data Reviewer also provides simple-to-use visual review tools. Users can identify missing or misplaced features, improperly attributed features, and other types of issues. Data Reviewer can also be used to detect anomalies with features, attributes, and spatial relationships in a database. Its data checks contain analysis rules that can be scheduled to run interactively or automatically as a recurring event. Depending on the type of analysis to be performed, the anomaly can be corrected as part of database maintenance or investigated further.

More specifically, Data Reviewer allows users to: (1) manage the quality control and analysis of their GIS data (for example, detecting a building in the river or on a highway would most likely be an error identified as part of quality control); (2) undertake spatial checks by analyzing the spatial relationships of features (for example, analyzing whether features overlap, intersect, reside within a specified distance of other features, or touch); (3) undertake attribute checks by analyzing the attribute values of features and tables (which can be simple field validation similar to a geodatabase domain or more complex attribute dependencies); (4) undertake feature integrity checks by analyzing the properties

of features—feature integrity checks ensure that the collection rules are followed for each feature class; (5) undertake metadata checks by analyzing the metadata information of the feature datasets and feature classes; (6) conduct a managed review of data through automated or visual checks to understand the integrity of the entire database; and (7) use interactive analysis tools that provide better communication about missing features and features with inaccurate shapes.[3]

Data Reviewer helps a user gain insight into sources of poor data quality and to identify error trends and monitor data health using reports, dashboards, and other automatically captured statistics.

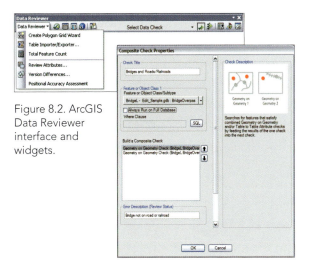

Figure 8.2. ArcGIS Data Reviewer interface and widgets.

Another tool that should be considered in the processing of data is ArcGIS® Workflow Manager. While Workflow Manager is useful for managing field operations, it extends ArcGIS by providing a centralized enterprise job management and tracking system to streamline daily tasks. Significant time savings and improved efficiency of GIS implementations can be achieved by enforcing standardized and repeatable workflows across the organization. Workflow Manager handles complex geodatabase tasks such as data access, version creation and management, and archiving behind the scenes by integrating with ArcGIS geodatabase tools. This ensures that the right person is working on the right data at the right time.

Aggregation

The creation of a digital census geographic database at the EA level serves the production of digital EA maps and reports at administrative and statistical units. This reporting can be done through geographic data aggregation. Based on a nested administrative hierarchy structured in the database, GIS-enabled spatial aggregation capacity allows the EAs to be aggregated to various reporting units, required for the countless geographic products for census dissemination. The aggregation process is required to preserve confidentiality, making census data available for spatial aggregates and not for

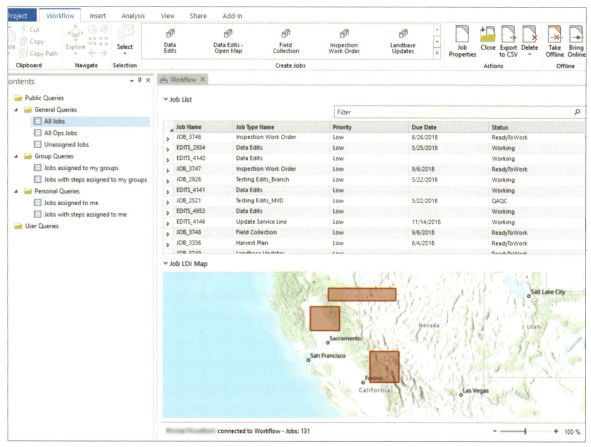

Figure 8.3. Example of an application of ArcGIS Workflow Manager.

individuals. Thus, the production of aggregated geographic areas enables NSOs to meet different user needs from different sectors (such as health, education, transportation, or environment). The data aggregation process is critical to the successful use of the data, in the near term and the distant future, because this will be the foundation for comparative purposes. Aggregation must be done at each level of geography to be published. It is often also necessary to the workings and needs of central and local governments. For example, for its 2016 census, Statistics Canada created a new census dissemination geographic area, a subprovincial census dissemination geography called *aggregate dissemination area* (ADA). The intent of the ADA geography is to ensure the availability of census data where possible, across all regions of Canada.[4]

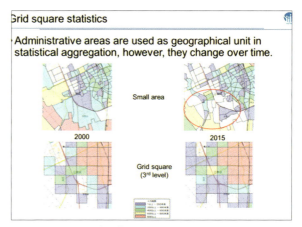

Figure 8.4. Example of aggregation: administrative areas and grid system. *Source*: National Statistics Center of Japan (NSTAC), Esri UC 2018 presentation "Utilizing grid square statistics."

The UN-EG-ISGI proposed the following definition: "Aggregated statistical information is aggregated from geocoded unit record level data into the dissemination geography, as opposed to disaggregated statistical information that is created using a spatial distribution model and larger statistical geographies as source data."[5] More specifically, the geocoding of the EAs, their geometrical representation, and topological structure in the database provide the basis for GIS to enact its spatial analysis capabilities and create various aggregations.

Spatial aggregations combined with overlay, distances, spatial selection, intersection, and other analytical techniques provide insights and useful knowledge about many geographically related issues. Obviously, aggregations require the boundaries and attribute data of the reporting units because this is the statistical data related to these units. This aggregate data related to the reporting can then be made available for use and reuse in appropriate open formats, such as comma-separated values (CSV), Extensible Markup Language (XML), and so on (see details in chapter 10).

While census data has been traditionally aggregated by various types of administrative units (villages, towns, cities, provinces, etc.), the increasing demands for small areas require aggregations of some EAs, local areas of interest, or very small units such as blocks or mesh-blocks. For some applications, the appropriate geographic units may be an *ad hoc* aggregation or an aggregation or group of local administrative units. However, when data is captured at the point level (dwellings or housing units, landmarks, addresses, etc.), grid systems may be used to aggregate this existing point-based data. Using a spatial reference system with squared grid cells allows for overlaying capabilities, comparisons, and other spatial analysis. Grids are covered in more detail in chapter 4.

Database archiving and maintenance

A population and housing census generates massive amounts of data and information that constitute a valuable asset for the country, which every NSO needs to preserve and sustain. Preserving the asset requires the setup of a data repository system enabling data to be safely stored and archived, and sustaining the system requires the maintenance of the master database, as its value increases through continual updates and long-term use.

Preserving and archiving census data and documentation related to their collection and processing contributes effectively to the data dissemination of the current census and for planning and implementing future censuses. Census data and documentation can also be used in conducting time-series or comparative analyses. Drawing lessons from records of how the census was planned, organized, and conducted, and guidelines and documents on past processes (e.g., how a specific technology was used in a previous census) could contribute to the success of a future census. Like many other census activities, the preservation procedures need to be raised early in the planning of census activities. This has become even more crucial with a technology-driven census, as rapidly changing technology affects digital files products and storage, which may require ongoing assessment to ensure access in the future.

While archiving census data is of critical importance, a survey led by UNSD during the 2010 Round of Censuses found that only 73 percent of the countries or areas responding to the questionnaire indicated that they will use a system to archive their census data. For example, only four African countries declared having a system to archive census data, but this number still reflects an increasing awareness that is promising for the 2020 Round of Censuses.[6]

Countries recognize that archiving a vast amount of data represents a considerable challenge, particularly when they deal with census individual records and related security and confidentiality. This challenge requires the NSO to develop a set of procedures and an archival program to ensure that the contents from data collection operations are maintained in formats that can be used by current and future censuses and for other statistical activities. In *Principles and Recommendations*, the UN recommends that "the national statistical authority needs to develop an institutional strategy for archiving based on three components: organizational infrastructure, technological infrastructure and resources." The organizational aspect generally refers to a centralized unit within the NSO that oversees archiving, maintenance, storage, and the possible release of census individual records. Technological infrastructure refers to the actual technology used for digital archiving, and resources are normally planned at an early stage of the census and needed for the archiving operation in the context of the organizational and technological infrastructures.[7]

A strong archival program includes not only the preservation of the current census data in a physical or logical space to protect it from loss, alteration, and deterioration,[8] but also the maintenance of the database, metadata, and census data products for future use, particularly for future census and statistical activities. Database maintenance is critical for ensuring that census data and information remain continually updated and accessible for long-term use. Database metadata, which explains the content and structure of the data, needs to be continually verified and completed to document any changes implemented in the database and keep up with any evolution in the definitions and related technical standards. NSOs should develop and implement database maintenance procedures immediately following a census, allowing for continuous updates of boundaries and other features as new information becomes available.

Maintaining the database also expands its use in the post-census evaluation of the census coverage and in the intercensal period, providing geospatial services for other statistical applications, such as sample surveys or sectoral applications. It also prepares the geographic base for the next census enumeration. As already stated, the benefits gained from using a GIS-based census database for many applications beyond the core tasks of a census, at the national level, outweigh the costs involved, thus greatly increasing the return on investment in opting for a digital geographic census infrastructure.

Open platform and system interoperability

As geographic information is increasingly distributed on the web and routinely integrated into thousands of applications and services, GIS has become more open. We all recognize the increasing importance of open data, open standards, data interoperability (e.g., open formats), open application programming interfaces (APIs), and specifications, all needed for easy access and sharing of data by an open community. All of these are required for an open platform that provides interoperability, an essential feature of any system to be able to interact with other systems during its mission to exchange and use information.[9] Indeed, a popular dissemination method today is open data using Internet protocols, which are usually configured to allow unrestricted access by people or other computers.

Esri has a longstanding commitment to standards and interoperability. As part of Esri's dedication to building an open and interoperable platform, its goal is to support appropriate technology specifications as they become finalized. The company also participates in the development of GIS standards through organizations like OGC and the ISO. By serving in leadership roles in many OGC initiatives and ISO/TC 211 committees, Esri contributes to a knowledge of interoperability to promote standards compliance across the ArcGIS platform.

ArcGIS supports more than 100 established standards, including data formats, metadata, and services. The ArcGIS platform conforms to open standards and enterprise IT frameworks that allow users to incorporate GIS into any application on a variety of computers and mobile devices. ArcGIS uses data format standards to store geospatial data in a common format or transfer data from system to system via ETL tools for data validation, migration, and distribution. Further, services standards are used to transfer data via the web or provide remote access to data stored on a web server. These standards allow users to interact with data, usually through simple web clients, on a live and real-time basis. This includes viewing maps, accessing and querying data, running analyses, and downloading data.

However, the trend today for open data and systems is bigger; it isn't just standards—it really is about integration. As we stated earlier, with the advent of open data, statistical organizations are facing new challenges: integrating the primary data (census and survey data) with secondary data sources (typically administrative datasets, geospatial data, and big data or any other nontraditional source of information for official statistics).[10] Having found the various data, the issue is how to integrate it into a form so that exploration, analytics, and visualization of the combined datasets can be performed. This integration is needed particularly in the context of the 2030 Agenda for Sustainable Development, where the delivery of indicators requires the combination of various multisource data.

In this regard, to fulfill its vision of openness, Esri has built ArcGIS as an open platform with the view that open systems encourage innovation, support interoperability, promote transparency, improve reliability, and increase collaboration. Indeed, the ArcGIS platform reflects Esri's relationship to all things open—standards, interoperability, data, APIs,

code, and the community. For example, the Esri platform-independent approach ensures interoperability because it supports industry and community standards, libraries in every major programming language, integration with common analysis and data management tools, and a growing repository of open-source software available on GitHub®.[11] For more information, see the 2017 Esri white paper *Esri Support for Geospatial Standards* at https://www.esri.com/~/media/files/pdfs/library/whitepapers/pdfs/esri-support-for-geospatial-standards.pdf.

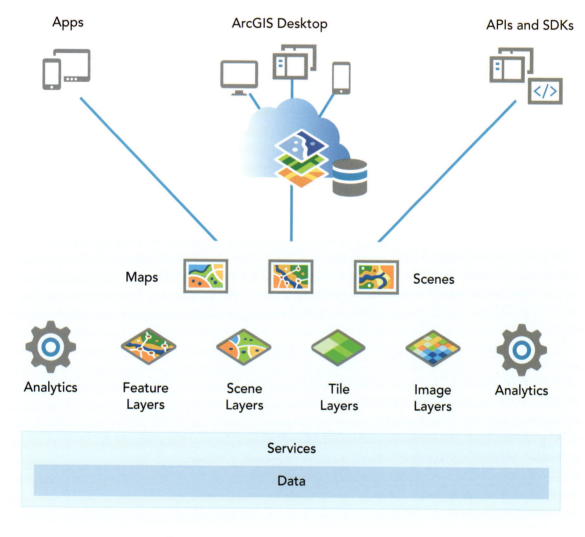

Figure 8.5. ArcGIS is an open platform for innovation.

Case study: Ireland

Joining forces, the Central Statistics Office of Ireland (CSO) and the Ordnance Survey Ireland (OSi) collaborated to make the country's 2016 census data more meaningful and accessible. The agencies launched two new data portals that are making information about Ireland's people, environment, and prosperity available in ways that previously were not possible.

Challenges

Every five years, the CSO conducts a census survey of the country's 4.8 million residents, at 1.5 million households, across an area of 70,000 km^2. Enumerators had been using the "long form" method to collect data about everything from people's employment status to their means of getting to work. The office traditionally presented this census data in statistical tables and published it in reports that contained a few maps and diagrams. Administrators realized, however, that they could add value to census data by presenting it in geographic context. Furthermore, if CSO provided GIS capabilities and interactive web applications, data users could make their own maps and do their own analysis.

CSO collaborated with OSi, the country's national mapping agency, via a formal memorandum of understanding. Both organizations had been playing active roles in the government's public-sector re-form plan; both organizations worked with data and analytics; and both organizations used the ArcGIS platform. The two organizations agreed to work together to create new channels for disseminating geospatially referenced data.

Just a few months after CSO and OSi had signed the memorandum, the United Nations and Esri invited the agencies to participate in a research project to develop and deploy a new method of monitoring the UN's Sustainable Development Goals (SDGs).

According to Esri, what makes data exploration like this feasible is having all the information in one place, which is what Esri and the UN Statistics Division (UNSD) are doing in their joint research exercise. For the project, participating member states use their existing data systems by deploying ArcGIS Hub in conjunction with ArcGIS Enterprise to help their national statistics offices integrate SDG-related data into their own work.

The exercise asks statistic offices to align their data and systems with other in-country SDG stakeholders, including National Mapping Agencies (NMAs), health ministries, natural resource and environmental agencies, and private-sector statistical data producers.

Ireland was one of seven countries selected for this groundbreaking initiative and the only country from Europe. The opportunity provided a clear focus for the partnership and provided the impetus for CSO and OSi to launch an ambitious, collaborative development project.

Solution

OSi had already developed a data-sharing platform called GeoHive®, based on the ArcGIS Hub solution, so CSO and OSi decided to use GeoHive as the technical platform for their collaborative projects. GeoHive acts as a "hub of hubs," allowing the same data to be presented to different audiences, with different views, in subportals known as *micro-hives*.

While working on the UN SDG project, CSO and OSi decided to create a micro-hive to present Ireland's Census 2016 Small Area Population Statistics (SAPS). For the first time, data would be geospatial and open. The resulting census portal (census2016.geohive.ie) allows data to be viewed, accessed, and downloaded in map form across 31 administrative counties, 95 municipal districts, 3,409 electoral divisions, and 18,641 small areas. Datasets include globally unique identifiers (GUIDs) to connect statistics and geography, which is a necessary step for using standard common IDs for spatial data in Ireland.

Using the Census 2016 portal, anyone can explore Ireland's latest census data by theme, combine multiple data layers to create maps, embed maps in other applications, and download data or connect to it via a series of open-standard application programming interfaces (APIs).

Four months later, in November 2017, CSO and OSi launched another micro-hive, this time for sustainable development statistics. The Ireland SDG portal (http://irelandsdg.geohive.ie) data specifically aligns to the UN's 17 development goals, 169 targets, and 230 indicators. The SDG portal incorporates Census 2016 variables from CSO as well as more than 100 spatial datasets ranging from biodiversity to traffic accidents. The portal provides over fifty indicators relating to Ireland's progress toward SDGs. Users can see very specific information such as the total unemployed females in each electoral ward.

As an extension to the two portals, the joint team created a series of ArcGIS Online story maps to highlight key issues indicated by the CSO Census 2016 data and other open-data sources. Its first story map addresses climate change and unemployment issues and brings together data, interactive maps, images, and narratives to tell the story behind the statistics. People don't need technical skills to use the story map. They simply access the map in their browsers and zoom to an area of interest to see how the issue affects that location.

Benefits

Improved ability to inform government policy decisions

By making it easier for policymakers, researchers, and government officials to visualize statistical information, the Census 2016 portal and Ireland SDG portal will play key roles in supporting government decision-making. Story maps will be particularly helpful in highlighting critical issues in society. For example, one recently completed story map, based on Census 2016 data, shows that 40 percent of children in Ireland live in rented accommodations and are therefore at risk of poverty and homelessness if rental prices increase. Story maps open issues for discussion and help to inform government policy.

Better information to encourage investment in Ireland's economy

The Irish agency responsible for attracting foreign investment to Ireland—the Industrial Development Authority (IDA)—uses the Census 2016 portal to identify the best locations for local and foreign business investments. For instance, the agency can map potential areas meeting the criteria for graduates, skilled labor force, and transportation links and use the maps to attract investors.

Easy access to transparent, meaningful data for all citizens

For the first time, anyone can access Ireland's 2016 census data in a geospatial format that is easy to understand and use. This improves public-sector transparency because any citizen can see the data on which government policies are determined. In addition, not-for-profit organizations can use the Census 2016 portal to see, for example, where there are high levels of unemployment. They can then better allocate their resources. They can also map areas with the greatest need and use them to lobby the Irish government to increase its support.

A powerful way to engage citizens in important issues

Story maps that link to the UN's SDGs, CSO, and OSi help the Irish government raise awareness of important issues that affect the country, such as the need to protect biodiversity and preserve water quality.

A cost-effective mechanism for meeting UN reporting requirements

Significantly, Ireland's new SDG portal will support the Irish government by making it easier for the government to meet the UN's SDG reporting obligations. Prior to the launch of the portal, there was no single repository for all the data that the Irish government would need to find and analyze to produce the reports. Now, government working groups responsible for UN reporting can more easily find the pertinent data without having to duplicate effort or waste time manipulating data. As a result, the agencies produce reports quickly, which will reduce costs by saving time.

The Irish government cites the Ireland SDG portal as a best-practice example of how public-sector organizations can share and use data. This country-owned, country-led project is a new strategy for the future development of Ireland's public service. It is opening the way for policies that envision shared data across government sectors that facilitate easier access to services, better service delivery, and better decision-making, and promises to drive government efficiency.

Notes

1. See the US Census Bureau report *New Technologies in Census Geographic Listing—Select Topics in International Censuses*. Available at https://www.census.gov/content/dam/Census/library/working-papers/2015/demo/new-tech-census-geo.pdf.

2. See the United Nations Economic Commission for Europe (UNECE) report *Conference of European Statisticians—Recommendations for the 2020 Censuses of Population and Housing*. Available at https://www.unece.org/fileadmin/DAM/stats/publications/2015/ECECES41_EN.pdf.

3. See the ArcGIS Desktop Help article "What is Data Reviewer?" at http://desktop.arcgis.com/en/arcmap/latest/extensions/data-reviewer/what-is-data-reviewer.htm and the ArcGIS Data Reviewer documentation at http://www.esri.com/software/arcgis/extensions/arcgis-data-reviewer.

4. See Statistics Canada note. Retrieved from https://www12.statcan.gc.ca/census-recensement/2016/geo/ADA/adainfo-eng.cfm.

5. See the document *Proposal for a Common Statistical-Geospatial Terminology Database* published by the UN-GGIM EG-ISGI. Available at http://ggim.un.org/meetings/2015-2nd_Mtg_EG-ISGI-Portugal/documents/UN-GGIM%20EG%20Lisbon%20meeting%20session%204%20background%20paper%20terminology.pdf.

6. See Jean-Michel Durr's *The 2010 Round of Population and Housing Censuses in the World*. Available at http://jmstat.com/publications/SINAPE%202010.pdf.

7. See additional details in the 2017 UN *Principles and Recommendations* publication.

8. See the book *Authentic Electronic Records: Strategies for Long-Term Access* from Charles M. Dollar.

9. See the book *System Interoperability: The Reliability Information Analysis Center (RIAC) Guide* from Chonchang Lee and Joseph Hazeltine.

10. See *Guide to Data Integration for Official Statistics: Introduction*. Available at https://statswiki.unece.org/display/DI/Introduction.

11. See *ArcGIS: An Open Platform for Innovation*. Available at http://www.esri.com/~/media/00C24660087A4EFB9F069148017EABD4.pdf.

Chapter 9

Post-enumeration— dissemination and analysis

This chapter addresses the use of geospatial information, GIS, and spatial analysis in support of data dissemination, the ultimate stage of a census. The need for meaningful presentation allowing for better interpretation and compelling insights of statistics is more critical than ever. The data user community continues to grow and includes new types of users who may be looking at this type of data for the first time. GIS has continued to advance in this area, as well, with an array of improved tools for spatial analysis, mapping, and graphing. GIS and the geographic database are at the forefront of dissemination in most NSOs. The widespread use of such tools has contributed to increased demand for census and geographic products that integrate statistical and geospatial information. This demand requires a dissemination strategy that is put in place prior to the census undertaking and takes into account multiple users' needs, multiple formats or mediums, and varying needs for data, including small area data, with the commensurate assurances of confidentiality.

Dissemination strategies

In conducting their census, NSOs expend a lot of effort to collect census data, and even more for their analysis. But these efforts will not bear fruit and influence policy decisions unless the census information is made available in a suitable format to the various users. The UN has put it clearly in these terms: "A census is not complete until the information collected is made available to potential users in a form suited to their needs."[1] Many countries in fact are bound by local laws or legislation to disseminate their data, and moreover feel the pressure from civil society to share data for the public good. Citizens today expect and demand more detailed and timely data and expect to access this data from any device, anywhere, anytime.

To maximize the use of census results, NSOs should develop a dissemination strategy that can be implemented through a sound dissemination program, with the objective of promoting the benefit and application of census data. The lessons learned from the country experiences in the recent round of censuses have clearly shown that the census dissemination program should be considered as an integral part of the overall planning process of the census. A census dissemination program should be user-centric and based on a detailed analysis of the various user needs and expectations, including the determination of the form and scope of census data. Users today must include government agencies and internal users, as well as citizens, civil society, researchers, academia, developers, and more. Considerations should also include determining the level of geography at which census data will be disseminated, timing the main dissemination operations, determining the mode of dissemination, determining estimated costs, and identifying the human and technological resources that will be needed.

As technological capabilities increase and digital products replace traditional publications, the dissemination strategy should consider the diversification of the means of distribution, taking advantage of existing and new technologies to enhance the process to reach a wider audience, including the media and the public. It should particularly address the challenge of developing cost-effective mechanisms for the marketing and continued delivery of useful census and geography products and services to a diverse customer base, which can go far beyond the first couple of years after the census. Some countries have stated that the primary goal of their census dissemination process is to ensure that census and geography products and services meet the primary needs of most of the data users.[2] In addition to the fact that the disseminated census products should be of sufficient quality to meet user needs, safeguards should be put in place to ensure that individual information is kept confidential.[3]

Another factor for a successful dissemination program requires the development of an outreach strategy that improves statistical literacy and awareness among users, policy makers, and the media. This includes making them aware of any limitations in the data and what can be delivered based on the level of detail of the data. Finally, one main benefit of developing an overall dissemination strategy at an early stage of the census planning is to draw the attention of the policy and decision makers and eventual donors to the facts that census funding is not centered only on the enumeration phase and that dissemination activities also need to be properly funded. The latter means that budget and human resources need to be determined and ideally secured from the beginning of the census project.

In designing and developing census information products for the 2020 Round of Censuses, the UN recommends considering the statistical framework of the 2030 Agenda for Sustainable Development, particularly the list of indicators modeled for the monitoring of the implementation of this agenda. The SDG Indicator Framework provides the final list of these indicators, which is now available at the UNSD website (https://unstats.un.org). Therefore, all efforts should be put in place to produce census statistics in line with this framework.[4] To help countries measure, monitor, and report their progress on achieving the SDGs within a geographic context, the UNSD has been teaming with Esri since May 2017 to develop a data hub, a web-mapping and data management platform that integrates various data systems using ArcGIS.[i] This Federated Information System for the SDGs (FIS4SDGs) is an example of tying census data directly to the goals,

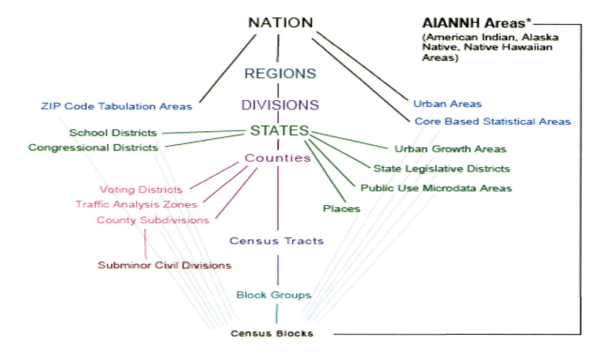

Figure 9.1. US Census standard hierarchy.

targets, and indicators and creating reports and information products to support the monitoring of the goals (see http://www.sdg.org).

Level of data release (geographic)

As previously mentioned, one of the earliest decisions in census planning relates to the administrative and geographic areas for which census data on diverse socioeconomic characteristics of the population will be reported and disseminated. This is generally based on consultations with stakeholders and various data users. The decision would consider a spectrum of geographic levels, from the highest level (country level) to the lowest geographic level (small areas), at which data can be disseminated with both a sufficient quality and flexibility to satisfy the needs of the various data users, and security measures to ensure that individual information is kept confidential.

Considering the dissemination geography at an early stage is important partly due to its relationships with the collection geography, because the geography on which the census is collected will affect the geography on which the census data can be disseminated (see chapter 4). In this context, there are two main methods for the dissemination geography, based on the geographic level of census data production, namely administrative method or grids. The traditional administrative method uses the EA as a basis to report census data in accordance with a hierarchical system of administrative units ranging from the local up to the country level. Using the administrative method and trying to offer a more flexible dissemination system, certain countries use a finer geography for their EAs to the level of a block, bounded by physical features such as streets or rivers, thus allowing reporting on data for small areas (see figure 9.2).

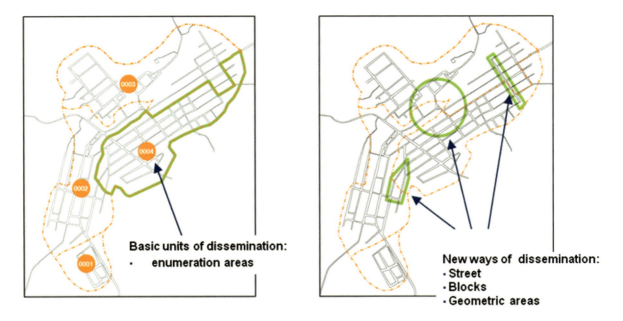

Figure 9.2. Example from the Instituto Brasileiro de Geografía e Estatística on dissemination possibilities.[5]

The second method relies on census data production at the point-based level (generally, buildings, businesses, and address registers geocoded with geographic coordinates to which the statistical information can be referenced), which can be aggregated at any spatial unit, administrative level, or even in a grid system, an inherently geographical output system[6] suitable to time series (for comparability) and environmental analysis. The population grid system is popular in Europe, particularly in the Nordic region. If census data is collected at the point level, new methods of dissemination are also possible, including *ad-hoc* shapes or units of dissemination based on local neighborhoods or other local criteria such as a drive-time polygon.

Each method has its advantages and disadvantages due to the different geographic levels at which census data can be disseminated. For example, the grid method requires the existence of georeferenced point datasets with high spatial accuracy, allowing NSOs to build small areas statistics, as well as delivering aggregations at various user-defined spatial units. In the absence of these point-based datasets, countries might opt for the administrative method that uses the EA as the key unit for the delivery of small area data. Administrative boundaries can also be superimposed on gridded maps, contributing greatly to their readability.

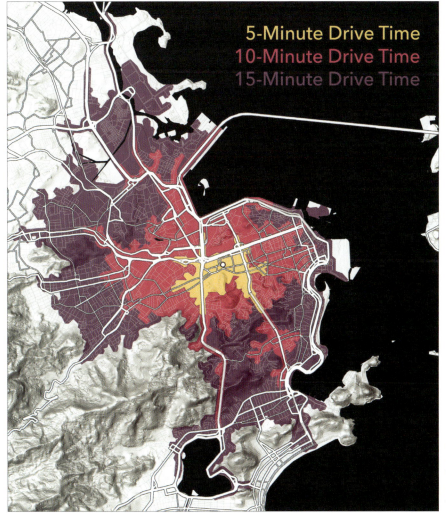

Figure 9.3. Brazil map showing drive-time polygons for five minutes, ten minutes, and fifteen minutes in Rio de Janeiro.

Pros and cons of administrative boundaries

This table is extracted from "The UN-GGIM Challenge to Develop Integrated Core Assets" presented by Tim Trainor, Retired Chief, US Census Bureau.[7]

PROS	CONS
Spatial accuracy of data	Comparability
Field verification	Boundary changes
Imagery verification	Traditional census data collection is becoming more infrequent for countries
Geocoding/address verification	Use of nonvisible boundaries
Authoritative sources	Number of different geographic areas
Local government involvement	Cartographic considerations/generalization of boundaries
Local knowledge	Varying participation
Nesting relationship with other geographic areas	Irregular sizes
Cadastral boundaries	Irregular shapes
Data thresholds	Variable density measures
Separate land and water area	High costs to maintain the data
Response rates	Legal variation
Response options	Regional variation
Response quality	Topographic variation
Sample frame	Insufficient understanding of microcharacteristics inside macroscale units
Controls on disclosure	Data integration is difficult

The statistical community has repeatedly debated whether to choose one or the other, although technology today supports both. The UN-EG-ISGI agreed on GSGF principle 2, which states: "The Global Framework recommends that the linkage of a geocode for each statistical unit record in a dataset (i.e., a person, household, business, building or parcel/unit of land) occurs within a data management environment . . . ."[8] However, it is also recognized that many countries are still collecting data only at EA level.

Each approach needs to consider user needs and maintain statistical and geospatial integration, bearing in mind that a single approach to the geographic dissemination of statistics may not be feasible. In this case, a hybrid solution combining the two methods is an option, depending on how transfer between the two approaches could be achieved.[9]

Pros and cons of grid-based statistical areas

This table is extracted from "The UN-GGIM Challenge to Develop Integrated Core Assets" presented by Tim Trainor, Retired Chief, US Census Bureau.[10]

PROS	CONS
Global and local scope—fully scalable	Disclosure control/cell size
Uniform scale conducive to cross-border studies	Grid cell sizes in rural areas
Comparability; better suited for Spatial Data Infra-structures (SDI)	When merging datasets, there is a need to change from one coordinate system to another before the data compilation into grids
More attention to problem-oriented science	European terrestrial reference system (ETRS80) is based on Lambert Azimuthal Equal Area coordi-nate reference system with fixed projection center; different projections may be needed in other parts of the world
Can locate people in space with more precision	Coding systems (scale intervals versus quadtree solutions)
Good territorial framework for sampling	Due to high data volume, errors are difficult to find and correct
Can aggregate to different kinds of territorial units	Various grids may be adopted within regions or countries
Ready to use with GIS analysis	Areas with dynamic or transient population fluctu-ations pose numerous complications for regional analysis
Easily generated from point-based georeferenced data	
Able to see clusters	
Easy and cost-efficient to collect	
Micro-scale analysis using flexible size grids	
Data integration is possible with newer data sourc-es, (i.e., ground-based, imagery, Internet)	
Stable over time; time-series not affected	

Data privacy and security during dissemination

The privacy and security of census data during dissemination is a major concern for national statistical authorities because one of the primary goals of confidentiality is to protect privacy by not allowing specific information related to an individual to be revealed or an individual observation to be identified, sometimes referred to as *personally identifiable information (PII)*. The concerns are even greater when the individual observation involves location information and the use of sophisticated technology to access and disseminate it. There are different measures to address and mitigate these concerns and protect the privacy of census and statistical data. For example, to prevent an individual or organization from being identified within the socioeconomic data and private information from being disclosed, the data being released may need to be de-identified and anonymized or "confidentialized."[11] In this section, we will focus on the confidential issues related to the geocoded census data and the use of geospatial technologies for census data dissemination.

Irrespective of the geographic unit and the method used for its geocoding, there is generally a difference between the level of data collection units, which can be a building or household, and data dissemination areas or levels of geography to which the data needs to be aggregated to ensure the confidentiality of individual information. The geography level at which a threshold of a number of persons can be released serves as an initial protection against disclosure. For example, the threshold can be set at a geography of 100 to 300 persons or 40 to 120 households, though there can sometimes be population or household counts available at lower geography.[12]

It is frequently argued that the development of a dwelling frame has elevated the issue of confidentiality due to concerns over the use of address data of housing units. While address data itself is not confidential and could be made available, confidentiality concerns are particularly raised when the address data is linked to data on individuals. To ensure preservation of data confidentiality, lower-level data would be available only to some authorized users. An acute issue of privacy protection arises when the names of household heads are included in the referencing of dwellings—a practice used to identify dwellings for which a formal address (such as street names and numbers) is missing. In such cases, we need to justify why it is necessary to collect identifying information about the head of household

and ensure that, to protect privacy, the data is anonymized when disseminated and identifying information about individuals is destroyed once it is no longer needed.

GIS data is generally not about specific individuals but rather about geographic locations and features such as addresses, coordinates (latitude/longitude), postal units, land parcels, settlements, administrative units, and so on. Database attributes are expected to require various levels of confidentiality. For example, the location of an individual's house and property tax, which are generally public records, are less sensitive than the individual's income and income tax. Although GIS can provide valuable insight into patterns of census data to the public, there is a legitimate concern involving the disclosure of confidential information through spatial display.

While the method of aggregating spatial data can mitigate these concerns, disclosure methods should be applied when the information is at the point level. ArcGIS technology is widely used today in secure enterprise solutions in both commercial and classified environments. Applying security controls to ArcGIS solutions is no different from securing any other IT solution. Security principles and controls can be applied at all levels of the architecture. Based on the security policies and requirements of the organization, ArcGIS security[13] can be applied at the application, network, operating system, and RDBMS levels.

NSOs should also consider the use of other data security methods such as remote wipe of data from a lost or stolen device or other enterprise security methods including firewalls, virtual private networks (VPNs), secure data encryption protocols, and more to secure confidential data and PII.

Another area for consideration of data privacy and security is the use of outsourced services or consultants. NSOs often need to outsource services in one or more tasks at the different census stages, including the dissemination operation. This may expose NSOs to potential confidentiality breaches for which they need safeguards by way of guidance and explicit provisions in the contract with the service providers, specifying contractor responsibilities for prompt notification to the agency if unauthorized disclosure or misuse occurs. NSOs should also be aware that implementation of such contract provisions will be enforced and monitored.

Open data considerations

As stated in chapter 3, the recent rise of the open data movement is at the forefront of the data revolution and has been particularly recognized by the UN within the context of the global SDGs. Countries are increasingly adopting open data policies, developing and executing open data strategies, and participating in initiatives in cooperation with international organizations[14] and civil society. Recognizing that the national statistical systems are concerned by this open data movement, the 2017 Cape Town Global Action Plan for Sustainable Development Data, endorsed by the UNSC, did "encourage national statistical offices to embrace the open data initiative and ensure stakeholders of the national statistical system as part of . . . the process."[15]

While data has been at the center of many systems and applications, most of the data, particularly that provided by governmental organizations, has been considered proprietary and subject to restrictions. Open data came out of a need for the access and use of data that is deemed to be in the public domain. While big data is defined by volume, velocity, and variety, open data is fundamentally defined by its use. Most definitions of open data include these basic features:

- Data must be publicly available, preferably online, and relatively easy to use to accommodate the largest number of users.
- It must be open-licensed to allow for its reuse and redistribution.
- It should be machine-readable so that datasets can be easily retrieved—downloaded in open formats and read by software—and analyzed.
- Datasets must be as complete as possible, documented, and available as a whole to render complete information about a subject.
- Data should be available free of charge, or at minimal cost, so that anyone can access.

There are significant benefits related to the use of open data for citizens and society in general: open data can help increase governmental transparency and social accountability, better target aid and public investments, and more effectively monitor service providers to deliver results. More specifically, there are economic benefits in terms of increased efficiency, new products and services, and the stimulation of economic development. Particularly, start-ups and small businesses are benefiting from the data-driven products and services they can generate and deliver. However, many governments have concerns about what data should be open to the public. What kind of procedures are needed to share this data? How should shared data be monitored and updated?

The biggest concerns that governments have expressed are related to confidentiality, privacy, and security. These concerns apply to census and statistical data. In this regard, the UNSD has stated: "Open data platforms can only achieve public support and success if proper precautions are taken to protect the privacy of individual persons, business and civil society organizations and we manage to ensure that data generated by administrative, civil and business registers could be made public by matching access with strict ethical and security protocols and secure technology platforms."[16] One example of security measures being taken are when open data catalogs implement security measures to protect data and metadata from being changed by unauthorized users.

With more countries adopting open data policies, particularly those promoted by the Open Government Partnership (OGP),[17] the access to geospatial information is being affected, increasing its use and value and benefiting a wider range of users (see the Census 2016 Ireland case study in chapter 8). However, since geospatial data is provided by multiple sources, some from official governmental agencies and others from nonauthoritative sources such as crowd-sourced data, the quality of open data varies considerably in terms of completeness and consistency. National statistical and geospatial agencies are uniquely placed to ensure data quality, and their responsibility will continue to grow as the volume of open data increases.[18] Governments are required to play a central role, not only to develop and implement policies but to mitigate the concerns about the misuse of open data. For example, the African Data Consensus has recommended: "African governments should acknowledge open data provided by credentialed data communities as acceptable sources of country statistical information."[19]

Many other considerations pertain to "open": open data, open specifications, open APIs, open source, and, most importantly, open systems that are standards-compliant and interoperable for an open community. The ArcGIS platform is an open platform with a platform-independent approach that ensures interoperability. ArcGIS supports industry and community standards, libraries in every major programming language, integration with common analysis and data management tools, and a growing repository of open-source software. Integrating open data sharing as a part of the platform achieves transparency and improves collaboration for all users.

Esri's open data strategy is built around geography, where ArcGIS technology can serve as the open data backbone for the organization, with a standard framework for unlocking and managing existing data, such as statistical, environmental, and health information.[20] The ArcGIS platform provides an easy way to integrate, manage, and publish this data for interagency collaboration and public consumption. Moreover, with the increasing use of GIS SaaS, we see solutions that can reduce the human and physical capital required to host geospatial data and reduce operational costs. Maps themselves provide an intuitive way to both share and analyze the data that the organization is providing.[21]

Figure 9.4. *Open Data for Census 2016 Ireland: Bringing Geography and Statistics Together.*[22]

Output needs—raster, CSV, tabular, maps

As noted previously, the identification of census output products in response to user needs, as part of the dissemination planning, should consider the available tools for wider publication. Typical census data outputs include tabular data, digital thematic maps, geographic files and other cartographic database dissemination products, digital imagery, digital interactive atlases, web-based mapping, and even APIs. We will elaborate on some of these in the next sections.

Dissemination of census and statistical data in digital form is ubiquitous and dominant today among users. Geospatial information too has evolved from files to databases and now to the web. Today, many census agencies use database management systems, such as Oracle, DB2, SQL or PostgreSQL, and the geodatabase to drive the creation of information products and the dissemination of data. In the past, we may have used a central database environment that helped us serve the needs of clients. Today, we need a system of distributed web services, feature services, and map services. We need to serve lightweight clients and custom applications on the web and on smart devices and desktops. GIS platforms are now more than ever a key part of the dissemination process.

An ArcGIS Server web service represents a GIS resource—such as a map, locator, or image—that is located on an ArcGIS Server site and is made available to client applications. Specialized GIS software to work with a service is not needed, and the service can be consumed within a web browser or custom application. This is a big change in the way that data users can consume and get access to information. In addition, ArcGIS applications, such as ArcMap and ArcGIS Pro, can also act as clients to web services, and census agencies can write their own apps to consume web services.

When working with a service hosted by ArcGIS Server, users have, in most cases, the same level of access to resources that they would have if those resources were located on their computer. A map service, for example, allows client applications to access the contents of a map on the server in much the same way that they would if the map were stored locally.

Much of the work in data dissemination today is actually in building and maintaining key foundational layers and basemaps that support the agencies' operations. These layers will find their way online as maps, as data layers, and even in analytical models. Statistical data can then come to life once joined to geographic data and be shared to users of all types. Information can be stored in ArcGIS as different types of geographic information such as web maps, scenes, layers, analyses, and apps.

Layers, one of the most important collections, can include streets, points of interest, parks, water bodies, and terrain. Layers are how geographic data is organized and are the basis for analysis.

Basemaps are another key. Today, the map mashup is more popular than ever. Basemaps can be as relatively simple as a street map, raster imagery, or a combination of the two (e.g., imagery with labels). GIS systems provide the ability to easily share data so that anyone can access and build on the work of others.

Not every census dataset appropriate for use with a GIS comes in a ready-to-use spatial format. Often, the data comes as a table or a spreadsheet, and it needs to be linked with existing spatial data or a geography boundary file.[23] Most GIS software can import spreadsheets and CSV files and read vector data out of these text files. For example, the software can read vector data out of GPX files, the popular format for GPS tracks, or CSV files that includes longitude (x) and latitude (y) columns. It can also convert, for example, raster data and export it to CSV and other tabular files that contain the x,y,z coordinates and all the attributes.[24] What's worth noting is that the divide between vector-based GIS and raster-based GIS is being increasingly blurred, and ArcGIS offers the tools to work with both.

Generally, the outputs are provided by the census database in the form of either tabular data or geographic products. Obviously, one of the important features of census outputs is to be easily accessible, retrievable, and usable. Data should be available for download in widely used formats to easily lend themselves to machine processing, such as CSV or XML, and as a single download file (with all data in a dataset) as much as possible.[25] For example, a data download for a specific area or region should include the geographic data and the attributes together, not as separate downloads.

Cloud/hybrid approaches

Chapter 3 touched on the growing use of cloud services in general. In this section, we will focus on the use of the cloud for dissemination purposes. As discussed earlier, cloud offerings can include public, private, or hybrid approaches. One hybrid approach that many GIS users take is to leverage ArcGIS Online along with the public and/or the private cloud.

The cloud can be useful in dissemination due to unpredictable spikes in load, for cost containment, or simply to provide a simple means of sharing and collaboration.

Often when setting up a service to make data accessible, it is hard to predict the demand and therefore scale that is necessary to support end users. By leveraging the cloud in data dissemination, organizations can better respond to demand spikes and therefore offer a stable service to data users while managing the costs associated with this service.

Metadata

The benefits of developing and implementing common standards and metadata are recognized by both statistical and geospatial communities because they enable interoperability and facilitate the use and integration of statistical and

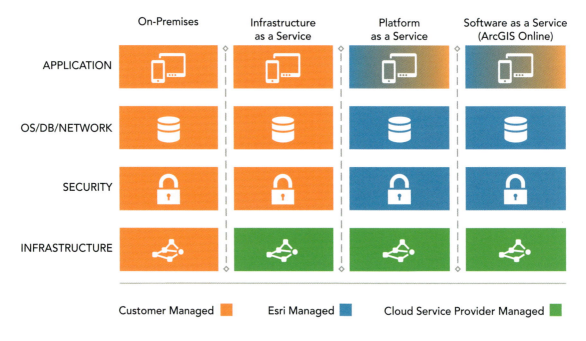

Figure 9.5. Cloud deployment options.

geospatial data and services in virtually all sectors of the economy. It is often noted that the development of common standards and metadata makes statistical and geospatial information more accessible, shareable, and relevant to a wider range of stakeholders and users.

We have already provided a definition and concepts of metadata in chapter 6 and noted that metadata is crucial for the management and maintenance of a digital GIS database, but its use spans all stages of the census and beyond. While its need for the geospatial database is more limited to the developers and those in charge of its maintenance, metadata needed for dissemination is designed for the different users of the census results. There is a growing need for comprehensive and easily accessible metadata to better understand the statistical data being presented.

The basic purpose of metadata is related to the production of census data and its documentation, processing, and interoperability. However, there are three major purposes for metadata related to data dissemination: facilitating the discovery of relevant data, supporting its correct use, and providing transparency in it. For example, metadata supports the correct use of data by providing contextual information and explaining the main relationships, causations, and trends in the data, including reference date, data source, data access conditions, release policy and confidentiality, and, when necessary, information on how the data was collected, compiled, processed, edited, and validated.[26]

In recognition of the important role of metadata for census data dissemination, the UN *Principles and Recommendations*, rev. 3, recommends the following: "Metadata are a key element of census dissemination to ensure that the underlying concepts are well understood and that the results are well interpreted." Further, it should be an integral part of statistical collection and dissemination processes. The UN also recommends that all tabulations should include some type of metadata or references to where this information can be obtained.[ii]

Based on lessons learned from the 2010 Round of Censuses and other reviews, it is agreed that metadata should be an integral part of the census process, including census dissemination. In this regard, the dissemination of metadata should be comprehensive and accessible. It was also recognized that there is a lack of common metadata standards and proper guidelines in terms of development and presentation of metadata. To address this issue, it was recommended that procedures for standardization be developed to respond to the needs expressed by many countries and to improve interpretation and facilitate sharing and comparability among countries. In this respect, international standards are emerging: for example, two international metadata standards being used today are the SDMX and the DDI (see additional details in chapter 6). The SDMX was approved by the ISO in 2013 as an international standard (ISO 17369:2013). A number of international agencies have endorsed SDMX, supported by the UNSC. The DDI,[27] which originated in 1995 and was initially aimed at social science research, is an international standard for describing surveys, questionnaires, and statistical data files.[iii]

The DDI is an international metadata standard designed to focus on describing microdata and the processing performed on the data as it is integrated and tabulated,[28] but the SDMX is designed to describe statistical data and standardize how that data and metadata are exchanged. The SDMX is particularly dedicated to handle large amounts of tabular data, some of which may have geographic meaning, through a location name (e.g., region/area) or a unique identifier (UID) that relates to a boundary (e.g., mesh-block, area unit, etc.). Likewise, in the geospatial world, international metadata standards, such as ISO-19115 or ISO-19139, do exist and are well established. ISO 19115-1:2014 is applicable to digital data and services, and its principles can be extended to many types of resources such as maps, charts, and textual documents as well as nongeographic data. While there is little reference to any specific geospatial component within the SDMX, recent efforts have been made by the European Union, through Eurostat, to integrate INSPIRE and SDMX data infrastructures for their 2021 population and housing censuses.

ArcGIS easily supports the metadata creation workflow. In ArcGIS, an item's metadata is created, edited, and viewed on the item page. Item details include the title, the type, the source, author, last modified date, thumbnail, and tags. It can also include additional information such as a summary and description, how accurate and recent the item is, restrictions associated with using and sharing the item, credits, and so on. This information can help others discover and validate the usefulness of the items. In ArcGIS, metadata is saved with the item it describes. It is copied, moved, and deleted with the item.

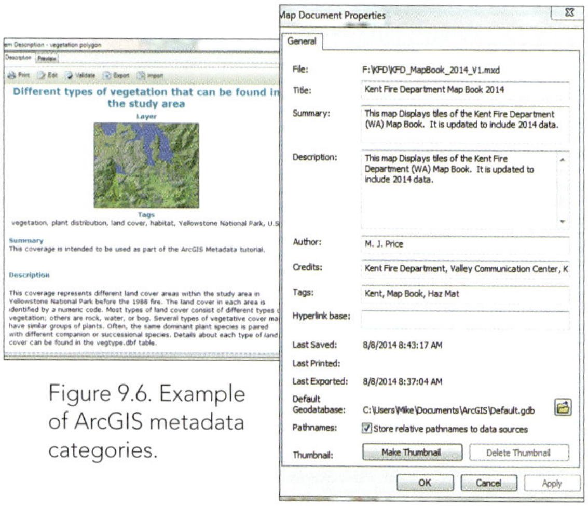

Figure 9.6. Example of ArcGIS metadata categories.

Organizations can enable metadata, which allows members of the organization to use the built-in metadata editor to include additional standards-based metadata for all item types. Metadata can be included for all items in a portal, including web maps, web scenes, and web apps. Organizations select a metadata style, which configures the organization's experience for editing and viewing metadata. In addition to determining the information available for viewing and editing, the metadata style identifies the metadata standard being followed and the schema used to validate an item's metadata for the standard. Regardless of the applied style, the metadata is always stored in ArcGIS metadata format. This means that metadata is not lost if the organization switches the metadata style.

The ArcGIS metadata format contains fields that can store all content in all metadata standards supported by ArcGIS, including all Federal Geographic Data Committee (FGDC) Content Standard for Digital Geospatial Metadata (CSDGM), all ISO 19139 metadata content, all North American Profile metadata content, and all INSPIRE metadata content. The ArcGIS format also stores item properties, such as thumbnails, that are not included in these official metadata standards and profiles.

Currently noticeable is the gap between the standards used for the dissemination of statistical data and those used for the geospatial information, making the link between statistical and geospatial information more challenging at the working level. Efforts are being made by the OGC, which recently developed the Table Joining Service (TJS) standard. This standard is designed to offer a web service interface that enables the automatic, service-oriented joining of tabular and geographic data across the web while keeping the data distributed at the data providers' source location.[29] As mentioned in

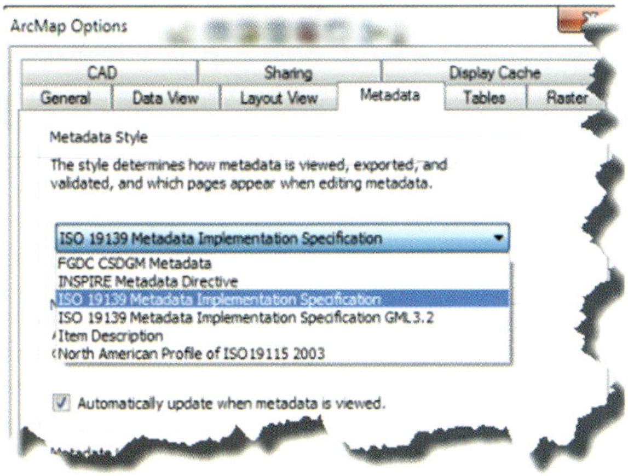

Figure 9.7. Metadata styles.

chapter 6, the UN-EG-ISGI has recommended, as a future area of standardization, to work on a statistical-geospatial metadata interoperability in integrating, for example, the SDMX and the DDI with ISO-19115. Furthermore, the Expert Group is developing the GSGF as a common standard allowing both statistical and geospatial communities to work together.

Data sharing

In a data-driven world, with the rapid emergence of technologies such as the cloud, the IoT, mobile technology, web GIS, and artificial intelligence, new horizons are opening for data analysis, accessibility, and sharing. Moreover, the increasing developments of open systems across organizations, applications, and industries attest to the vital importance of data sharing. In this context, sharing statistical data has been a rallying cry among development partners in statistical development and among many users more at ease with these advanced technologies.

In response to the needs for sharing data, and in addition to the adoption and building of technical capacities, NSOs should include in their overall data policy specific provisions for data sharing, including institutional arrangements and

agreements with other governmental organizations defining custodianship, rights and responsibilities; preparation of guidelines containing general advice and guidance on data sharing; and particularly measures and procedures with regard to the protection of individual privacy and data confidentiality. There is increasing recognition that responsible data sharing, allowing the maximum use of data for statistical purposes while taking into consideration security concerns, contributes to the evidence-based decision-making capability of both governments and communities.

At the national level, with the large number of players involved in data production, requests for data sharing are affecting NSOs and exposing them to challenges in terms of coordination and security concerns but also providing opportunities for adding value to their data. NSOs are embracing the need to share data in line with the existing institutional arrangements in their countries. For example, it is now widely accepted that developing NSDIs better facilitates the availability, access to, and effective sharing of geospatial data among geospatial information authorities and other governmental organizations, including NSOs, the private sector, universities, and citizens in general.

Sharing data is also needed at the regional level, particularly to assist in the formulation of community policies across boundaries. One example is the INSPIRE initiative to build a European Union spatial data infrastructure to enable the sharing of harmonized and qualitative geospatial information among public sector organizations and facilitate public access to geospatial information across Europe. Furthermore, developing a global strategic framework for statistical and geospatial information has been a goal for both the statistical and the geospatial communities. Such a framework constitutes a foundation for building geospatial information infrastructure at all levels and provides reference framework, allowing the integration and sharing of various data to support decision-making for sustainable development.[30]

With respect to the geospatial technology in support of data sharing, many organizations expressed the need for a GIS capable of integrating services and data from multiple sources and in different formats. In this regard, Esri technology and products support interoperability, and Esri plays an active role in the development of open standards, which has helped ensure that data can be easily accessed by other technologies and applications. Esri products support numerous data converters and direct read access, including Spatial Data Transfer Standard (SDTS), Vector Product Format (VPF), imagery, CAD files, digital line graph (DLG), and TIGER®. The ArcGIS system supports more than 100 formats and continues to add more as the industry demands. Of equal importance, Esri systems enable organizations to share GIS services and communicate across different vendor implementations. An open, distributed, and networked GIS architecture provides the framework for sharing data.

GIS role in creating products for dissemination

GIS has been widely used in the dissemination of census and statistical data. Even without initiating a full digital census-mapping program, many NSOs had been using GIS for dissemination purposes, as GIS software packages offer simple and easy methods for putting census data on maps that enhance their understanding and enable users to visualize statistical information. Moreover, GIS enables the presentation of census results in different forms—maps, charts, graphs, map

applications, and story maps—and maps can be customized and dynamically presented with links to the charts, graphs, and other media. In addition to the capacity of producing maps in traditional paper formats, GIS enables maps to be easily exchanged in digital format on an intranet, the Internet, or other storage media.[31] With the building of a geospatial census database at the EA level, GIS provides powerful tools to proceed with spatial analysis, allowing the user to create various products to be disseminated. In addition, with the use of mobile technology and the web, the census data dissemination has reached new horizons, putting census data at the fingertips of the users and the public in general. We will elaborate on the various media of presentation of census products created using GIS in the subsequent sections.

Thematic maps

Consider the following definition of geographic maps: "A map is a symbolised image of geographical reality, representing selected features or characteristics . . . ."[32] A thematic map for statistical data dissemination is an even greater simplification of reality, designed to show the geographical distribution of a statistical variable for selected geographic areas, leaving out all irrelevant details. Thematic maps for dissemination are generally produced not only for the major census data users, but also for a wider, nonspecialist audience. Thus, they should be designed carefully and of a quality that meaningfully illustrates census results and makes them easily understandable. Thematic maps are also often meant to support textual information, accompanying census reports.

Since a thematic map shows the geographic distribution of one or more specific data themes for standard geographic areas, GIS, with its data structure organized by layers or themes, can straightforwardly represent the various statistical variables through maps. In addition, with an ability to combine a variety of datasets in an infinite number of ways, GIS is useful for representing the results of the combination of many themes at once. Generating graphic outputs in the form of thematic maps requires that GIS software have a wide variety of graphic symbols and format options. GIS tools offer mapping functionalities to customize the design of the output, including cartographic symbols and insets, as well as text options for labeling and annotating the map legend and other metadata.

Creating a good thematic map takes thought. Before creating one, consider some simple questions such as the following:

- What is the story you are trying to tell?
- What is the intended message?
- Who is the intended audience?
- What do they know about the topic?
- What do you want them to understand?
- What data do you need to tell this story?

A thematic map can be qualitative or quantitative in nature.[33] Thematic maps can also provide insights on change over time by showing comparisons of topical indicators in a time series, provided that comparable indicators are available from previous censuses.

Many types of maps can be made from a single dataset and a single theme of data. Maps can also be symbolized in many ways, including point symbols, proportional symbols, graduated symbols, heat maps, clustering, and more. The traditional choropleth (graduated color) map is what many typically choose, but today, many other choices allow us to communicate the data.

However, there are many other traditional choices, including 3D, dot density, cartograms, contours, multivariate symbol, proportional symbol, predominance, and even bivariate mapping.

Even more exciting are some of the modern ways of engaging users with maps. Maps like predominance maps and smart maps provide visual storytelling, build trust, and engage users.

Many other types of maps might be considered for publications on special topics or to highlight interesting aspects of census results in regions of the country. Since tabulations of census data can be disaggregated by statistical variables such as age and sex, population, level of education, or urban/rural, GIS-based thematic maps for census dissemination can represent these variables geographically. In other words,

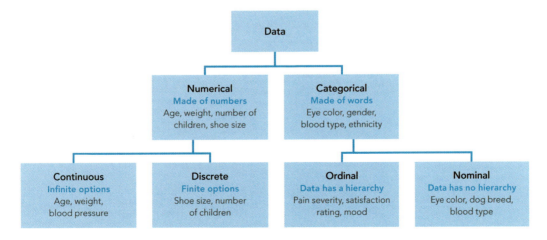

Figure 9.8. Types of data.

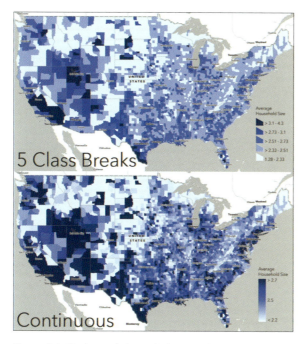

5 Class Breaks

Continuous

Figure 9.9. Traditional choropleth map. These two maps compare a five-class natural breaks map to a continuous ramp map using the 2018 average household size in each county.

a thematic map can show the spatial distribution of one or more specific data themes for standard or selected geographic areas.[34] While a thematic map may be univariate (dealing with one data attribute or one variable), bivariate (combining two data themes and modeling their correlations), or even multivariate (two or more datasets), the majority of thematic maps today are for a single purpose: showing the spatial distribution of one particular theme (e.g., population density map, land use map, and so on). However, innovation in technology is changing this and making it easier for the noncartographer to create beautiful maps easily.

The ability to map two attributes from your data within a single map in ArcGIS is possible today. Comparing two attributes or understanding relationships is important. A relationship map combines two data patterns to see whether those patterns converge geographically. Sometimes, pat-

Figure 9.10. Predominance map.

terns look similar; relationship mapping allows the combining of two map patterns to explore where patterns overlap or diverge. Combining two color ramps to show a combination of the patterns would yield a grid and map like this image.

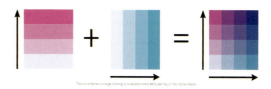

Figure 9.11. Color ramps combined to understand a pattern.

In figure 9.12, the corners convey a great deal of information. The purple values show high rates of both obesity and diabetes. The darkest pink values show the areas with a high amount of diabetic population but fewer people with obesity. The darkest blue values show where people are most likely to be obese but less likely to have diabetes.

This type of map is valuable, especially when exploring data. It can help users quickly assess whether two attributes might be related.

Traditionally known as bivariate choropleth maps, these maps have always been possible in ArcGIS but required a great deal of customization and forethought. Now, these maps can be created in minutes and easily modified while the user explores the data. Using color ramps inspired by Dr. Cynthia A. Brewer,[35] these bivariate choropleth

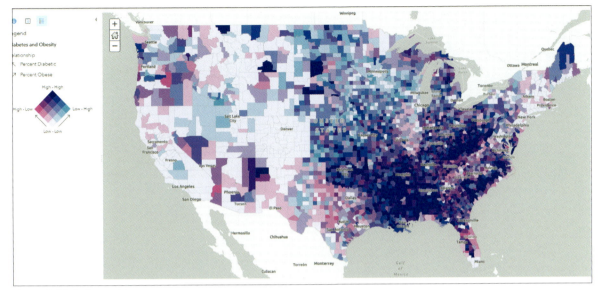

Figure 9.12. Relationship map.

maps show how two data patterns overlap (or don't overlap).[36]

Atlas products

An atlas traditionally is defined as a book of maps and charts. It is a way to assemble a collection of maps and show selected topics or themes of the census at the national and subnational levels. As a way of disseminating the census, many NSOs in the past would create a census atlas to provide a broader picture of the population in the country and the living conditions, economic conditions, geographical distribution, urban/rural spatial patterns, and disaggregation of data by gender and other categories. Generally, thematic maps in an atlas present census data at a country level, or major civil divisions (provinces or states), urbanized regions, large cities, and human settlements. However, for the big cities and urban agglomerations, the maps of the census atlas would present data at a lower geographic level—small areas such an aggregation of EAs (e.g., the US Census Atlas presents data at the "census tract" for the largest cities and metropolitan areas).

Historically, NSOs published census atlases, generally high-quality large-format maps in color, and in some cases do so today. However, with the use of GIS-based systems and the growth of the Internet, the traditional paper-based atlas is increasingly being replaced by an atlas in digital form that is published online. The production of a web-based atlas requires a team with subject matter expertise in data, mapping, and GIS skills. A digital atlas can include static or interactive images. A static digital atlas provides thematic maps, uploaded in various formats (e.g., PDF, BMP) to a website as a repository, allowing the user to view them as static web pages.

Online atlases today can be much more interactive and can serve multiple users, from GIS and statistics subject matter experts to citizens and civil society, academia, and research. Publishing digital maps and data with a modern GIS can allow users to produce custom maps of census data and indicators, constituting what is a dynamic or interactive census atlas. This interactive census atlas has the advantage of being able to serve the needs of users without GIS expertise, users who want more

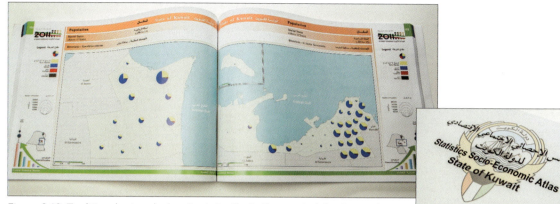

Figure 9.13. Traditional printed atlas: *Statistics Socio-Economic Atlas State of Kuwait.*

information than is possible with a prepackaged static census atlas. It may include digital boundary files, layers, and some major ratios, indices, or averages such as population densities appropriate for mapping already calculated; it may also provide tools for creating maps on the fly.

An interactive atlas should be oriented to a broad audience of users. It needs to be user-friendly, allowing users the option of choosing between different themes for display and presentation by geographic area and allowing for exploration of the data. More specifically, it needs to allow users to perform their own query of the database and dynamically customize the maps and views according to their needs. GIS query tools are often used to search for data in the database and display results in both map and tabular formats. An interactive atlas can also offer users various delineation options by selecting, for example, schools or health-care facilities in a district as seed points to create a report or map or to define *ad hoc* areas by drive time or hand-drawn polygon. GIS web maps provide an interactive experience. A GIS-based web atlas offers tools that enable users to view the data by interacting with the map. A user may pan a map in any direction, zoom in or out to view specific areas in more or less detail, pan to areas of interest, layer

different indicators on top of one another, create composite indicators, modify colors and symbols, and generate a range of charts and graphs.[37] An online atlas can also allow the user to change methods for data display—e.g., quantile or equal interval—and interact with or interrogate the data to better understand what is being represented using smart mapping and other new methods.

An interactive atlas in the past was a serious undertaking that required planning and understanding the data users. A multidisciplinary team with expertise in statistics, mapping, and usability were all important. Until recently, many NSOs, particularly those in developing countries, may not have had the in-house skills to perform this kind of work. Today, however, with advancements in technology, these types of projects are not only within reach but are obtainable for any organization. The tools have become simpler to use and understand and yet much more sophisticated in functionality.

Gazetteers

A gazetteer is a geographic index or dictionary that helps to identify the geographic location associated with a place name. Place names matter for a census, particularly for two main operations: enumeration and dissemination. At the enu-

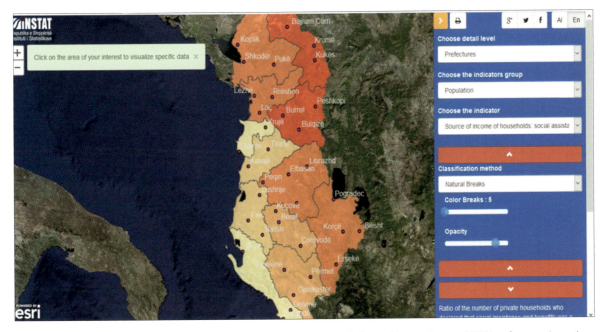

Figure 9.14. Sample online atlas: *Statistical Atlas of Albania* by INSTAT (https://instatgis.gov.al/#!/l/prefectures/population/prefpop1).

meration stage, one of the biggest challenges for the NSO is the multiplicity of names that enumerators find when identifying their EAs and collecting data. In addition to the names of cities, towns, villages, and settlements, the geographic names of reference features are needed, such as rivers, roads, forests, mountains, ridges, shoreline features, and so on. At the dissemination stage, standardized place names are needed for reporting and communicating census data about the right places. The UN has recommended that, for all census products, the NSO should "adopt a standardized approach to place names and codes" to "allow for easy comparability by data users."[38] In addition, place names have a cultural influence and the ability to present the heritage inherent in the place they identify. It is critically important to report census data with the correct name of a village or a settlement; an error may cause an emotional response if the place name is a cultural reference and the community has an emotional attachment to it.

The UN Group of Experts on Geographical Names (UNGEGN),[39] which addresses the national and international standardization of geographic names, has been promoting and encouraging member states to create their national gazetteers for standardized geographical names. UNGEGN defines a gazetteer as a "list of toponyms arranged in alphabetic or other sequential order, with an indication of their location and preferably including variant names, type of topographic feature and other defining or descriptive information."[40] The gazetteer is used in conjunction with a map as a reference document. However, geographic names are not only a part of a map, but they constitute an important communication tool reflecting the historical and cultural heritage of the country.

Many countries have their national gazetteers in print or online, and some have developed online searchable geographic name databases that have their gazetteer as part of their national atlas.[41] Gazetteers are generally made in the native language of the country, though names of places often differ between languages. For example, an Italian gazetteer may use the name Milano (in Italian) for that city, while in English or French the name used is Milan. In geographic name terminology, a word that describes a geographic place using native terminology (an internal name) is referred to as an *endonym*, while using non-native terminology (external name) is referred to as an *exonym*. In our example, Milano is an endonym, and Milan is an exonym. Therefore, some countries and even regional organizations have developed or are developing multilingual gazetteers.[42] Generally, national gazetteers are created by the National Commission on Toponymy or the NMA or any other national organization in charge of geographic names. It is therefore advisable that the NSO inquire about the existence of a national gazetteer within the country before proceeding with developing a gazetteer on its own. This avoids duplicating effort and allows the NSO to use the standardized geographic names used within the country and at the international level. As for the classification of the places by code, where the place code should be a UID for every level of geography, the NSO could adopt a similar approach used for the coding scheme of the national administrative hierarchy: "A popular method is to classify each level of geography using a two or three digit code. For nested geography, e.g. a district within a province within a region, the individual codes are concatenated together to form a unique national code for that geographic unit."[43] Place names are generally considered attributes of the geographic units of the GIS database.

In addition to using a gazetteer as a companion document with a map or for census dissemination, it can be used for disaster management and humanitarian purposes. A national gazetteer including geographic names and coordinates of population settlements, referred to as *P-codes* in the UN humanitarian community, can be paired with population estimates and used by humanitarian organizations for development and emergency response.[44]

ISO/TC 211 has developed an international standard, namely ISO 19112:2003, that defines the essential components of a gazetteer, enabling gazetteers to be constructed in a consistent manner. A gazetteer conforming to ISO 19112:2003 meets the following requirements.[45]

1. The gazetteer is described by at least the following four attributes:
   - Identifier
   - Territory of use (i.e., the geographic domain covered by the gazetteer)
   - Custodian (i.e., the organization responsible for maintaining the gazetteer)
   - The location types for which instances are recorded in the gazetteer
2. Optionally, the gazetteer may also be described by the following two attributes:
   - Scope (i.e., description of the location types in the gazetteer)
   - Coordinate reference system (i.e., name of the coordinate reference system used to describe positions of location instances in the gazetteer)
3. The gazetteer is versioned; a new version is created whenever any location instance is added, removed, or replaced with a new version of a location instance. The version information is included in the name attribute.
4. All location instances are recorded in the gazetteer and location instances conform to ISO 19113:2003.

Esri offers an online World Gazetteer as part of ArcGIS Online.

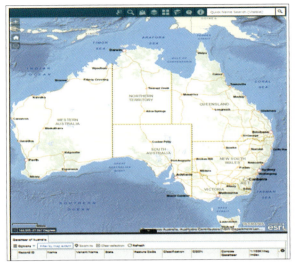

Figure 9.15. Gazetteer of Australia. The gazetteer provides information on the location and spelling of more than 370,000 geographic names across Australia and its external territories.[46]

Infographics

Infographics are visual graphic representations of information, data, or knowledge intended to present information quickly and clearly. Every NSO aims to present large amounts of census data in a compelling way so that users can have a quick and clear insight into the post-census state of population and housing conditions in their country. Data producers understand that the use of infographics is the most efficient way to create visual presentations and comparisons of census data that is otherwise hard to fully understand or interpret when shown in tabular form. Infographics are typically consumed by all categories of users who usually glance quickly at the data and information. Infographics can also be used to create dashboards (see figure 9.16), which are typically designed for a category of users, such as business experts who can perform simple analysis (such as ranking and filtering) or managers and decision-makers who want to have an overall high-level understanding of the data being reported.

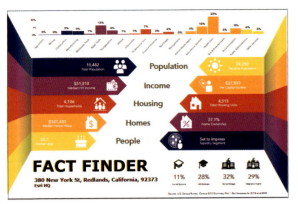

Figure 9.16. Example of an infographic in a dashboard.[47]

Furthermore, when census data is visualized with graphs, charts, tables, and graphics in combination with a map, the outcome is more telling and engaging, which can raise public awareness of and interest in the usefulness of census data. Given the web's graphical nature, the combination of web mapping and infographics fits well in the design and creation of attractive websites and portals. One of the major capabilities of a GIS is to enable users to create, display, and visualize information in different forms—maps, charts, graphs, and other graphics (such as histograms or scatter charts). GIS maps that are dynamically linked to charts, graphs, and other media allow greater exploration of spatial data and enable census data to come to life (see figure 9.17 of the UNSD SDG hub with infographics).

Figure 9.17. Infographics in new UNSD SDG website (www.sdg.org) showing the use of infographics to help understand SDGs using statistical data combined with geospatial data.

What many users would like to ideally have is business-like dashboards, with the ability to ask questions using GIS and then present the results and communicate them in a captivating and effective manner. In the past, the concern and challenge were how to create engaging graphics with maps in a balanced way that fits with cartographic presentation principles.[48] Today with modern GIS, this is no longer a challenge. The focus is instead on a successful communication of insightful information through compelling visualization and engaging stories.

According to Jim Herries, an applied geographer with Esri in Redlands, California: "The most valuable maps are information products. They are visually interesting the very first time you see them, and they reward you with additional information."

Smart mapping

This book has consistently stressed the importance of mapping for the census and the useful information that maps convey to the many users of census data. The book has also highlighted the importance of the dissemination of census data through thematic maps, atlases, map applications, web mapping, and infographics. In the past, this may have required classically trained cartographers with experience and a certain set of tools and knowledge. Today, maps are a commodity; every person is becoming a cartographer, zooming and panning, turning layers on and off to create the desired experience. In this context, the need is growing to create meaningful yet accurate maps easily. The challenge for the GIS community is how to create and deliver tools that everyone can use—even someone not familiar with GIS or statistical data. Users want to create interactive web maps that communicate meaningful stories from their data. This challenge has been met in part with the introduction of smart mapping by Esri.

The mission of smart mapping is to provide a kind of strong "cartographic artificial intelligence" that enables virtually anyone to visually analyze, create, and share professional quality maps in just a few minutes, with minimal mapping knowledge or software skills.[49] Put simply, smart mapping is about using computation and analysis to automate the creation of easy-to-use maps that are both beautiful and meaningful. Smart mapping, introduced by Esri in 2015, is a capability that is built into ArcGIS Online and ArcGIS Server technology, enabling users to create with just a few clicks the kind of map they want to create and the kind of story they want to tell. One of the critically important capabilities of smart mapping is the added ability to interactively explore data layers—for example, users can explore the range of values for median household income within each US block group in a map by interacting with the histogram of median income values. The ability to interact with the data behind each map layer provides deeper insights into the questions users are trying to answer.[50] Thus, smart mapping can bring census data to life, making it real, relevant, and meaningful to users.

Smart mapping can be performed in three simple steps:

1. Choose an attribute to show.
2. Select a drawing style.
3. Explore the options.

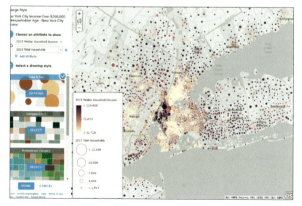

Figure 9.18. The simple steps in smart mapping.

Once a drawing style is chosen, users are given a set of options for customizing their map. Clicking the Options button allows users to explore their data and make additional cartographic changes. Depending on the attribute and data type, the following elements can be changed:

- The data classification method
- The symbol size
- The symbol color and shape
- The transparency of the features
- The rotation of the symbols

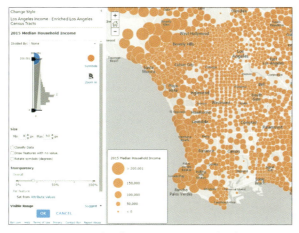

Figure 9.19. Example of smart mapping with a histogram.

A histogram is included to help users understand how the data is distributed. The x̄ symbol allows users to quickly see the average value within the attribute being used. By default, the map is set to highlight statistically significant high and low values. Dragging the handles or type in a specific value changes the representation of the data values. The classification can also be changed to use common methods: natural breaks, equal interval, quantile, and standard deviation.

Smart mapping will help make suggestions as the map is edited. For example, if the basemap is changed, smart mapping will automatically adjust the available color ramp options so the data will contrast well with the map's background.

Smart mapping will suggest options that work with a specific combination of data and attribute choices.

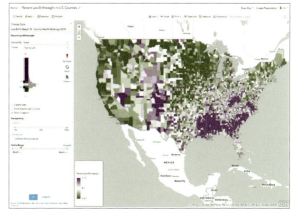

Figure 9.20. Example of above and below capability available in ArcGIS.[51]

As Esri looks to the future, it must continue to develop tools such as this because the layperson will become a "cartographer." It is incumbent on cartographers and GIS professionals to simplify the process and teach data users how to make accurate, compelling maps.

Mobile applications

There is no other technology that spread worldwide as rapidly as mobile technology. Mobile applications have proliferated, and today, there is an application or "app" for almost anything you can think of. The mobile device is now not only a phone but also a calculator, an alarm clock, a camera, a GPS device, a compass, a map, a calendar, a watch, a currency converter, a tape measure, and more. A mobile application is generally defined as a software application developed specifically for use on mobile devices, such as smartphones, tablets, and more. Mobile applications are distinguished from those running on desktop or laptop computers or on the web. There are generally three categories of mobile applications: (1) native apps that are developed specifically for a given platform (working with a specific operating system such as Android or iOS) and that can be accessed only from the dedicated application store (such as Google® Play or Apple's App Store), taking full advantage of all the device features; (2) web-based apps that refer to the mobile apps that run in mobile web browsers rather than directly on the mobile device; and (3) hybrid apps that combine elements of both native and web apps.[52]

What is obvious about the mobile app development trends is that location-based services, with mapping and GPS capabilities, are now mainstream. This development is made possible by the fact that nearly all smartphones come with GPS and Bluetooth low-energy capabilities to provide applications with location-based services (LBS). These LBS are positioned to grow owing to their increasing popularity not only for weather, navigation and routing, tracking, and finding the nearest store or restaurant, but especially for location-based offers, advertisements, and services—which even offer deals to app users depending on their location. This mapping revolution has been underway for some time, from the early days of MapQuest® and Microsoft Earth to Google Maps, Bing, Yahoo!®, and Apple Maps® today. The industry has paved the way for mobile mapping apps. Location technology is being applied in numerous ways today, and yet we have probably just begun to scratch the surface.

Developers can create apps in several different ways. Traditionally, developers might build an app from scratch, which takes time and requires expertise. Today, the industry is changing and moving toward toolkits that help develop apps quickly. AppStudio for ArcGIS® is a good example of this and a groundbreaking tool in the GIS app revolution. It allows users to convert their maps into beautiful, consumer-friendly mobile apps ready for Android, iOS, Windows, Mac OS X, and Linux. It also allows users to publish the maps using their own brand to all popular app stores; no developer skills are required.

One great example is the winner of the AppStudio for ArcGIS "App Challenge." In a disaster, Evacu8® helps locate, check, and preregister to evacuation centers prior to arriving. This type of application brings data and maps together in a useful tool for citizens and agencies alike. Apps allow us to deliver the experience that users need—with authoritative data, thereby enhancing decision-making.

The following case study is an example of architecture leveraging modern GIS technologies. For more information, see the Esri 2015 white paper *Modernization of National Statistical Organization (NSO) Business Processes Using GIS* available at https://www.esri.com/library/whitepapers/modernization-national-statistical-organization-business-processes.pdf.

| 1. Write an App | 2. Test on Devices | 3. Generate Installation Files | 4. Distribute in the Enterprise, or Publish to App Store |

Figure 9.21. Custom apps for the enterprise.[53]

Case study: Nepal

The Government of Nepal's Central Bureau of Statistics (CBS) provides government agencies data for planning, policy-making, and economic growth measurements. Using household surveys and national census methods to collect data, CBS assesses Nepal's socioeconomic conditions and measures economic growth. Within the government services, the bureau is a technology leader. It investigates new technologies to improve methods for more scientific and reliable data collection, processing, and analysis.

In 2018, CBS conducted its first economic census to count all entrepreneurial units in the country. The information provides the government insight into the status and financial aspects of the nation's enterprise business activities. In addition, the census establishes a baseline for measuring business growth and gives entrepreneurs intelligence for creating better business strategies.

CBS asked its GIS team to produce enumerator area (EA) maps for the entire country. The team, consisting of two GIS professionals, faced multiple challenges. GIS data about the country is scarce. In urban areas, landscapes rapidly change. Internet connections are not stable and power outages are common. Because Nepal's street systems are not built on a grid, defining specific EAs is complicated. The team could not reuse the EAs outlined in the previous census because new government leaders had changed administrative boundaries. What's more, streets do not have names, making it difficult for enumerators to navigate streets.

The team used ArcGIS to complete the task. To edit enumeration boundaries, they used the platform's basemaps and satellite imagery for urban areas. They also accessed OpenStreetMap data, which contains content contributed by users from around the world. The interface map is written in the country's official language and script, Nepali. The team chose ArcGIS Pro to output maps because of its high-performance capability.

Although Nepal's Internet infrastructure is improving, it is not yet reliable for large projects. When the connection is working, the team downloads geospatial data, such as Esri's satellite imagery, and performs editing tasks offline. Because administrative boundaries tend to change, CBS uses statistics software to process attribute values. Using these values, ArcGIS dissolves and merges old boundary polygons to update the boundaries.

Using ArcGIS Online, the GIS team built a web application that helps enumerators use their tablets in the field to navigate through mazes of nameless streets. The app identifies EAs by area number and lays out a route to the location.

During the spring, CBS conducted Nepal's National Economic Census 2018 in about six weeks. The GIS team used imagery and open content to create enumerator maps for the country. It also built mobile apps that helped enumerators navigate locations and enabled them to survey businesses throughout the country.

Web-based mapping

In this era of GIS, the Internet, the cloud, open data, and social media, census data dissemination and communication have become even more important and challenging. The web lends itself as a key medium to the dissemination of census data, allowing all standard geographic products and major tabular data to be disseminated to a wider audience. Web-based mapping has simplified access and allows us to easily discover, use, make, and share maps and data with others. It is a user-oriented approach *par excellence*, aiming to respond to the high expectation of "anywhere, anytime, any device" access.

NSOs are increasingly making census data available via the Internet with web apps, maps, and various information products. Some country experiences with the use of web-based mapping for census data dissemination clearly show the benefits of web dissemination. This can be summarized as: (1) improved timeliness; (2) increased accessibility; (3) broader reach; (4) increased utilization; and (5) increased awareness of the value of census statistics. NSOs opting for web-based dissemination must consider the same concepts as in the past when publishing via paper or simple CSV files but also must consider the diversity of users and experience with data and user needs. Checking the quality of census data before publishing the results continues to be the priority. However, we should also consider the users and their level of experience with data. We see increased user expectations and the need to enhance accessibility and discoverability as well as the need for clear metadata. NSOs must also consider the need for a mechanism to respond to queries from users, who will have questions on the data—for example, data aggregation and disaggregation methods, margin of error and more—and will require regular interaction over time to adjust to these new methods.

Every NSO has an official website which is used to provide information about the NSO's activities and conventional statistical indicators. In some countries, the website also provides census data to the public, civil society, academia, researchers, and developers. Often, the NSO will dedicate a specific website for the census data dissemination itself. What varies from one country to another is the scope of the census products provided and the level of sophistication of the tools, particularly web maps and apps, offering the users access to the data.

As stated previously, the use of the web as a dissemination medium for maps has been popularized by Google Maps and other mapping applications such as Bing Maps. This represented a major advancement in the awareness of geography and underscored the importance of spatial thinking. In addition, it allowed for major advancement and innovative approaches in generating, publishing, and delivering maps and data in a much more user-friendly way.

The other major development has been in APIs, which enables users and developers to create custom applications.[54] An API is a set of functions, procedures, methods, or classes used by computer programs to request services from the operating system. Computer programmers use APIs to make applications.

ArcGIS provides tools for app builders and developers alike such as Web AppBuilder for ArcGIS. This is an intuitive what-you-see-is-what-you-get (WYSIWYG) application that allows one to build 2D and 3D web apps without writing a single line of code. It includes powerful tools to configure fully featured HTML apps. As the map and tools are added, they can be seen in the app and used right away.

Maps can be incorporated in apps to add functionality in many ways. For example, a map

Figure 9.22. Kuwait Finder and Kuwait Stats apps.

can be added to a dashboard app that displays key indicators for the area of interest, or to a time-series app that lets users cycle through data from past surveys.

APIs provide new ways to access and disseminate data, including providing access to census data for application developers both inside and outside the census organization.[55] GIS-based APIs are designed to manage data for its delivery to a web browser client from a GIS server. Some NSOs have already begun using these methods of data dissemination to deliver their census data directly from their GIS database.

Another popular idea is that of the mashup, a web application that combines data from more than one source into a single integrated tool. An example of a mashup is the use of data from Google Maps to add location information to statistical data, thereby creating a new and distinct map that was not originally provided by either source. Another example would be to overlay life expectancy at birth (for both sexes) from one source (UNdata®) over the world map from Google Maps. In figure 9.23, World Bank data that displays the proportion of national parliament seats held by women at the country level from 2012 to 2015 is overlaid on an Esri basemap. According to Webopedia, "this capability to mix and match data and applications from multiple sources into one dynamic entity is considered by many to represent the promise of the Web service standard . . . ."[56] Mashups exemplify a captivating way to integrate statistical and geospatial information.

Figure 9.23. Example of a mashup using data from World Bank on national parliament seats held by women overlaid on an Esri basemap.

As mentioned in chapter 6, there are international standards for web-based mapping services—for example, a Web Map Service (WMS) that has been developed by the OGC and adopted by the ISO as a standard protocol for serving georeferenced map images over the Internet that are generated by a map server using data from a GIS database. WMS is a widely supported format for maps and GIS data accessed via the Internet and loaded client side into GIS software. Most GIS software supports WMS. Other open standards such as Web Feature Service (WFS) and Web Coverage Service (WCS) also support web-based data, services, and systems interoperability.

As we think about web-based mapping for census data dissemination, in the past the implementation of a comprehensive dissemination system would have required substantial human resources with skills in web design, GIS, and mapping. Today, with new tools and advancements in technology, this is becoming simpler and more manageable for the NSO. It still requires important work to be carried out to make census products accessible, share methods and metadata, and interact with users. An additional issue for some countries is the limited accessibility of tools in areas with limited connectivity or a low bandwidth.

Findings of the evaluation of the 2010 Round of Censuses have shown that the use of the Internet to disseminate static web pages was well established, but only half of the countries or areas were planning to disseminate interactive online databases, making it possible for users to make their own requests.[iv] It was also found that the use of GIS web-based mapping tools was growing, and half of the countries expressed intentions to move ahead in this domain.[57] Today, this trend has been confirmed, and the use of GIS web-based tools is the goal for all countries (see figure 9.24). In summary, the use of GIS benefits all the stages of the census.

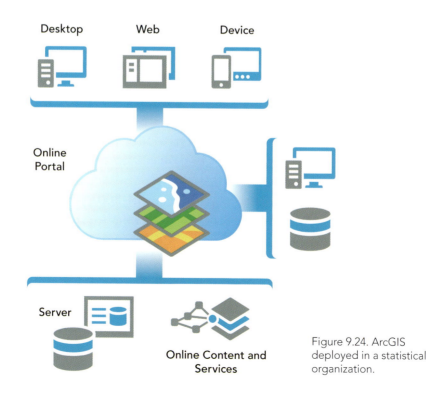

Figure 9.24. ArcGIS deployed in a statistical organization.

Case study: Canada

Statistics Canada (StatCan) conducts a census every five years and runs approximately 350 active surveys on nearly all aspects of Canadian life. StatCan has made census data easier to view and understand through online interactive maps and dashboards. Census statistical information provides elected representatives, businesses, unions, nonprofit organizations, and citizens with a solid foundation for informed decision-making.

Beginning with the 2001 Census of Population, StatCan introduced new ways to view census data with a series of data visualization tools, such as age pyramids. In 2011, the agency introduced the Focus on Geography Series. This tool presented data as tables, texts and maps that showed population, age and sex, language, etc. Canadians could also see how the population had changed over time. By the 2016 Census, StatCan had rolled out more advanced data visualization tools. These tools included a variety of interactive charts and a new statistical dashboard—the Census Program Data Viewer (CPDV), an advanced web-based data visualization tool.

The CPDV makes data easier to interpret. It shows basic geographic and sociodemographic data categorized by statistical indicators. Users can easily find statistical information about a geographic location using the thematic map. At a glance, users can compare statistical values for different locations and identify relationships between indicators.

The CPDV helps people answer fundamental questions related to places in Canada, including the following:

- What are the top five ethnic origins reported in each of the census metropolitan areas of Montréal, Ottawa–Gatineau, Toronto, Calgary, and Vancouver?
- What are the top ten municipalities where a language other than English or French is spoken most often at home?
- How does the average age for my municipality compare with that for my province, my territory or the nation?
- Is there a relationship between level of education and average income?

The CPDV is built using ArcGIS and Geocortex software. The platform's dashboard technology was used to feature a map that could display different levels of geography to show Canada's diversity at general and more detailed levels.

The platform has met StatCan's goals: it displays more than 5,000 geographic locations in a single chart and includes charting indicators that have extreme outliers (e.g., population changes). Corporate formatting standards can be applied to data so that the data is usable across the agency. The dashboard fits into the web template designed by the Government of Canada.

The result is shown in figure 1.

The simplicity of the user experience conceals design complexities that are managed behind the scenes. For instance, developers followed an iterative process to make corrective changes as they encountered issues. They created a new data model that supported the efficient mapping and charting of an unlimited number of indicators.

For the 2016 Census, StatCan mapped approximately 100 indicators at seven different levels of geography, ranging from provinces and territories to cities and neighborhoods. The CPDV generated dynamic layers by joining indicator data to spatial features. Without geographic information system automation, StatCan staff would have had to build 700 individual data layers. Because of these dynamic layers, the CPDV is capable of supporting approximately 5,000 users viewing the dashboard at any one time. In addition to the mapped indicators, an extra 400 indicators are used to generate charts.

As a member of the United Nations Statistical Commission, StatCan endorses the Fundamental Principles of Official Statistics, and built its census system accordingly. The agency also designed the CPDV to meet all Government of Canada standards for accessibility, interoperability, security and web usability. Its adaptive design enables users to view data on desktops, tablets, and smartphones.

The CPDV, along with other data visualization tools, provides new ways to visually communicate statistical information and engage data users. The system demonstrates the importance of statistics in the economic and social development of Canada.

Figure 1. Statistics Canada's Census Program Data Viewer is a dashboard that shows statistical indicators and locations.

References

i. UNSD launched this research exercise to test a data hub with a pilot group of fourteen countries representing all the regions of the world, namely Brazil, Colombia, Ireland, Kenya, Mexico, Morocco, Palestine, the Philippines, South Africa, Qatar, Senegal, Tanzania, UAE, and the United Kingdom. See details in "A Data Hub for the Sustainable Development Goals" in the Spring 2018 issue of *ArcNews* at http://www.esri.com/esri-news/arcnews/spring18articles/a-data-hub-for-the-sustainable-development-goals.

ii. The UN *Principles and Recommendations* have also recommended that "all tabulations should include the following metadata or references to where this information can be obtained: census questions; reasons why they are asked; conceptual definitions (census dictionary); geographic hierarchies used; changes since the previous census with regard to content, operational methods or geographic boundaries; and quality indicators such as coverage rates and item non-response. . . . If a long-form sample is used in the census, metadata should also provide information on the sampling variability of the results. When the census tabulations include suppressed data cells due to small numbers, the metadata should also include a methodological note on the rules and methods of suppression." The UN document also states that the type of metadata items includes population groups included, source of statistics (type of census), type of population count, classifications, definitions of urban/rural, duration of residence, etc.

iii. The International Household Survey Network (IHSN) Microdata Management Toolkit uses the DDI metadata standard.

iv. For example, South America appeared to be keeping abreast with the technological advances in this domain as all the nine responding countries plan to offer online databases. In Africa, where the access to high-speed Internet was still limited, only one third of the countries intended to develop such interactive online databases. See *The 2010 Round of Population and Housing Censuses in the World* by Jean-Michel Durr.

Notes

1. See p. 1.206 in the UN's *Principles and Recommendations for Population and Housing Censuses*, rev. 2. ST/ESA/STAT/SER.M/67/Rev.2. Available at https://unstats.un.org/unsd/demographic-social/Standards-and-Methods/files/Principles_and_Recommendations/Population-and-Housing-Censuses/Series_M67Rev2-E.pdf.

2. An example is Statistics Canada.

3. See the UN *Principles and Recommendations for Population and Housing Censuses*, rev. 3. ST/ESA/STAT/SER.M/67/Rev.3. Available at https://unstats.un.org/unsd/publication/seriesM/Series_M67Rev3en.pdf.

4. See the UNSD *Handbook on the Management of Population and Housing Censuses*, rev. 2. Available at https://unstats.un.org/unsd/publication/seriesF/Series_F83Rev2en.pdf.

5. See the UN Economic and Social Council's report *National Statistical and Geographical Institute of Brazil: Global Geographic Information Management*. Available at https://unstats.un.org/unsd/statcom/41st-session/documents/2010-13-Brazil-GGIM-E.pdf

6. Proponents of the grid method would argue that even in the absence of a point-based statistical data as a source data for statistical grids, grids might be produced from disaggregated larger statistical geographies using auxiliary information (see the in-depth review of developing geospatial information services based on official statistics—Note by the United Kingdom Office for National Statistics, ECE/CES/2016/7).

7. See the presentation slides for "The UN-GGIM Challenge to Develop Integrated Core Datasets" at http://ggim.un.org/meetings/2015-2nd_Mtg_EG-ISGI-Portugal/documents/Tim_Trainor_Grid_v_admin_Lisbon_2015.pdf.

8. See the GSGF principles in the "What is the GSGF?" box in chapter 2.

9. See the UN-EG-ISGI Second Meeting Report. Available at http://ggim.un.org/meetings/2015-2nd_Mtg_EG-ISGI-Portugal/documents/EG-ISGI-Second%20Meeting-Summary-.pdf.

10. See "The UN-GGIM Challenge."

11. See the in-depth review of developing geospatial information services based on official statistics—Note by the United Kingdom Office for National Statistics (ECE/CES/2016/7).

12. For instance, the New Zealand threshold is set at "meshblocks," which average 100 people, while UK output areas are at least 100 persons and forty households (average size is 300 persons and 125 households). See the Note by the United Kingdom Office for National Statistics.

13. For the most up-to-date information on ArcGIS security, see the ArcGIS Trust Center at https://doc.arcgis.com/en/trust/documents. The site provides white papers on security, implementation patterns with ArcGIS, mobile applications, and detailed security answers relative to ArcGIS Online for information security professionals.

14. See the World Bank Open Government Data Toolkit at http://opendatatoolkit.worldbank.org/en.

15. See the Cape Town Global Action plan at https://unstats.un.org/sdgs/hlg/Cape-Town-Global-Action-Plan.

16. See the UNSD forty-eighth Session Statistical Commission Friday Seminar on emerging issues at https://unstats.un.org/unsd/statcom/48th-session/side-events/documents/20170303-1M-Stefan-Schweinfest.pdf.

17. The OGP, initially launched in 2011, has grown from eight participating countries to seventy-five in 2017. The OGP was established to bring governments and civil societies working together to develop and implement open data reforms.

18. See *Future Trends in Geospatial Information Management: The Five to Ten Year Vision*. Available at http://ggim.un.org/documents/UN-GGIM-Future-trends_Second%20edition.pdf.

19. See *African Data Consensus*. Available at https://www.uneca.org/sites/default/files/PageAttachments/final_adc_-_english.pdf.

20. Included with ArcGIS Online, ArcGIS® Open Data lets users instantly unlock their data for the public in just a few clicks.

21. See *An Open Data Approach That Works* at http://www.esri.com/library/brochures/pdfs/open-data-government.pdf. Also see *ArcGIS: An Open Platform for Innovation* at https://www.esri.com/~/media/00C24660087A4EFB9F069148017EABD4.pdf.

22. See Census 2016 Open Data Site, Ordnance Survey Ireland: "On this site, Census 2016 datasets [from Central Statistics Office (CSO) Ireland] have been combined with Ordnance Survey Ireland's (OSi) official boundary data as part of a collaborative project between the Central Statistics Office (CSO) and OSi to link geography and statistics. . . . [This site] was created to promote the use of Geography and Statistics to support evidence based decision making across the Irish Public Sector and among Civil Society. This site and the data it presents are Open, Public and Free to Use." Available at http://census2016.geohive.ie. See also the Census 2016 Ireland case study in chapter 8.

23. For example, we may be working with census data for a country in which the data is in a table, CSV, Microsoft Excel file, Microsoft Access database table, or other geospatial format. To map this data with ArcGIS software, we need to merge it with a shapefile containing boundaries of census tracts. The operation is known as a *table join*.

24. Convert raster to a CSV values and latitude–longitude based on raster value in ArcGIS.

25. According to the World Bank Open Data Toolkit: "Open Data catalogues typically make each dataset available as a unique and permanent URL, which makes it possible to cite and link to the data directly."

26. See also the Australian Bureau of Statistics's *1500.0 - A Guide for Using Statistics for Evidence Based Policy, 2010*. Available at http://www.abs.gov.au/ausstats/abs@.nsf/lookup/1500.0chapter92010.

27. See http://www.ddialliance.org.

28. See the Open Data Foundation's *The Data Documentation Initiative (DDI): An Introduction for National Statistical Institutes*. Available at http://odaf.org/papers/DDI_Intro_forNSIs.pdf.

29. See *UN-GGIM Future Trends*, second ed.

30. See the "What is the GSGF?" box in chapter 2.

31. See the 2012 Esri white paper *What is GIS?* Available at http://www.esri.com/library/bestpractices/what-is-gis.pdf.

32. The International Cartographic Association has developed the following definition of geographic maps: "A map is a symbolised image of geographical reality, representing selected features or characteristics, resulting from the creative effort of its author's execution of choices, and is designed for use when spatial relationships are of primary relevance."

33. See the Pennsylvania State University's College of Earth and Mineral Sciences article *Mapping Our Changing World: 3.2 Thematic Maps*. Available at https://www.e-education.psu.edu/geog160/c3_p14.html.

34. In 1854, John Snow, a London doctor, created the first thematic map used for problem analysis when he mapped the spread of cholera throughout the city.

35. Dr. Brewer is professor of geography at Pennsylvania State University and a renowned expert in color theory in cartography.

36. To learn more about this mapping style and to see examples, see the ArcGIS Blog articles *How to Make a Relationship Map in ArcGIS Online (https://www.esri.com/arcgis-blog/products/arcgis-online/mapping/how-to-make-a-relationship-map-in-arcgis-online) and What Is a Relationship Map?* (https://www.esri.com/arcgis-blog/products/arcgis-online/mapping/what-is-a-relationship-map).

37. See the Esri *ArcUser®* article "Making Census Data More Useful." Available at http://www.esri.com/esri-news/arcuser/summer-2013/making-census-data-more-useful.

38. See the UN's *Handbook on the Management of Population and Housing Censuses* rev. 2. Available at https://unstats.un.org/unsd/publication/seriesF/Series_F83Rev2en.pdf.

39. See details about UNGEGN at https://unstats.un.org/unsd/geoinfo/UNGEGN/geonames.html.

40. See the UN's *Glossary of Terms for the Standardization of Geographical Names*. Available at https://unstats.un.org/unsd/geoinfo/UNGEGN/docs/pdf/Glossary_of_terms_revised.pdf.

41. Consider the case of Sweden, *National Atlas of Sweden—The Swedish Gazetteer* at http://www.sna.se/gazetteer.html.

42. "A multi-lingual gazetteer (service) shall most probably be established as a part of INSPIRE." Available at http://inspire.ec.europa.eu/theme/gn.

43. See the UN's *Handbook on Census Management*, rev. 2.

44. See the UN's *Handbook on Geospatial Infrastructure in Support of Census Activities*. Available at https://unstats.un.org/unsd/demographic/standmeth/handbooks/series_f103en.pdf.

45. See details at https://www.iso.org/standard/26017.html.

46. See http://www.ga.gov.au/placename.

47. See http://mediamaps.esri.com/Infographics/SideBanners.html to interact with this example.

48. See the Esri *ArcUser* article "Make Maps People Want to Look At," available at http://www.esri.com/news/arcuser/0112/make-maps-people-want-to-look-at.html.

49. See the book *The ArcGIS® Book, Second Edition: 10 Big Ideas about Applying The Science of Where™* from Esri Press.

50. See *The ArcGIS Book*.

51. See https://www.esri.com/arcgis-blog/products/arcgis-online/mapping/better-breaks-define-your-maps-purpose for details.

52. See the Nielsen Norman Group article "Mobile: Native Apps, Web Apps, and Hybrid Apps," available at https://www.nngroup.com/articles/mobile-native-apps.

53. See https://appstudio.arcgis.com for details.

54. Some depict this trend as a move from maps to apps.

55. See, for example, the US Census Bureau's API at http://www.census.gov/developers (reported in the UN's *Handbook on Census Management*).

56. See https://www.webopedia.com/TERM/M/mash_up.html.

57. See *The 2010 Round of Population and Housing Censuses in the World* from Jean-Michel Durr. Available at http://jmstat.com/publications/SINAPE%202010.pdf.

Chapter 10
Marketing geographic products and data

Marketing communication plans

The previous chapter stressed the critical importance of developing a census dissemination strategy and its implementation through a dissemination program to promote the use and benefit of census data. A key component of the dissemination program is the marketing of census data and products. This component requires a dissemination data policy that guides the NSO on any data pricing, data formats, and measures to protect data privacy. The organization also needs to consider methods in which to conduct a marketing campaign either alone or with possible partners. Generally, NSOs initiate communications activities in the buildup to and execution of the census but begin with intense follow-up communications once the enumeration has been completed. In this chapter, we will focus on the post-enumeration promotion and marketing of census products as part of the dissemination phase activities and how GIS can add value.

Census marketing activities aim to promote to and inform a wide range of potential users about the availability and access of census data and products. The ultimate objective is to raise awareness about the importance of census and statistical data. A marketing campaign generally focuses on three main elements: identifying the target audience to whom census products are marketed; choosing media channels; and developing the messages to best engage the community.

We also need to consider which media and mode will be needed to help us best present statistical information and facilitate its access, including the use of the data. We need to understand the market demand for the type of data that is most requested and the level of geography, as well as access (apps, maps, web, and mobile).

Figure 10.1. Audience, media, and message are critical factors in a marketing campaign.

All products that are developed must also meet brand standards and require the supporting systems that are appropriate for the selected channels of communication.

Most statistical agencies have a marketing unit in charge of promoting census products, communicating with the media, and maintaining a relationship with the data user community. Typically, the data user community consists of citizens, civil society, academia, research organizations, government agencies, and the private sector, each with their own unique needs. The marketing unit must promote census data and products in a user-friendly way, increasingly with a compelling message,[1] so that the user community can be engaged and encouraged to use statistics. This unit manages and conducts communication campaigns that raise the profile of the census and the NSO itself,[2] and consequently improves public awareness of the importance and relevance of statistics in general.

An NSO's marketing units usually carry out promotional activities using many different forms of media, including traditional print outlets such as magazines, newspapers, or newsletters; broadcast media such as radio or television; websites; blogs; and newer outlets such as YouTube® or Twitter®. They will conduct public advertising campaigns (including in schools) and run promotional events and national and interna-

2020 US Census—future data dissemination and integrated communication plan

Excerpted from the US Census Bureau, *The Future of Data Dissemination.*[3]

- The focus is on user-centric capabilities and dissemination as a business function with a major information technology component.
- An enterprise-level dissemination system, the Center for Enterprise Dissemination Services and Consumer Innovation (CEDSCI), will provide access to prepackaged data products via an interactive website. Data users will have access to the prepackaged data products, APIs, and metadata documentation. This system replaces the previous dissemination system, known as American FactFinder.
- For digital advertising, the approach will determine the appropriate mix of display, search, video, social, mobile, email, text messaging, and audio streaming advertising. Especially on the local level, digital advertising—more than any other medium—can deliver tailored messaging to target audiences and can be optimized based on real-time results.
- Based on insights from campaign research, self-response propensities, and previous successes working with media, the US Census Bureau will bring to life the stories that generate interest in the census process and raise awareness about the mission. Storylines will be organized around distinct themes; for example, one could explore the value of the census to local neighborhoods, and another could make the value of census data clear to the news media. This approach will be designed to demonstrate the relevance of Census Bureau data to citizens' daily lives, connecting messages and calls to action with trending topics, relevant news cycles, and the previous reporting of targeted journalists.

tional statistical days to raise awareness. Products needed to support these efforts may include posters, press releases, reports, audio-video broadcasts, web applications, maps, atlases, and more. Market research in support of the development of census products is critically important. Organizations typically look to better understand or segment their users to tailor the census products to their different demands and needs, and then follow up the promotional activities to evaluate their impact and adjust accordingly.

As stressed in chapter 9, in line with UN recommendations, the country's dissemination plan should cover the costs of the full range of dissemination activities, including costs associated with marketing and ongoing support of all census products through the complete census cycle.[4] It is important to remember that census data marketing and dissemination are typically carried out with public funding, as are all costs of planning, operations, and census data collection. Some NSOs may offer free access and opt not to sell census products with any kind of profit, while others may have a profit recovery policy. Opting for a user-centric dissemination strategy with the view of dissemination itself as a business function[5] may require partnerships with other data producers—for example, partnering with agencies such as mapping, environmental, or health ministries that are also data providers (see the Census 2016 Ireland case study in chapter 8).

Modern GIS make it possible today to serve the data needs of many different types of users, including the dissemination of small-area statistical data disaggregated at various levels of geography.

Since the 2010 Round of Censuses, major developments in the landscape of marketing and advertising have occurred and are important to consider. Two key developments are the ubiquity of mobile and web-based technologies and the strong demand for location-based information. A third trend to consider is the development of social media platforms that communicate compelling messages and stories about the census and reach out to various users and members of the media.

The use of online social media to engage audiences continues to rise, competing with the traditional channels of communication. For example, a recent Pew Research Center report about today's digital news media landscape found that "digital news and social media continue to grow, with mobile devices rapidly becoming one of the most common ways for Americans to get news. . . . More than eight-in-ten US adults (85%) now get news on a mobile device, up from 72% in 2016."[6] Furthermore, marketing and social research studies have shown that among societal changes, owing to the impact of the pervasive use of mobile devices and social media, today's consumers are self-sufficient and more prone to research a brand on their own. Social influencers have taken on a more prominent role in the marketing strategies of brands and in effectively getting products and messages out to the consumers, particularly among millennials.

Consequently, it is essential that NSOs emphasize the use of web-based and mobile tools and leverage the location component of the data collected. Maps, applications, and other information products need to be optimized for mobile and online use.

The list of potential products that the NSO should consider publishing as covered in the previous chapter includes reference maps, dynamic and static atlases, gazetteers, thematic maps, map applications, smart maps, and story maps. These products all need to be marketed

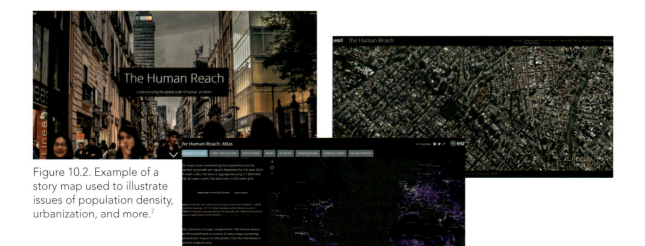

Figure 10.2. Example of a story map used to illustrate issues of population density, urbanization, and more.[7]

to the appropriate audience. A modern GIS aids in the marketing of these different types of products. By using a map services–based approach, NSOs can produce and share products with different users with varying needs in a more cost-effective manner.

New tools such as story maps can also be used as effective marketing tools to educate the public, other government agencies, researchers, and data users from all sectors.

Esri® Story Maps allow for combining authoritative maps with narrative text, images, and multimedia content. These tools make it easy to harness the power of maps and geography to tell a story to data users from all sectors. To use story maps effectively, consider, as with any information product, the audience, user experience, maps needed, and ease of use. One should avoid jargon and use easily understood language. It's not about "dumbing down"; it's about striving for clarity and simplicity. The more nonessential elements are removed, the more effectively the story is conveyed. Remember that attention spans are short in the digital age.

Once a story map is finished, it can be shared either publicly or with restricted access to allow only certain people in the organization to view it. After user restrictions are applied, the story map can be linked to or embedded in an organization's website. Story map authors can write a blog post about it, share it on social media, and so on.

With respect to location-based information, the building and developing of a full, digital GIS-based census database allows the creation of census geographic products. This data and the products produced from it can be used by many different industries, such as retail, financial services, manufacturing, and health care. In fact, marketing data to these industries can be made easier via web and mobile GIS-based applications and APIs. For example, a health-care organization may want to consume information on income, education, and average family size to build its own application for serving its customers. By marketing not only the data but new means of access to this information (via APIs), NSOs can increase the use and demand for census data overall. Many agencies are looking at commoditizing data and building spatially enabled government services. By building this type of system, we bring together data producers and consumers and create a network.

Census data has been used for years in market research, especially for demographic segmentation, understanding customers, market expansion opportunities, and attracting customers to stores or purchasing online. By allowing users to generate reports and data around a specific location while still protecting privacy and confidentiality, you are creating increased market demand and affecting the economy. Integrating geographic and demographic information with business data provides insights, otherwise hidden, for business intelligence solutions. This has been labeled *location intelligence*, considered by some a new disruptive technology.[8]

Companies from many sectors rely on GIS technology to help them understand market potential and customer needs, including major brands such as Starbucks®, Walmart®, Cirque du Soleil®, Petco®, and Chick-fil-A®[9] as well as smaller retailers such as Lululemon Athletica®. By using demographic data with their own internal customer data, these organizations can make better business decisions, making a positive impact on the local economy.

Some statistical agencies are even beginning to offer applications to help small-business owners and economic developers alike to easily gain access to data, thereby affecting local economies.

The US Census application Census Business Builder (CBB) was created specifically to make census data available to these users in an easy-to-use web-based application. The CBB Small Business Edition allows individual small-business owners to access key data needed to make smart decisions, including demographic and socioeconomic indicators, helping them understand the market demand.

The US Census Bureau also makes this data available for regional economic developers via its Regional Analyst Edition (see https://cbb.census.gov/rae/#).

Traditional publication and advertising methods will continue to be used, but with the significant increase in electronic dissemination and digital advertising and marketing, we expect to see the decrease in hard-copy publications to continue. This trend means that census products will gain use by focusing on web, mobile, infographics

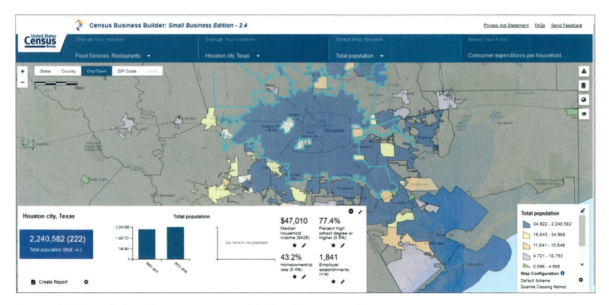

Figure 10.3. Example from Census Business Builder Small Business Edition.

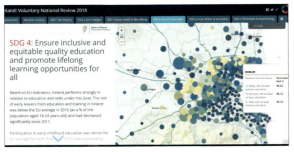

Figure 10.4. CSO Ireland story map. *Ireland: Voluntary National Review 2018* is a report on various SDG indicators.

and animated graphics, interactive web-based smart mapping, and other apps. Statistical data enriched with location data offers visual patterns and insights and helps tell stories that mainstream viewers can benefit from.

Notes

1. For example, the US Census Bureau used the expression "It's in our hands" as the key message of its 2010 Census Integrated Communications Campaign, and Statistics South Africa used "The South Africa I know, the home I understand" for its 2011 Census user segmentation and preparation of products.

2. For example, we can cite the use of SMS to announce census results in Kenya, the use of PDAs for data collection in Cape Verde, and the use of smartphones to collect point-based data in Poland. These innovative practices during the 2010 Round of Censuses have contributed to the visibility and reputation of the corresponding NSOs and their countries.

3. US Census Bureau sources: *The Future of Data Dissemination*, available at https://www2.census.gov/about/partners/sdc/events/steering-committee/2015-04/2015-blash.pdf; *2020 Census Integrated Communications Plan* version 1.0, available at https://www2.census.gov/programs-surveys/decennial/2020/program-management/planning-docs/2020_integrated_COM_plan.pdf.

4. See the UN *Handbook on the Management of Population and Housing Censuses* rev. 2. Available at https://unstats.un.org/unsd/publication/seriesF/Series_F83Rev2en.pdf.

5. See the US Census Bureau white paper *The Future of Data Dissemination*, available at https://www2.census.gov/about/partners/sdc/events/steering-committee/2015-04/2015-blash.pdf.

6. See the Pew Research report "Key Trends in Social and Digital News Media," available at http://www.pewresearch.org/fact-tank/2017/10/04/key-trends-in-social-and-digital-news-media/.

7. For more information, see *The Human Reach*, a story map in the *Living in the Age of Humans* series, available at https://arcg.is/1XjzKC.

8. Listen to the Esri podcast "Why Location Intelligence Is a Disruptive Technology," available at https://www.esri.com/about/newsroom/podcast/why-location-intelligence-is-a-disruptive-technology.

9. See the Esri case study "Reliable Growth in the Restaurant Market," available at https://assets.esri.com/content/dam/esrisites/media/pdf/chick-fil-a-case-study.pdf.

Chapter 11

Contemporary ideas

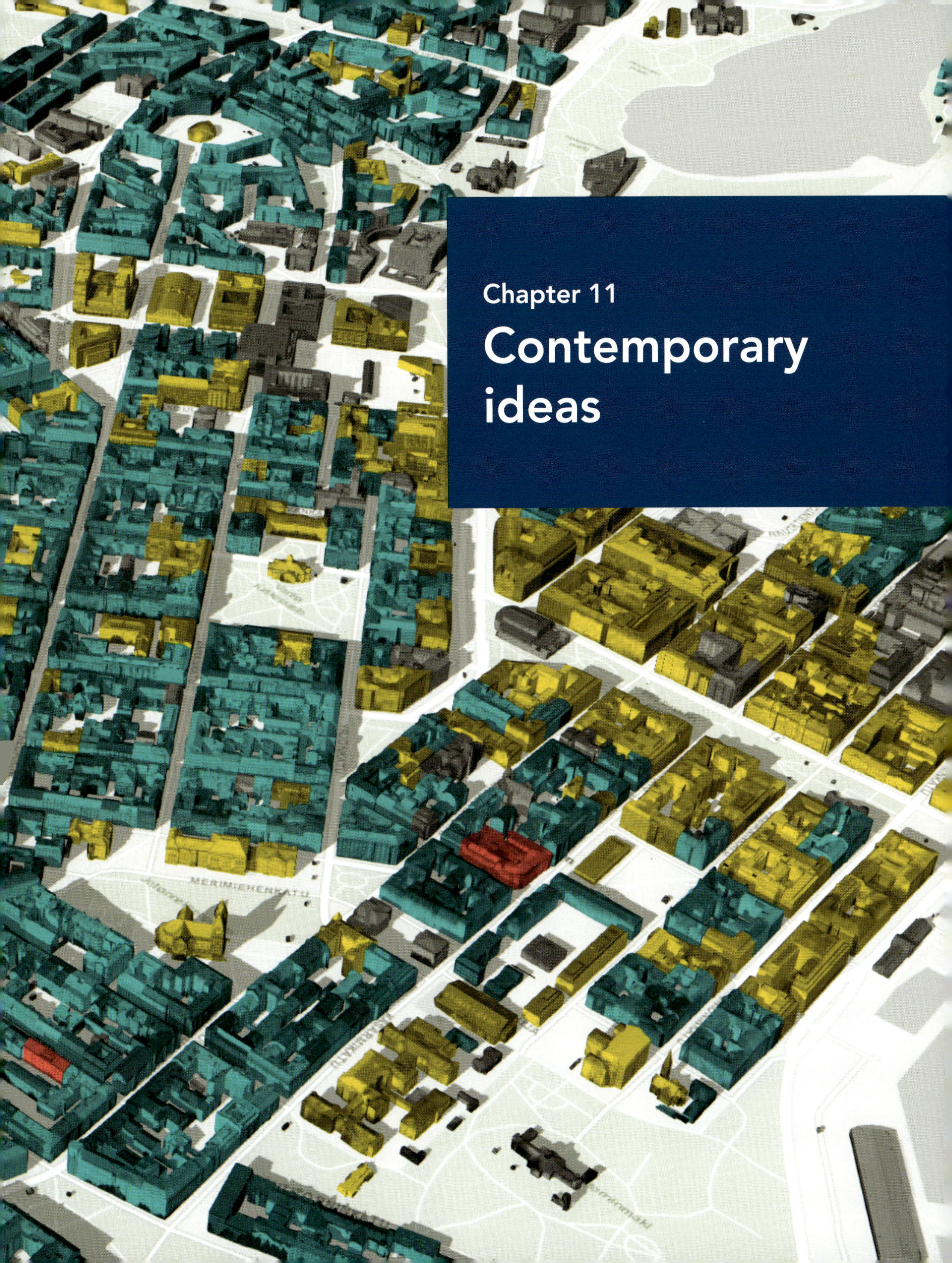

The future is here. If you read this far, you are aware of the massive changes underway affecting GIS and statistics. The pace of adoption of new innovations such as ML and drones has been faster than expected. Some say that we are entering the human era of GIS. A modern GIS is about participation, sharing, and collaboration. It allows us to share information with anyone we choose and consume information we need that has been published by others. This chapter will expand on some of the ideas presented earlier on dissemination and spatial analytics and provide you with information about leveraging these and other new technologies in your organization.

ArcGIS® Hub

According to the Pew Research Center, 65 percent of Americans search online for information about their government, yet less than 10 percent report finding what they need.[1] Citizens need and want information, and leaders need input from society. With data-driven citizenship as a top priority, ArcGIS Hub engages governments and communities around policy initiatives to tackle pressing issues. It is important to understand the issues your country identifies as significant, and equally important to have the input of citizens, civil society, and academia to help solve those issues. ArcGIS Hub brings top priorities into focus by helping to define initiatives and the data needed to better understand the issue. What is an initiative? We all need our local governments to take initiative to solve key critical issues. Initiatives usually are focused on a certain topic, such as decreasing traffic congestion, improving access to health care, or decreasing unemployment. These issues can be understood by combining different types of data and by using mapping and visualization tools to

tell the story. Initiatives help support the overall goals of your government and focus on improving the lives of its citizens.

Initiatives work in ArcGIS Hub by combining data, visualization, and analytics with collaboration technology. Getting citizens to participate is often the key—by engaging and informing your citizens, organizations can achieve better involvement and therefore success. One good example comes from the city of Los Angeles called "Vision Zero." The goal of this initiative is to reduce severe injuries and deaths in roadway collisions. Data needed to understand this issue includes basemap data, transportation network information, POIs (e.g., hospitals, retail centers, industrial centers), traffic data, and demographic data. Finally, information about the accidents themselves is needed—the type of vehicle involved, the location of the accident, the time of the accident, and the injuries or fatalities that were sustained. This data may come from various sources, including the Department of Transportation, the NSO, the NMA, or even local jurisdictions. The idea behind Vision Zero is that these deaths are both unacceptable and preventable, so the initiative strives to take a data-driven

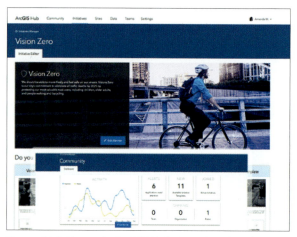

Figure 11.1. Example ArcGIS Hub site—Los Angeles, Vision Zero initiative.[2]

approach to reducing severe and fatal injuries.

This idea can also be applied to the SDGs. The goals as defined include targets and indicators that can guide initiatives. Imagine setting up an initiative for your country focused on reducing poverty in all its forms, everywhere. The data needed to understand many of the goals comes primarily from the NSO, though collaboration with other organizations is needed if we are to gain true understanding and take action.

Goal 1. End poverty in all its forms everywhere	
Goals and targets (from the 2030 Agenda for Sustainable Development)	**Indicators**
1.1 By 2030, eradicate extreme poverty for all people everywhere, currently measured as people living on less than $1.25 a day	**1.1.1** Proportion of population below the international poverty line, by sex, age, employment status, and geographical location (urban/rural)
1.2 By 2030, reduce at least by half the proportion of men, women and children of all ages living in poverty in all its dimensions according to national definitions	**1.2.1** Proportion of population living below the national poverty line, by sex and age **1.2.2** Proportion of men, women and children of all ages living in poverty in all its dimensions according to national definitions
1.3 Implement nationally appropriate social protection systems and measures for all, including floors, and by 2030 achieve substantial coverage of the poor and the vulnerable	**1.3.1** Proportion of population covered by social protection floors/systems, by sex, distinguishing children, unemployed persons, older persons, persons with disabilities, pregnant women, newborns, work-injury victims and the poor and the vulnerable
1.4 By 2030, ensure that all men and women, in particular the poor and the vulnerable, have equal rights to economic resources, as well as access to basic services, ownership and control over land and other forms of property, inheritance, natural resources, appropriate new technology and financial services, including microfinance	**1.4.1** Proportion of population living in households with access to basic services **1.4.2** Proportion of total adult population with secure tenure rights to land (a) with legally recognized documentation, and (b) who perceive their rights to land as secure, by sex and type of tenure
1.5 By 2030, build the resilience of the poor and those in vulnerable situations and reduce their exposure and vulnerability to climate-related extreme events and other economic, social and environmental shocks and disasters	**1.5.1** Number of deaths, missing persons and directly affected persons attributed to disasters per 100,000 population **1.5.2** Direct economic loss attributed to disasters in relation to global gross domestic product (GDP) **1.5.3** Number of countries that adopt and implement national disaster risk reduction strategies in line with the Sendai Framework for Disaster Risk Reduction 2015–2030 **1.5.4** Proportion of local governments that adopt and implement local disaster risk reduction strategies in line with national disaster risk reduction strategies

Figure 11.2. Example of goals, targets, and indicators from the UNSD. Excerpted from a UNSD report on final goals, targets, and indicators. *Source*: UNSD.[3]

Indicators such as these all require basic demographic data, including disaggregations (e.g., by sex or age), income data, and location information at a minimum. In some cases, information from other local agencies such as the Ministry of Health or a disaster agency may be needed.

ArcGIS Hub allows any organization to tell compelling stories with data. By using story maps, dashboards, and infographic reports, data can be presented in intuitive ways. ArcGIS Hub allows any organization to share information, measure progress, and show accountability. It is the engagement focal point for top issues and a place to publish the work the community creates together.

As mentioned in an earlier chapter, UNSD has used hub technology to create the FIS4SDGs. This system allows for collaboration across the UN and with member states, creating transparency and empowering the community.

Figure 11.3. UNSD hub implementation dedicated to the SDGs from the UNSD SDG website (https://www.sdg.org).

Hubs are just beginning to grow in popularity and are allowing nations to create a network of networks—bringing data from various agencies together to solve problems, innovate, and inspire.

Smarter maps

As you have learned, hubs should tell compelling stories with data. Smart mapping, which was described earlier, allows just that: telling the story of the data. Smart mapping provides better initial parameters, such as colors, scale, and styling, that fit the data and map's story. This functionality is why smart mapping benefits novices and experts, making both more productive.

Continuous color ramps and proportional symbols, improved categorical mapping, heat maps, and new kinds of bivariate maps that use transparency are delivered through a streamlined and updated user interface.

As technology continues to evolve, maps get even smarter. One of the newest features in ArcGIS is called ArcGIS® Arcade expressions. Arcade is a portable, lightweight, and secure expression language. Like other expression languages, it can perform mathematical calculations, manipulate text, and evaluate logical statements. Arcade was designed specifically for creating custom visualizations and labeling expressions in the ArcGIS platform. It allows users to write, share, and execute custom expressions in ArcGIS Pro, ArcGIS® Runtime, ArcGIS Online, and the ArcGIS® API for JavaScript™.

What makes Arcade particularly different from other expression and scripting languages is its inclusion of feature and geometry data types. Though one of Esri's newest scripting languages, Arcade is not a full programming or scripting language for creating stand-alone apps; nor is it a replacement for automation. It is a focused, intuitive, JavaScript-like language for creating expressions that customize visualization and labeling. Think of it more like a spreadsheet formula.

With Arcade, calculations with layer fields can be easily performed, and the result for label expressions or data-driven visualizations can be easily used. This means that when making a map and the layer being used doesn't contain the exact attribute field needed, data can be generated on the fly without editing source data, adding a field, or permanently calculating values. Simply put, Arcade expressions allow map-making from simple calculations, functions, data conversions, and brand-new representations of the data.

With Arcade, created expressions can be used without modification across the platform. For example, visualizations can be based off values returned from custom calculations in ArcGIS Pro and saved as web map items, and those custom visualizations can be shared for use in other web, desktop, and mobile applications.

Figure 11.4. Map of solar potential of rooftops in Bristol, United Kingdom, created using ArcGIS Arcade expressions. The values are recorded in kWh per year and represent PV generation potential. The map uses an Arcade expression to color each polygon.

Esri provides a public gallery of Arcade expressions to give some good ideas on how this works. This collection of maps is available as examples of Arcade expressions within the smart-mapping interface. These maps can be viewed along with the expressions used to create the cartography.[4]

Arcade is purposefully simple. Instead of the many programming constructs found in other languages, it has a rich library of data, logical, mathematical, geometry, date, and text functions that make it easy to do complex calculations.

Spatial analysis

We touched a bit on spatial analysis earlier in the book when we spoke about using analysis for optimizing EAs or for use in siting field offices. However, it's a very broad topic. Spatial analysis is the process of examining the locations, attributes, and relationships of features in spatial data through overlay and other analytical techniques to address a question or gain useful knowledge. Spatial analysis extracts or creates new information from spatial data. More simply put, spatial analysis is how we understand our world—mapping where things are, how they relate, what it all means, and what actions to take.

Consider the following six categories of spatial analysis:
- Understanding where
- Measuring size, shape, and distribution
- Determining how places are related
- Finding the best locations and paths
- Detecting and quantifying patterns
- Making predictions

Each of these categories has a set of related topics or questions, as shown in figure 11.5.

A quick guide to spatial analysis

Understanding where
- Understanding where things are (location maps)
- Understanding where the variations and patterns in values are (comparative maps)
- Understanding where and when things change

Measuring size, shape, and distribution
- Calculating individual feature geometries
- Calculating geometries and distributions of feature collections

Determining how places are related
- Determining what is nearby or coincident
- Determining and summarizing what is within an area(s)
- Determining what is closest
- Determining what is visible from a given location(s)
- Determining overlapping relationships in space and time

Finding the best locations and paths
- Finding the best locations that satisfy a set of criteria
- Finding the best allocation of resources to geographic areas
- Finding the best route, path, or flow along a network
- Finding the best route, path, or corridor across open terrain
- Finding the best supply locations given known demand and a travel network

Detecting and quantifying patterns
- Where are the significant hot spots, anomalies, and outliers?
- What are the local, regional, and global spatial trends?
- Which features/pixels are similar, and how can they be grouped together?
- Are spatial patterns changing over time?

Figure 11.5. Categories of spatial analysis of spatial analysis (from the 2013 Esri workbook *The Language of Spatial Analysis*)[5]

Many different tools are available that allow one to conduct spatial analysis. For example, ArcGIS® Spatial Analyst™ provides a rich set of spatial analysis and modeling tools for both raster (cell-based) and feature (vector) data.

The capabilities of Spatial Analyst are divided into categories or groups of related functionalities. This functionality can be accessed in several ways, including through a tool dialog box, Python™, or a model. Traditional operations and workflows using map algebra or analysis using the Raster Calculator can also be performed.

Space-time analysis continues to advance as well. Creating a space-time cube allows one to visualize and analyze the spatiotemporal data in the form of time-series analyses, integrated spatial and temporal pattern analysis, and powerful 2D and 3D visualization techniques.

The ArcGIS Space Time Pattern Mining toolbox contains statistical tools for analyzing data distributions and patterns in the context of both space and time. ArcGIS allows the creation of space-time cubes and the conducting of emerging hot spot analysis.

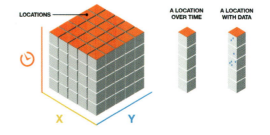

Figure 11.6. Space-time cube.

The Emerging Hot Spot Analysis tool identifies trends in the data. It finds new, intensifying, diminishing, and sporadic hot and cold spots, for example. It takes as input a space-time Network

Common Data Form (NetCDF) cube created using either the Create Space Time Cube By Aggregating Points tool or the Create Space Time Cube From Defined Locations tool. It then uses the conceptualization of spatial relationships values provided by the user to calculate the Getis-Ord Gi* statistic (Hot Spot Analysis tool) for each bin.[6]

Tools such as these can be used to detect and

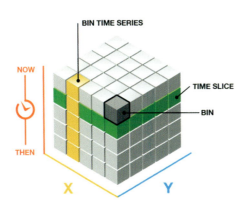

Figure 11.7. Time slice and bin time series.

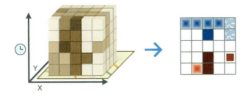

Figure 11.8. Space-time cube and emerging hot spot.

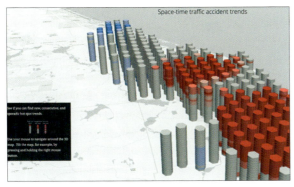

Figure 11.9. Analyzing traffic accidents in space and time.

quantify patterns and make predictions. Many others are available that allow ArcGIS users to perform time-series clustering, outlier analysis, network analysis, or even 3D analysis. The power of spatial analysis does not stop there, and new developments in geospatial artificial intelligence (GeoAI) will continue to push the boundaries of what is possible.

GeoAI

To understand GeoAI, we need to first understand AI. AI has been defined as the "broadest way to think about advanced computer intelligence . . . anything from a computer program playing a game of chess to a voice-recognition system . . . interpreting and responding to speech."[7]

According to the company McKinsey,[8] AI is trending now owing to the convergence of algorithmic advances, data proliferation, and tremendous increases in computing power and storage, propelling AI from hype to reality. Think big data, IoT, and the cloud.

Another part of the equation here is ML. ML can be done in a supervised or unsupervised mode or by using something called *re-enforcement learning*. ArcGIS provides built-in ML tools such as clustering, classification, and prediction, bringing the "geo" to ML. According to Joseph Sirosh, corporate vice president of artificial intelligence and research for Microsoft Azure, "Integrating geography and location information with AI brings a powerful new dimension to understanding the world around us."[9] Further, "This has a wide range of applications in a variety of segments, including commercial, governmental, academic or not-for-profit. Geospatial AI provides robust tools for gathering, managing, analyzing and predicting from geographic and location-based data, and powerful visualization that can enable unique insights into the significance of such data." Microsoft and Esri are partnering in this area,[10] intending to bring AI, cloud, geospatial, and visualization aspects together in one application.

The areas of application of this type of technology seem to be almost limitless. One example might be in land change. What if you could predict land desertification based on the rate of change using models using data from historical imagery, weather, and tidal information? Or consider being able to predict agriculture and land efficiency from elevation, weather, crop yield, and soils information? The GeoAI, ML, and big data expert Mansour Raad tells us this is possible. Raad, who is the lead on advanced spatial analytics and the big data subject matter expert at Esri, challenges us to think about other areas of application, such as predictive incident analysis, and to consider the data needed for this type of analysis.

Think of the implications for this in official statistics. According to Raad, "When data volume swells beyond a human's ability to discern the patterns in it—when a company is faced with truly big data—we need a new form of intelligence. GIS, infused with artificial intelligence, can help executives make better decisions."[11]

Whether it's the use of data from mobile phones to understand movement or some of the new streaming data from the IoT world, statisticians and geographers both face the challenge of determining how best to apply this data and create meaningful information from it.

Geoblockchain

In a 2018 survey of global executives, Deloitte found that 65 percent of US organizations plan to invest more than $1 million in blockchain technology in 2019.[12] A blockchain is a growing list of records, called *blocks*, which are linked using cryp-

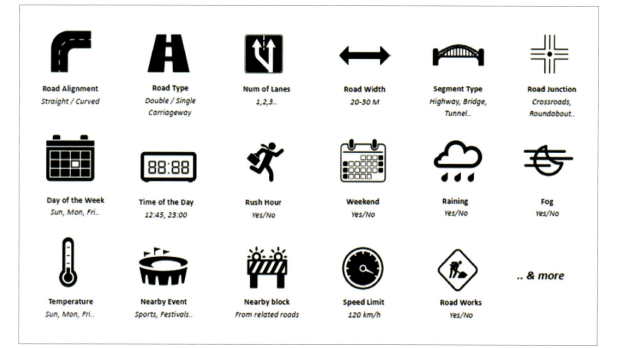

Figure 11.10. Spatiotemporal variables that may correlate to accidents.

Figure 11.11. Blockchain transactions can be understood using spatial analysis.

tography. Each block contains a cryptographic hash of the previous block, a timestamp, and transaction data. It is a ledger that records transactions in a verifiable, permanent way.[13] If only 2 percent of all servers one day run on blockchain, Bank of America estimates that it will represent a $7 billion market.[14] Geography is critically important to capture in a blockchain record, which is why we are now calling this a *geoblockchain*.

What do we as statisticians need to think about regarding geoblockchain? How will this new technology affect our work? Today, the answers are not clear, but what is certain is the potential for this new innovative technology. One example of the potential is an application by the UN World Food Program (WFP). The UN WFP blockchain system combines biometrics with blockchain technology to help those without an identification. For example, refugees, separated from their families, often have no public records or identification. It is difficult if not impossible to conduct normal daily transactions—such as

buying food, withdrawing cash, or getting a credit card—with no identification. By combining biometrics with blockchain technology, WFP helps provide monetary aid to these displaced people; they save money on bank-related fees and can track daily transactions, just as they could with a credit card.[15] This information can be used to better understand needs and inform other needed services.

Another example of a real-world application is from India, where blockchain is being used to make land registry more reliable. The idea here is to create a single source of truth of ownership status and a property history. The buyer is assured that the land being bought is the correct plot and that the seller is unequivocally the owner.[16]

Adding location to the blockchain would provide enhanced security and validation because the same transaction cannot happen in two places at the same time. Use cases for blockchain being explored today include land title, supply

Understanding where

If you don't know where you are, you are lost. Understanding where is about putting the world in context. Where are you? What is around you? Very similar to when you were two years old, your journey of spatial analysis requires an understanding of how you fit into your geography.

Understanding where includes geocoding your data, putting it on a map, and symbolizing it in ways that can help you visualize and understand your data. Within the taxonomy of spatial analysis, the first category of understanding where contains three types of questions.

TYPES

- Understanding where things are (location maps)
- Understanding where the variations and patterns in values are (comparative maps)
- Understanding where and when things change

Measuring size, shape, and distribution

The task of measuring size and shape is a common requirement in the spatial analysis process. You may want to know how large an object is, or you may want to describe an object in terms of its geometric properties, such as area, perimeter, length, height, and volume.

When there are multiple objects, the set of objects takes on additional properties, including extent, central tendency, and other characteristics that collectively define the distribution of the entire dataset.

The process of measuring and describing these characteristics constitutes the second category of spatial analysis questions.

TYPES

- Calculating individual feature geometries
- Calculating geometries and distributions of feature collections

Determining how places are related

Answering spatial questions often requires not only an understanding of context (understanding where), but also an understanding of the relationships between features. Take any two objects: How are they related in space?

How are they related in time? These relationships in space and time include associations such as proximity, coincidence, intersection, overlap, visibility, and accessibility.

Determining how places are related includes a set of questions that help describe and quantify the relationships between two or more features.

TYPES

- Determining what is nearby or coincident
- Determining and summarizing what is within an area(s)
- Determining what is closest
- Determining what is visible from a given location(s)
- Determining overlapping relationships in space and time

Finding the best locations and paths

A very common type of spatial analysis, and probably the one you are most familiar with, is optimization and finding the best of something. You might be looking for the best route to travel, the best path to ride a bicycle, the best corridor to build a pipeline, or the best location to site a new store.

Using multiple input variables or a set of decision criteria for finding the best locations and paths can help you make more informed decisions using your spatial data.

TYPES

- Finding the best locations that satisfy a set of criteria
- Finding the best allocation of resources to geographic areas
- Finding the best route, path, or flow along a network
- Finding the best route, path, or corridor across open terrain
- Finding the best supply locations given known demand and a travel network

Detecting and quantifying patterns

In the fifth category of the spatial analysis taxonomy, the keyword is patterns.

These spatial analysis questions go beyond visualization and human interpretation of data (from the understanding where category) to mathematically detecting and quantifying patterns in data. For example, spatial statistics can be used to find hot spots and outliers; data mining techniques can be used to find natural data clusters; and both approaches can be used to analyze changes in patterns over time.

TYPES

- Where are the significant hot spots, anomalies, and outliers?
- What are the local, regional, and global spatial trends?
- Which features/pixels are similar, and how can they be grouped together?
- Are spatial patterns changing over time?

Making predictions

The last category includes questions that use powerful modeling techniques to make predictions and aid understanding. These techniques can be used to predict and interpolate data values between sample points, find factors related to complex phenomena, and make predictions in the future or over new geographies. Many specialized modeling approaches also build on the physical, economic, and social sciences to predict how objects will interact, flow, and disperse.

Despite their differences, all these questions share the same principles: they are used to predict behavior and outcomes and to help us better understand our world.

TYPES

- Given a success case, identifying, ranking, and predicting similar locations
- Finding the factors that explain observed spatial patterns and making predictions
- Interpolating a continuous surface and trends from discrete sample observations
- Predicting how and where objects spatially interact (attraction and decay)
- Predicting how and where objects affect wave propagation
- Predicting where phenomena will move, flow, or spread
- Predicting what-if

Figure 11.12. Six categories in spatial analysis.

chain, and data exchanges. The amount of data that will become available with systems like these is worth consideration and needs research.

This is an exciting and challenging time for those of us engaged in the data revolution. Technology continues to advance, and with it the potential to expand the use and application of statistical and geospatial data. The future is within our grasp, and data truly can help us understand the pressing questions of the present and the future. The more accessible that data is, the more important it will be to understand it. Maps are the visual language for understanding the context of data.

Notes

1. See the Pew Research Center Internet & Technology's *Americans' Views on Open Government Data*, available at http://www.pewinternet.org/2015/04/21/open-government-data.

2. See the Los Angeles GeoHub at https://geohub.lacity.org for more information.

3. See the UNSD SDGs website at https://unstats.un.org/sdgs/indicators/indicators-list for more information.

4. See *Arcade Expressions and You*, available at https://arcgis-content.maps.arcgis.com/apps/PublicGallery/index.appid=8951b538362b492cadadf7ede1b85c21.

5. This workbook is available at https://www.esri.com/library/books/the-language-of-spatial-analysis.pdf.

6. See Esri documentation at https://pro.arcgis.com/en/pro-app/tool-reference/spatial-statistics/h-how-hot-spot-analysis-getis-ord-gi-spatial-stati.htm and https://pro.arcgis.com/en/pro-app/tool-reference/spatial-statistics/hot-spot-analysis.htm for more information.

7. See the 2017 TechRepublic® article *Understanding the Differences Between AI, Machine Learning, and Deep Learning* by Hope Reese, available at https://www.techrepublic.com/article/understanding-the-differences-between-ai-machine-learning-and-deep-learning.

8. McKinsey (https://www.mckinsey.com) is a global consulting company that conducts qualitative and quantitative analysis to evaluate management decisions across the public and private sectors.

9. See the 2018 Microsoft article *Microsoft and Esri Launch Geospatial AI on Azure* by Joseph Sirosh, available at https://azure.microsoft.com/en-us/blog/microsoft-and-esri-launch-geospatial-ai-on-azure.

10. See *Microsoft and Esri Launch*.

11. See the Esri Newsroom article "A new business intelligence emerges: Geo.AI" by Mansour Raad, available at https://www.esri.com/about/newsroom/publications/wherenext/new-business-intelligence-emerges-geo-ai.

12. See the 2019 Esri article *Think Tank: Blockchain Evolves into Geoblockchain*, available at https://www.esri.com/about/newsroom/publications/wherenext/geoblockchain-think-tank.

13. See https://en.wikipedia.org/wiki/Blockchain.

14. See the CNBC article *Blockchain Could Be a $7 Billion Market and a Major Book to Amazon, Microsoft, Bank of America Says*, available at https://www.cnbc.com/amp/2018/10/02/blockchain-could-be-a-major-boost-to-amazon-microsoft-analyst-says--.html.

15. See *Blockchain Could Be a $7 Billion Market*.

16. See the 2018 UNDP article *Using Blockchain to Make Land Registry More Reliable in India* by Alexandru Oprunenco and Chami Akmeemana, available at http://www.undp.org/content/undp/en/home/blog/2018/Using-blockchain-to-make-land-registry-more-reliable-in-India.html.

Appendix: Acronyms

3G	third generation
ABS	Australian Bureau of Statistics
ADA	aggregate dissemination area
AI	artificial intelligence
API	application programming interface
ARD	analysis-ready data
AWS	Amazon Web Services
BGE	Buildings Geographic Database
BLOB	binary large object
CAD	computer-aided design
CAPI	computer-assisted personal interviewing
CAPMAS	Central Agency for Public Mobilization and Statistics
CARICOM	Caribbean Community
CATI	computer-assisted telephone interviewing
CAWI	computer-aided web interview
CBB	Census Business Builder
CBS	Central Bureau of Statistics
CEDSCI	Center for Enterprise Dissemination Services and Consumer Innovation
CES	Conference of European Statisticians
CIESIN	Center for International Earth Science Information Network
CPDV	Census Program Data Viewer
CPH	Census of Population and Housing
CPU	computer processing unit
CSDGM	Content Standard for Digital Geospatial Metadata
CSO	Central Statistics Office
CSV	comma-separated values
DBMS	database management system
DDI	Data Documentation Initiative
DEM	digital elevation model
DF	dwelling frame
DGGS	discrete global grid system
DLG	digital line graph
EA	enumeration area
ECA	Economic Commission for Africa
ECE/CES	Economic Commission for Europe—Conference of European Statisticians

EG-ISGI	Expert Group on the Integration of Statistical and Geospatial Information
ELF	European Location Framework
EO	earth observation
ESA	European Space Agency
ETL	extract, transform, and load
EU	European Union
FGDC	Federal Geographic Data Committee
FIS4SDGs	Federated Information System for the Sustainable Development Goals
GBDX	Geospatial Big Data Platform
GEO	Group on Earth Observations
GeoAI	geospatial artificial intelligence
GFM	General Feature Model
GIS	geographic information systems
GLONASS	Russia's Global Navigation Satellite System
GML	Geography Markup Language
GNSS	Global Navigation Satellite System
GPS	Global Positioning System
GSBPM	Generic Statistical Business Process Model
GSGF	Global Statistical Geospatial Framework
GSIM	Generic Statistical Information Model
IaaS	infrastructure as a service
IDA	Industrial Development Authority
IHSN	International Household Survey Network
INSPIRE	Infrastructure for Spatial Information in Europe
INSTAT	Institute of Statistics
IoT	Internet of Things
ISO	International Organization for Standardization
ISO/TC	International Organization for Standardization Technical Committee
ITU	International Telecommunications Union
JRC	Joint Research Center
LaaS	location as a service
LAS	LASer (industry-standard binary-format file used for storing airborne lidar data)
LBS	location-based services
LDC	least developed country
lidar	light detection and ranging

LoT	Location of Things
LTE	long-term evolution
ML	machine learning
NAIP	National Agriculture Imagery Program
NDVI	normalized difference vegetation index
NetCDF	Network Common Data Form
NIR	near-infrared
NMA	National Mapping Agency
NSDI	National Spatial Data Infrastructure
NSO	National Statistical Office
NSTAC	National Statistics Center of Japan
OGC	Open Geospatial Consortium
OGP	Open Government Partnership
OODBMS	object-oriented database management system
OSi	Ordnance Survey Ireland
PaaS	platform as a service
PAPI	paper-and-pencil interviewing
PCBS	Palestine Central Bureau of Statistics
PII	personally identifiable information
POI	points of interest
POPGRID	(data consortium hosted by the CIESEN)
PSA	Philippine Statistics Authority
RCMRD	Regional Centre for Mapping of Resources for Development
RDBMS	relational database management system
REST	Representational State Transfer
RFID	radio-frequency identification
ROI	return on investment
RS	remote sensing
SA	supervisory area
SaaS	software as a service
SAPS	Small Area Population Statistics
SC	Statistics Canada
SDGs	Sustainable Development Goals
SDI	spatial data infrastructure
SDMX	Statistical Data and Metadata eXchange
SDTS	Spatial Data Transfer Standard
SMS	short message service

SOAP	Simple Object Access Protocol
SP	Statistics Portugal
SQL	Structured Query Language
TIN	triangulated irregular network
TJS	Table Joining Service
UAV	unmanned aerial vehicle
UID	unique identifier
UN	United Nations
UNECE	United Nations Economic Commission for Europe
UN-EG-ISGI	UN Expert Group on the Integration of Statistical and Geospatial Information
UNGEGN	UN Group of Experts on Geographical Names
UN-GGIM	UN Committee of Experts on Global Geospatial Information Management
UNGIWG	UN Geographic Information Working Group
UNSC	UN Statistical Commission
UNSD	UN Statistics Division
UNWDF	United Nations World Data Forum
URL	uniform resource locator
USB	universal serial bus
VGI	volunteered geographic information
VPF	Vector Product Format
VPN	virtual private network
WCS	Web Coverage Service
WFP	World Food Program
WFS	Web Feature Service
WMS	Web Map Service
WMTS	Web Map Tile Service
WPE	World Population Estimate
WYSIWYG	what you see is what you get
XML	Extensible Markup Language

Index

size of, 71–72, 104, 124; use of imagery in updating, 109–18

enumeration geography, 66–67

Esri, 126, 171, 172, 188, 194

Esri geodatabase, 62

Esri imagery basemap, 94–95

Esri Story Maps, 221

Esri World Population Estimate (WPE), 31–33

Evacu8, 204

evidence-based decision-making, 5

exonyms, 200

Expert Group on the Integration of Statistical and Geospatial Information (EG-ISGI), 3

Extensible Markup Language (XML), 168, 190

F

feature classes, 55

feature data, 128

Federated Information Systems for the SDGs (FIS4SDGs), 182, 228

field data collection, 145–152

field data verification, 142

field office site placement, 129–30

field operations management, 152–53, 157, 158, 168

fieldwork: benefits of using GIS/GPS and imagery in, 142–44; EA delineation process and, 104, 105, 116–18; imagery and, 112–13

First Law of Geography (Tobler), 5

G

Galileo (GNSS), 45

gazetteers, 22, 198–201

General Features Model (GFM), 27

General Statistical Information Model (GSIM), 27

Generic Statistical Business Process Model (GSB-PM), 12

GEO. See Group on Earth Observations

GeoAI, 231–32

GeoAnalytics Server, 41

geoblockchain, 232–35

geocodes, 5, 74

geocoding, 25–26, 72–76; additional reference information, 75–76; boundary changes and, 124; definitions of, 74–75

geodatabases, 52–83; archiving and maintenance, 170–71; attributes, 55; basemaps, 63–65; case study: Albania, 76–79; census geography, 65–70; database modeling, 59–65; datasets, 54–55; defined, 52–53; design of, 59; enumeration areas, 70–72; feature classes, 55; fieldwork and, 116–18; geographic coding, 72–76; integration of existing data into, 108–9; spatial data models, 56–59; spatial data structures, 53–55; topologies, 57–59; updating and verifying changes to, 166–68

GeoEvent Server, 41

geographic attribute tables, 62

geographic boundaries, 123–24

geographic boundary files, 21

geographic classifications, 66, 72–73

geographic coding, 72–76; additional reference information, 75–76; coding scheme, 73–74; definitions of, 74–75

geographic information systems (GIS), 2, 4, 6; applications of, 16; census process planning with, 10–16; cost-benefit analysis, 20; data dissemination and, 194–208; design of, 52; EA delineation process and, 104–5; enterprise, 15, 127; fieldwork benefits of using, 142–44; geodatabases, 52–83; key trends in, 38–48; optimizing capital and asset distribution using, 130–31; optimizing field office placement using, 129–30; planning considerations, 15–16; real-time, 42; technological change and, 30–31; training and awareness programs for, 16; use and application of, 38

geographic products, marketing of, 218–223

196; offline, 128–29; online, 144; ortho, 88, 97, 110; smart, 202–3, 228–29; thematic, 194–97; types of, 106; univariate, 196; updating, 142–43; using offline, 118, 144; web-based, 206–8; *see also* basemaps

map services, 43, 127–28, 143

marketing communication plans, 218–23

market research, 220, 222

mashups, 207

MDA/DigitalGlobe Imagery + Analytics (I+A), 95–96

MDA NaturalVue, 32

Measuring the Information Society Report (ITU), 42

metadata, 21–27, 64, 107–8; data dissemination and, 190–93; maintenance of, 170–71; purpose of, 191; standards, 121–23, 191–93

Microsoft Azure, 46, 125, 126, 127, 231

Microsoft Earth, 204

Microsoft Windows, 148, 151, 204

miniature satellites, 113

ML. *See* machine learning

mobile applications, 149, 157, 203–4

mobile devices, 42, 105, 145–50, 156, 157, 166

mobile map packages, 128–29

mobile technology, 156, 158, 220

mobility, 42

multivariate maps, 196

N

National Institute of Statistics of Albania (INSTAT), 76–79

National Mapping Agencies (NMAs), 15

National Spatial Data Infrastructure (NSDI), 15

National Statistical Offices (NSOs), 2, 4, 6

National Statistics Center of Japan (NSTAC), 69

natural disasters, 5

natural resource assessment, 87

Navigator for ArcGIS, 155

needs assessment, 16–22

Nepal, 205

Netherlands, 70

NetSuite, 125

Network Common Data Form (NetCDF), 230–31

nodes, 58

O

object-oriented database management system (OODBMS), 60, 62

object-oriented models, 60, 62–63

obliquity, 93–94

offline maps, 128–29

on-demand workflow, 129

online atlases, 197–98

online questionnaires, 152

open data, 47–48, 187–88

Open Geospatial Consortium (OGC), 123, 128, 171

Open Government Partnership (OGP), 188

open platform, 171–72

open-source software, 172

operational dashboards, 22, 153, 156

optimization: of capital and asset distribution, 130–31; EA, 132–33; of field office placement, 129–30; route, 154–55; workload, 153–54

ortho mapping, 88, 97

ortho-mapping tools, 110

orthophoto maps, 65, 110–111

output needs, 188–90

outreach strategy, 181

outsourced services, 186–87

P

paper-and-pencil interviewing (PAPI), 143, 145

P-codes, 200

personally identifiable information (PII), 185–86

Philippine Statistics Authority (PSA), 134–35

physical models, 59

pixels, 56

NEW RELEASE